Simplifying Inclusive Leadership

Simplifying Inclusive Leadership is a practical text that brings together the scientific evidence behind the concept of inclusive leadership, presenting this in an accessible, easy-to-read, and engaging format.

Combined with tips and recommendations, the book supports leaders embracing what it means to practise inclusive leadership and subsequently to behave more inclusively.

Fulfilling five key objectives, it:

- Explains what is meant by inclusive leadership and why it is important.
- Presents a scientifically grounded model of inclusive leadership that brings the concept to life in a practical and tangible way.
- Explores the components of the model (leader wellbeing, drivers of inclusive leadership, and inclusive leader behaviours).
- Provides the evidence supporting each of these components with engaging case examples to bring the topic to life.
- Translates the research into practical recommendations and actions leaders can take to apply what they have learned and practise inclusive leadership.

Simplifying Inclusive Leadership is the ideal introductory text for managers and leaders at any level who wish to enhance their leadership practice and support their team members to thrive.

Rebecca J. Jones is co-founder of the Inclusive Leadership Company. She is also a Professor of Coaching & Behaviour Change at Henley Business School, UK. She is a chartered psychologist and is committed to utilising the science of behaviour change to create inclusive workplaces and conducting robust and rigorous research into a variety of inclusion and behaviour change topics.

Priscila Pereira is co-founder of the Inclusive Leadership Company. She is also an EDI research director for an award-winning gender consulting firm and has a PhD in Gender Studies. She has significant in-house practitioner experience in the field of inclusion and diversity and leadership development across Europe in a variety of projects within global corporate settings, matrix teams, and multidisciplinary teams.

Simplifying Inclusive Leadership

Recommendations for Everyday Practice

REBECCA J. JONES AND PRISCILA PEREIRA

Routledge
Taylor & Francis Group

LONDON AND NEW YORK

Designed cover image: Getty Images @wildpixel

First published 2026
by Routledge
4 Park Square, Milton Park, Abingdon, Oxon OX14 4RN

and by Routledge
605 Third Avenue, New York, NY 10158

Routledge is an imprint of the Taylor & Francis Group, an informa business

For Product Safety Concerns and Information please contact our EU representative GPSR@taylorandfrancis.com. Taylor & Francis Verlag GmbH, Kaufingerstraße 24, 80331 München, Germany.

Trademark notice: Product or corporate names may be trademarks or registered trademarks, and are used only for identification and explanation without intent to infringe.

British Library Cataloguing-in-Publication Data
A catalogue record for this book is available from the British Library

ISBN: 978-1-032-98308-0 (hbk)
ISBN: 978-1-032-96855-1 (pbk)
ISBN: 978-1-003-59802-2 (ebk)

DOI: 10.4324/9781003598022

Typeset in Dante & Avenir
by SPi Technologies India Pvt Ltd (Straive)

Contents

Introduction

When we feel included, we feel that we are a valued member of the team and organisation. These feelings of inclusion stem from feeling seen and appreciated by others for what makes us unique and that we belong as an important member of the group. When we belong to a group, we have robust and stable relationships with other members of the group, consequently fulfilling one of our most basic human needs: to be connected to others. This basic need to belong is so strong that research from neuroscience has demonstrated that social isolation causes cravings for social interaction in the same way that fasting causes hunger.[1] Researchers believe that reactions to rejection and social isolation operate via the same mechanisms as physical pain,[2] demonstrating that people are so important to one another that social needs are ingrained in our biology. This evidence makes a clear link between inclusion, wellbeing, and performance.

Leaders play a critical role in enabling inclusion because they influence culture (i.e., what it feels like to work here) and decision-making, they control resources and access to these resources, they set the scene for how we should treat one another including how psychologically safe it feels to work here, and so on. Leaders can be either accelerators or blockers of inclusion. Inclusive leadership is not static. Instead, we can consider it as a practice, and inclusive leaders are individuals who are committed to this practice. Inclusive leaders nurture the mindset, develop the knowledge, and focus on behaviours that satisfy team members' paradoxical needs for belonging in social groups and their desire to be seen with distinctive qualities and uniqueness. Therefore, when we refer to inclusive leaders in this book we refer to leaders who practise inclusive leadership.

DOI: 10.4324/9781003598022-1

We can all be inclusive sometimes – and even the most inclusive leaders, despite their best efforts, will exclude. We know that our brains have limited capacity to process information: therefore, we have evolved to rely on mental shortcuts, known as heuristics, to process information and make decisions quickly. Unfortunately, these shortcuts are prone to bias. Our brains are also wired to keep us safe. As social animals, safety is traditionally within our own social groups (the ingroup), therefore bias-driven judgements are made about people not in our own social group (the outgroups) and they might be subconsciously seen as social threats. Hence, we all exclude and are excluded more often than we think. Feeling uniquely valued and like you belong does not happen automatically for marginalised employees because, as confronting as this may feel, if we are not consciously including, this means by default that we are excluding.[3]

Despite our biological limitations, we believe that experiencing something different to what we are used to can be reframed from being a potential threat to a reward, consequently creating a positive automatic response to difference. Therefore, we propose that inclusive leadership can (and should) be learned and developed as a practice and the Inclusive Leader System can help us to do that. The Inclusive Leader System is the framework that we developed to help us to understand what it takes to practise inclusive leadership and this framework provides the basis for this book.

What are "marginalised" employees?

You will notice that throughout this text we will often use the terms "marginalised employees/individuals" or "marginalised groups". When we refer to marginalised groups, we are referring to people who have been marginalised in that context (i.e., pushed to the edges, experiencing systemic inequalities, discrimination, and historical disadvantages). This does not necessarily mean that they are in the minority. For example, women are often marginalised despite making up half of the population and as a consequence are underrepresented in leadership roles.

There are multiple ways in which individuals can become excluded, marginalised, and underrepresented in decision-making and positions of power and this often includes, but is not limited to gender, ethnicity, race, sexual orientation, disability, religion/faith, and age. Marginalised groups can also experience the compounding impact of discrimination when they hold multiple characteristics that are subject to systems of oppression (i.e., when racism and sexism intersect).

If you are not familiar with some of this terminology, you may wish to skip ahead and read Chapter 14 where we cover knowledge of topics and issues relevant to inclusion, before returning back to continue with the rest of the book.

Why inclusive *leadership*?

In this book, we focus on what it takes to practise inclusive *leadership* and therefore the target reader for our book is anyone who operates in a people leadership role. We argue that it is critical to focus on the leader as, even within an inclusive organisation, individuals can still feel excluded because of the impact of their line manager on their team's subculture. For example, data indicate that anything from 45 per cent[4] to 70 per cent[5] of employee experiences of inclusion are explained by their line managers' inclusive leadership behaviours. Data collected from online recruitment websites with employee reviews about their experiences of inclusion in the firms they work for showed that, on average across industries, 51 per cent of the total mentions related to leadership and 56 per cent of those mentions had negative sentiment.[6] This highlights the need for leaders to be accountable for their impact on people in relation to inclusion. Leaders are role models and set the tone for the team, and inclusive leaders create the environment for all team members, including those from diverse backgrounds, to thrive and reach their full potential, maximising their contribution to their organisation.

Critically, research indicates that we are not very accurate at measuring our own inclusive leader capability. For example, a third of leaders believe they are more inclusive than they are perceived to be by those around them, while a third lack confidence in their inclusive leadership capability and so do less than they could to actively guide others and challenge the status quo.[7] This data is backed up by research that found that just one-third (36 per cent) of leaders could accurately judge their inclusive capabilities as others saw them, with a third (32 per cent) overestimating their effectiveness.[8] Similar findings have been seen in research assessing 1,825 senior leaders on their effectiveness at valuing diversity.[9] Leaders who were rated in the bottom quartile by their direct reports on valuing diversity rated themselves at the 42nd percentile; therefore, those leaders who were the poorest at valuing diversity were more likely to overrate their capability. Our own experience of working with leaders in our consultancy practice at Inclusive Leadership Company, reflects this. We find that most leaders are well intentioned and have a strong desire to practise inclusive leadership, yet they have a poor understanding of what inclusive leadership is and how to be inclusive in different work contexts, and they generally overestimate their own inclusive leader capability. This is why we developed our inclusive leader assessment which uses a 360-rater approach to gather feedback from others on inclusive leader behaviours.

Our connection to inclusive leadership

Together, we are co-founders of Inclusive Leadership Company, and our purpose in our work is to transform leadership to build an inclusive and sustainable world. We believe organisations can be both financially successful and responsible for their people and the planet if they have inclusive leaders. Our ambition is to ignite one million leaders to embrace inclusion as their core value as leaders, creating a ripple of positive impact on business performance, innovation and people's lives.

We both have a deep connection to inclusion, albeit stemming from very different lived experiences.

Priscila grew up in São Paulo, Brazil. As a white,[10] heterosexual Brazilian of Portuguese descent in a socioeconomically disadvantaged area of the city, she witnessed the routine discrimination and marginalisation of Black people around her. At the same time, she faced gender-based discrimination within her nuclear family, which shaped her early understanding of inequality. Priscila's values of solidarity and fairness were grounded by the influence of her maternal aunts and grandmother. In her mid-20s, Priscila moved to the UK, where her immigration status introduced new layers of challenge. Priscila overcame early setbacks, through social mobility, made possible by key sponsors who opened doors and supported her pursuit of an MBA, a Master's in Human Resources Management (HRM), a PhD in Gender Studies, and a Chartered Institute of Personnel and Development (CIPD) fellowship, many of which were employer-funded, as she would not have been able to afford them otherwise. Today, she draws on her lived experience and privileges to drive change and advocate for inclusive leadership.

Rebecca was born and raised in the UK, and her lived experience includes the power of inclusion to create career opportunities. In 2011, when she was heavily pregnant, Rebecca was interviewed (in person) by a prospective PhD supervisor. Rebecca had not mentioned that she was pregnant before the interview out of fear that the supervisor would not consider her a viable candidate for the PhD scholarship she was applying for. This supervisor exemplified inclusion: Rebecca felt seen and heard rather than judged on her identity at the time as a heavily pregnant woman. This supervisor's actions not only opened doors to allow Rebecca entry into a career path but also gave her the confidence to be herself without fear of judgement or retribution. Rebecca successfully completed her PhD in under four years (after having a healthy baby boy). As an occupational psychologist, Rebecca has been committed to improving the experience of work. However, as her knowledge and understanding of privilege, systemic oppression, and barriers to equality has grown, she has recognised the extent of the disparities in the experience of work (and beyond). Rebecca's strong desire for fairness and equality drives her work in the space of inclusion and inclusive leadership.

Our purpose for this book

Topics like inclusive leadership, which are rooted in historical social structures and dynamics, are complex and challenging to understand and to apply. Likewise, oversimplifying them risks missing the nuances, tensions, and complexities necessary to truly understand what inclusive leadership is. To address this, our ambition for this book was to distill the principles of inclusive leadership while providing practical examples throughout, making them accessible and applicable. The simplicity comes from the day-to-day examples that leaders do to practise inclusive leadership. Inclusive leadership is not an inert form of being a leader, instead, it is a daily practice where we will inevitably sometimes get it wrong, while striving to keep improving.

Throughout the book, we explore inclusive leadership in bite-size chunks. We address five key core principles of practising including leadership:

- Explain what is meant by inclusive leadership and why it is important.
- Present a scientifically grounded model of inclusive leadership that brings the concept to life in a practical and tangible way.
- Explore the components of the model (leader wellbeing, drivers of inclusive leadership, and inclusive leadership behaviours).
- Present the evidence supporting each of these components with examples from our own practice.

- Translate the research into practical recommendations and actions leaders can take to apply what they have learned to practise inclusive leadership.

We recognise that most leaders are time-constrained, and therefore, there is a need for an accessible book that brings the concept of inclusive leadership to life, taking an evidence-based approach to understand in a practical way how to lead inclusively. In developing our framework, the Inclusive Leader System, we conducted an extensive review of the corporate and academic literature and built on our research and experience from working with leaders and organisations. A core guiding principle that has shaped the development of our framework and the content for this book is that theory and research from psychology tells us how complex human behaviour change is. Our attitudes do not always predict our behaviour[11] and the way that we learn new information is in "knowledge chunks": simple components of more complex knowledge.[12] Therefore, the content of this book has been shaped by these principles. Creating a positive attitude to change is not enough: we must understand how to change, and this means breaking down what it means to be an inclusive leader into manageable chunks. This inevitably means that there are elements of inclusive leadership that we have not focused on. Instead, we have reviewed the breadth and depth of inclusive leadership research and practice and highlighted the areas we believe are the most important for leaders to focus their attention and efforts. It is also important to acknowledge our identities as the authors and how this will have shaped and influenced our view of this topic. For example, we are both white and this can mean that we may unintentionally centre the white experience of inclusive leadership. We have sought advice and guidance in authoring the book to minimise this risk, however, we acknowledge that there will be instances where this has still occurred.

Overview of the book structure

The book is split into two parts. Part One contains three chapters where we set the scene for the rest of the book. In Chapter 1, we define what inclusive leadership is, in Chapter 2 we explore why inclusive leadership is important and in Chapter 3 we discuss the concept of psychological safety and how this underpins inclusive leadership.

Part Two presents the exploration of the inclusive leader system and consists of three sections. In Section One we explore leader wellbeing with

Chapters 4 to 8. Section Two explores the drivers of inclusive leadership with Chapters 9 to 14. Finally, Section Three presents inclusive leadership behaviours with Chapters 15 to 21.

Finally, we share our concluding thoughts in Chapter 22.

Notes

1 Tomova, L., Wang, K. L., Thompson, T., Matthews, G. A., Takahashi, A., Tye, K. M., & Saxe, R. (2020). Acute social isolation evokes midbrain craving responses similar to hunger. *Nature Neuroscience, 23*(12), 1597–1605.

2 MacDonald, G., & Leary, M. R. (2005). Why does social exclusion hurt? The relationship between social and physical pain. *Psychological Bulletin, 131*(2), 202.

3 Lieberman, M. D., Rock, D., Halvorson, H. G., & Cox, C. (2015). Breaking bias updated: The seeds model. *Neuroleadership Journal, 6*, 4–18.

4 McKinsey. (2020). *Diversity wins: How inclusion matters.* Accessed from https://www.mckinsey.com/~/media/mckinsey/featured%20insights/diversity%20and%20inclusion/diversity%20wins%20how%20inclusion%20matters/diversity-wins-how-inclusion-matters-vf.pdf. Retrieved 14 September 2024.

5 Bourke, J., Titus, A., & Espedido, A. (2020). The key to inclusive leadership. *Harvard Business Review, 6*, H05GLB.

6 McKinsey. (2020). *Diversity wins: How inclusion matters.* Accessed from https://www.mckinsey.com/~/media/mckinsey/featured%20insights/diversity%20and%20inclusion/diversity%20wins%20how%20inclusion%20matters/diversity-wins-how-inclusion-matters-vf.pdf. Retrieved 14 September 2024.

7 Bourke, J., Titus, A., & Espedido, A. (2020). The key to inclusive leadership. *Harvard Business Review, 6*, H05GLB.

8 Bourke, J., & Dillon, B. (2018). The diversity and inclusion revolution: Eight powerful truths. *Deloitte Review*, Issue 12.

9 Zenger, J., & Folkman, J. (2021). *How 360 processes support diversity, inclusion and belonging.* Accessed from https://zengerfolkman.com/articles/how-360-feedback-processes-support-diversity-inclusion-and-belonging/. Retrieved 14 September 2024.

10 You will notice throughout our text that we capitalise the word "Black" however "white" is not capitalised. We follow other authors who have adopted this practice to acknowledge a shared history, culture, and identity among Black people. It signals that Blackness is more than just a skin colour, it includes collective experiences shaped by slavery, colonisation, and systemic racism. Using lowercase for "white" avoids lending legitimacy to white supremacist movements, which have historically capitalised it to signal racial pride or superiority.

11 Ajzen, I., & Fishbein, M. (2005). The influence of attitudes on behaviour. In D. Albarracin, B. T., Johnson, & M. P. Zanna (Eds.), *The handbook of attitudes* (pp. 173–221). Mahwah, NJ: Lawrence Erlbaum Associates.
12 Anderson, J. R. (1996). ACT: A simple theory of complex cognition. *American Psychologist, 51*, 355–365.

Part One

Foundations of inclusive leadership

In Part One, we lay the foundations for the rest of the book, ensuring that we outline the key principles that will influence the implementation of inclusive leadership in practice. We provide a comprehensive overview of how inclusive leadership is defined, we explore why inclusive leadership is important, and finally we discuss psychological safety as a critical construct to understand in the context of inclusive leadership.

DOI: 10.4324/9781003598022-2

What is inclusive leadership?

1

Leadership is about empowering others, enabling them to perform their jobs to the best of their ability. When we add inclusion into the mix, we recognise that, in enabling our people to do their best work, we must appreciate that each individual is unique. We also recognise the importance of enabling people to feel they belong as part of the team and organisation.

Belonging is often rooted in a shared sense of identity related to culture, values, and experiences, which can create challenges for those from marginalised groups. Furthermore, different people need different things to enable them to feel valued, accepted, and connected. Therefore, belonging alone is problematic: valuing diversity and uniqueness is at the core of true inclusion. Finally, we also recognise the role of an inclusive leader in shaping systems. By understanding the system and how different parts of the system interact, we can explore root causes of prejudice and inequality, and strive to influence and ultimately reform the systems we are part of.

In this book, we will break down what individual leaders need to do to practise inclusive leadership. However, first, in this chapter, we explore what we mean when we say "inclusive leadership". The concept of inclusive leadership has been the focus of both corporate and academic literature. Here we present a brief summary of some of the key themes from the literature before sharing our definition of inclusive leadership that forms the basis for the rest of this book.

DOI: 10.4324/9781003598022-3

Corporate perspective to inclusive leadership

A range of reports showcasing sector-based knowledge has been published by corporate organisations on the topic of inclusive leadership. Much of this literature emphasises the importance of inclusive leadership for retention of diverse talent[1] and in harnessing diversity of thought.[2] A range of models and approaches to inclusive leadership are offered in the corporate literature, however the essence of how inclusive leadership is defined is the assertion that inclusive leaders foster feelings of both belonging and uniqueness in their people. For example, we belong not *despite* our differences, but *because* of them. Catalyst (2014)[3] do a great job of describing the seemingly paradoxical nature of belonging and uniqueness. They state that inclusion means: "Employees feel included when, simultaneously, they perceive they are both similar to and distinct from their coworkers. Perceiving similarities with coworkers engenders a feeling of belongingness while perceiving differences leads to feelings of uniqueness." Inclusive leadership means working with individuals and systems to enable this outcome.

Authenticity, inclusion and respect

Authenticity is a word frequently used in the context of inclusive leadership. If we understand inclusive leadership to include valuing the uniqueness of the individuals in our team, then it follows that those working in an inclusive environment will be able to be their authentic selves at work. However, the concept of authenticity can be somewhat problematic in the context of equity, diversity, and inclusion (EDI). For example, some individuals have weaponised "authenticity" to justify being offensive when expressing their beliefs or disagreement. Equally, many individuals from marginalised groups know that if they bring their authentic selves to work, they will experience a backlash as they are expected to fit in with the majority within their work system.

In any system, it is our responsibility to understand the impact of our words and behaviour on other people. Many of us will have personal beliefs, communication styles, or language that might be offensive to others. For example, someone might hold sexist, racist, ableist, or homophobic beliefs, consequently being their authentic self might mean expressing those sexist, racist, ableist, or homophobic beliefs to others!

This is why, when we consider authenticity, we must consider how we can be authentic while also behaving in a way that is respectful.

A great way of thinking about this is reflecting on the difference between doing things *with* people and *at* people. If we behave in a way which unintentionally upsets someone, then we notice a change in the dynamics and *yet* we continue to behave in the same way, this becomes doing things *at* people. This is the difference between communicating *with* someone versus communicating *at* someone. There is no respect when we are communicating *at* them.

Equally, if someone uses language or behaves in a way that is offensive to us, we need to highlight the issue to this person as they might not be aware of their impact. If they continue, then we know they are now being intentionally offensive. At this point we have to set boundaries for the interaction to continue. If they still fail to adjust, we can disengage or, if the interaction cannot be paused, escalate the concern. Hence, we always recommend teams "contract" up front to set the ground rules for the interaction to avoid unnecessary misunderstanding in relation to communication styles and preferences. Contracting can happen before a meeting starts, when you first meet someone, or even as part of a reset when things are not going well (*see Chapter 15 for more on contracting*).

Therefore when we consider authenticity in the context of inclusion, we must always prioritise care and respect.

Academic perspective to inclusive leadership

While much of the corporate literature originates from the USA, inclusive leadership has been explored academically from a range of locations including Canada,[4] China,[5] Egypt,[6] Holland,[7] India,[8] Iraq,[9] Pakistan,[10] Palestine,[11] Turkey,[12] UK,[13] USA,[14] and Vietnam,[15] thus offering a cross-cultural perspective to inclusive leadership. When we consider the academic perspective to defining inclusive leadership, the majority of research draws on a few key definitions.

Nembhard and Edmondson (2006)[16] define inclusive leadership as "words and deeds by a leader or leaders that indicate an invitation and appreciation for others' contributions". Another frequently cited definition from the academic literature emphasises that inclusive leadership denotes leaders who demonstrate their visibility, accessibility, and availability during interactions with direct reports.[17] These definitions propose that inclusive leaders invite interactions with their direct reports and make themselves open and available to their people. However, a major criticism of these approaches to inclusive leadership is that they approach the concept of inclusion from a dominant group's perspective, with little to no acknowledgement of diversity in the context of inclusion. Without this emphasis on diversity, inclusive leadership only serves to enable dominant groups to feel even more included, especially as feeling included is easy when everyone is similar.

An alternative academic definition is provided by Shore et al. (2011)[18] who emphasise that inclusive leaders create inclusive environments for diverse groups. Similar to the corporate literature, Shore et al. argue that inclusive leaders' efforts are specifically focused on fostering group members' perceptions of both belonging and value for uniqueness. A distinction with this definition is that it incorporates the leaders' pro-diversity beliefs (recognising and appreciating the value of difference) in their definition of inclusive leadership. Therefore, in addition to supporting group members, engaging in shared decision-making and helping group members to fully contribute, Shore et al. suggest that inclusive leaders also ensure justice and equity and encourage diverse contributions.

Psychological safety and inclusion

Psychological safety describes perceptions of the consequences of taking interpersonal risks in a particular context such as a workplace.[19] It is deeply interconnected to inclusion. For example, inclusive leaders must create a psychologically safe environment to enable people from all backgrounds to feel free to hold differing views, make mistakes without being penalised, and feel secure enough to address tough issues or take risks.[20] Psychological safety is also an outcome of inclusive leadership: when you are led by an inclusive leader, you are more likely to experience high levels of psychological safety.[21] However, when we consider psychological safety and diversity, psychological safety is more problematic for marginalised employees due to systemic biases and the formation of outgroups. *Psychological safety and inclusion are explored in greater detail in Chapter 3.*

Inclusive leadership versus traditional theories of leadership

Our understanding of what it means to be an effective leader is deeply influenced by historical leadership theories, which have shaped widely held stereotypes that define what we implicitly believe leaders should "look like". The earliest theories of leadership focused on personality traits that predicted leadership effectiveness. The premise here is that leaders who held certain personality traits such as intelligence, task-relevant knowledge, assertiveness, and need for power[22] were more effective leaders. Yet, these historical theories of leadership were based on workplaces that look very different to the workplace of today.

If we think back to when these trait theories of leadership in management studies were initially developed, well over 100 years ago, the focus at that time was on individual productivity and efficiency, often in more manual occupations. The "rules" for productive and efficient work rarely took into account the need to work more cognitively, the needs of employees who differed from the prototypical worker (i.e., white, male, heterosexual, non-disabled), or the collective needs for organisations to work responsibly, innovatively, and with a focus on sustainable growth (rather than growth at all costs).

Understanding this historical context can help us to appreciate why sometimes it can be hard to be valued as an inclusive leader. However, it is our collective responsibility to challenge these outdated assumptions about effective leaders and create a new prototype for leadership that embodies more contemporary traits and embraces inclusion.

Inclusive leadership, diversity and uniqueness

You may ask yourself, what is so difficult about being yourself at work? If you find this question occurring to you as you read this, it is likely that you have benefitted from the privilege of being a member of the dominant group within your organisation. The reality is that this experience of being yourself is not as easy for everyone, with 66 per cent of employees reporting feeling pressure to mute some aspect of their identities at work, consequently significantly undermining their sense of self.[23] Although we position diversity and uniqueness as separate constructs (diversity being based on aspects of identity such as race and uniqueness on the individual's distinct perspectives, experiences, and ideas, beyond just identity), both are equally compromised when the environment is not inclusive.

In addition, while there is a strong business case for increasing diversity within the workforce (*more on this in Chapter 2*), research indicates that it is not a simple case of adding diversity to the mix of a team and expecting people to automatically collaborate, connect, or innovate as a cohesive unit.[24] Without inclusion, diverse teams have a high chance of becoming chaotic, leading to lower productivity and engagement, higher turnover, and litigation.[25] When organisations embrace diversity without also pursuing inclusion, they can end up with workers who never quite feel accepted, valued, and supported – and who thus rapidly exit the organisation[26]. Therefore, diversity without inclusion is an incubator for prejudice. Consequently, inclusive leadership is crucial to support these groups who are at a greater risk of exclusion.

This is why simply increasing diversity will not make a difference unless people also feel included. It is, after all, much easier to manage a group of people with similar backgrounds and experiences than it is to convince teams made up of diverse individuals to understand their varying thought patterns and behaviours and value them at a deep and personal level.[27] For example, data from McKinsey and Company (2020)[28] illustrates the challenge that even organisations with higher levels of diversity face in tackling inclusion. They found that while the overall sentiment from employees they surveyed was 52 per cent positive and 31 per cent negative in relation to diversity, sentiment on inclusion was markedly worse at only 29 per cent positive and 61 per cent negative. Consequently, hiring diverse talent is not enough, it is the experience individuals have in the workplace that shapes whether they remain and thrive.

Our definition of inclusive leadership

Throughout the rest of this text, we adopt the broad definition that inclusive leadership describes leaders' practice of enabling others to experience belonging and that they value their people for both their diversity and uniqueness. Inclusive leaders have strong pro-diversity beliefs. This goes beyond a focus on "diversity of thinking" and uniqueness alone, with inclusive leaders actively prioritising diversity of groups (including but not limited to disability, sex, gender reassignment, race, sexual orientation, neurodiversity, age, marriage and civil partnership, pregnancy, and maternity). Inclusive leaders are proactive in creating inclusive systems, dismantling deeply embedded prejudice and discrimination that perpetuates the uneven playing field for these groups.

In this book, we bring this concept to life, elaborating on the characteristics of leaders who practise inclusive leadership and breaking down the actions inclusive leaders take to enable their people to experience belonging and being valued for their diversity and uniqueness.

Chapter 1 in summary

- An extensive body of corporate literature, predominantly from the US, defines inclusive leadership as a practice that enables the experience of belonging while being valued for diversity and uniqueness.

- Inclusive leadership has been researched across multiple cultural contexts and the academic literature generally defines it in a similar way to the corporate literature, namely with the emphasis on enabling belonging across diverse groups and being uniquely valued.
- While there are clear benefits to diversity for individuals and organisations, these only exist when inclusion is present, hence the criticality of considering diversity and inclusion.
- We define inclusive leadership as a practice of enabling a sense of belonging across diverse groups while valuing what makes individuals unique. Inclusive leaders proactively work to disrupt systemic biases and prejudice that hinder inclusion for diverse marginalised groups.

Notes

1 Catalyst. (2020). *Getting real about inclusive leadership: Why change starts with you.* Accessed from https://www.catalyst.org/wp-content/uploads/2020/03/Getting-Real-About-Inclusive-Leadership-Report-2020update.pdf. Retrieved 13 September 2024.

2 Deloitte. (2016). *The six signature traits of inclusive leadership.* Accessed from https://www2.deloitte.com/us/en/insights/topics/talent/six-signature-traits-of-inclusive-leadership.html. Retrieved 13 September 2024.

3 Catalyst. (2014). *Inclusive leadership: The view from six countries.* Accessed from https://www.catalyst.org/research/inclusive-leadership-the-view-from-six-countries/. Retrieved 13 September 2024.

4 Javed, B., Abdullah, I., Zaffar, M. A., ul Haque, A., & Rubab, U. (2019). Inclusive leadership and innovative work behavior: The role of psychological empowerment. *Journal of Management & Organization, 25*(4), 554–571.

5 Ahmed, F., Zhao, F., Faraz, N. A., & Qin, Y. J. (2021). How inclusive leadership paves way for psychological well-being of employees during trauma and crisis: A three-wave longitudinal mediation study. *Journal of Advanced Nursing, 77*(2), 819–831.

6 Elsaied, M. M. (2020). A moderated mediation model for the relationship between inclusive leadership and job embeddedness. *American Journal of Business, 35*(3/4), 191–210.

7 Ashikali, T., Groeneveld, S., & Kuipers, B. (2021). The role of inclusive leadership in supporting an inclusive climate in diverse public sector teams. *Review of Public Personnel Administration, 41*(3), 497–519.

8 Panicker, A., Agrawal, R. K., & Khandelwal, U. (2018). Inclusive workplace and organizational citizenship behavior: Study of a higher education institution, India. *Equality, Diversity and Inclusion: An International Journal, 37*(6), 530–550.

9 Bannay, D. F., Hadi, M. J., & Amanah, A. A. (2020). The impact of inclusive leadership behaviors on innovative workplace behavior with an emphasis on the mediating role of work engagement. *Problems and Perspectives in Management, 18*(3), 479.

10 Fatima, T., Majeed, M., & Zulfiqar Ali Shah, S. (2021). A moderating mediation model of the antecedents of being driven to work: The role of inclusive leaders as change agents. *Canadian Journal of Administrative Sciences/Revue Canadienne des Sciences de l'Administration, 38*(3), 257–271.

11 Aboramadan, M., Dahleez, K. A., & Farao, C. (2022). Inclusive leadership and extra-role behaviors in higher education: Does organizational learning mediate the relationship? *International Journal of Educational Management, 36*(4), 397–418.

12 Cenkci, A. T., Bircan, T., & Zimmerman, J. (2021). Inclusive leadership and work engagement: The mediating role of procedural justice. *Management Research Review, 44*(1), 158–180.

13 Javed, B., Abdullah, I., Zaffar, M. A., ul Haque, A., & Rubab, U. (2019). Inclusive leadership and innovative work behavior: The role of psychological empowerment. *Journal of Management & Organization, 25*(4), 554–571.

14 Hassan, S., & Jiang, Z. (2021). Facilitating learning to improve performance of law enforcement workgroups: The role of inclusive leadership behavior. *International Public Management Journal, 24*(1), 106–130.

15 Choi, S. B., Tran, T. B. H., & Kang, S. W. (2017). Inclusive leadership and employee well-being: The mediating role of person-job fit. *Journal of Happiness Studies, 18*, 1877–1901.

16 Nembhard, I. M., & Edmondson, A. C. (2006). Making it safe: The effects of leader inclusiveness and professional status on psychological safety and improvement efforts in health care teams. *Journal of Organizational Behavior, 27*(7), 941–966.

17 Carmeli, A., Reiter-Palmon, R., & Ziv, E. (2010). Inclusive leadership and employee involvement in creative tasks in the workplace: The mediating role of psychological safety. *Creativity Research Journal, 22*(3), 250–260.

18 Shore, L. M., Randel, A. E., Chung, B. G., Dean, M. A., Ehrhart, K.H., & Singh, G. (2011). Inclusion and diversity in work groups: A review and model for future research. *Journal of Management, 37*, 1262–1289.

19 Edmondson, A. (1999). Psychological safety and learning behavior in work teams. *Administrative Science Quarterly, 44*(2), 350–383.

20 Catalyst (2020). *Getting real about inclusive leadership: Why change starts with you.* Accessed from https://www.catalyst.org/wp-content/uploads/2020/03/Getting-Real-About-Inclusive-Leadership-Report-2020update.pdf. Retrieved 13 September 2024.

21 Carmeli, A., Reiter-Palmon, R., & Ziv, E. (2010). Inclusive leadership and employee involvement in creative tasks in the workplace: The mediating role of psychological safety. *Creativity Research Journal, 22*(3), 250–260.

22 Woods, S. A., & West, M. A. (2019). *The psychology of work and organizations.* Andover, UK: Cengage Learning EMEA.

23 Yoshino, K., & Smith, C. (2014). Fear of being different stifles talent. *Harvard Business Review, 92*(3), 27–28.

24 Catalyst. (2020). *Getting real about inclusive leadership: Why change starts with you.* Accessed from https://www.catalyst.org/wp-content/uploads/2020/03/Getting-Real-About-Inclusive-Leadership-Report-2020update.pdf. Retrieved 13 September 2024.

25 Korn Ferry. (n.d.). The five disciplines of inclusive leaders: Unleashing the power of all of us. Accessed from https://www.kornferry.com/insights/featured-topics/diversity-equity-inclusion/5-disciplines-of-inclusive-leaders. Retrieved 13 September 2024.

26 NeuroLeadership Institute. (2019). *NLI perspectives: Cultures of inclusion.* Accessed from https://hub.neuroleadership.com/nli-perspectives-cultures-of-inclusion. Retrieved 13 September 2024.

27 Korn Ferry. (n.d.). The five disciplines of inclusive leaders: unleashing the power of all of us. Accessed from https://www.kornferry.com/insights/featured-topics/diversity-equity-inclusion/5-disciplines-of-inclusive-leaders. Retrieved 13 September 2024.

28 McKinsey. (2018). *Delivering through diversity.* Accessed from https://www.mckinsey.com/capabilities/people-and-organizational-performance/our-insights/delivering-through-diversity. Retrieved 13 September 2024.

Why is inclusive leadership **2** important?

The moral case for EDI is undeniable. It is a call to action grounded in our evolutionary history, the hard-fought gains of civil rights movements and decolonisation, and the pressing need for social and environmental justice. This evolution is also marked by more recent social movements (such as Black Lives Matter in 2020 and #MeToo in 2017) that have led to growing expectations for organisations to demonstrate their commitment to social and corporate governance.

Despite this, the fact remains that we do not live in a fair and equal world. For example, women account for 42 per cent of the global workforce[1] yet hold just 28 per cent of management positions.[2] Global data from the United Nations (2024)[3] shows that one person in six continues to encounter discrimination, with racial discrimination and discrimination based on age, gender, religion, or belief remaining pervasive. Data on the ethnicity pay gap in the UK indicates that white people earn more on average than people from almost all of the other ethnic groups[4] with data from the US indicating that in 2022 Black women earned just 70 per cent and Hispanic women 65 per cent as much as white men[5]. Unfortunately, systemic discrimination continues to be prevalent in all aspects of our society. (*We will unpack many of the important concepts that we must understand in relation to systemic discrimination in Chapter 17.*)

Although progress has been made in legislative responses and employment practices and governance, the landscape has unfortunately regressed significantly since COVID-19. Crises tend to exacerbate existing inequalities, and disproportionately affect marginalised groups and COVID 19 was no different.[6] Compounding the effects of the pandemic, an anti-EDI movement fuelled by political rhetoric, particularly in the United States, has gained traction. Political campaigns have increasingly targeted LGBTQ+

DOI: 10.4324/9781003598022-4

(lesbian, gay, bisexual, transgender, queer or questioning, and others (including intersex, asexual, non-binary, pansexual, and other identities that fall outside heterosexual and cisgender norms)) communities and the case for positive action, further undermining efforts towards equity and inclusion (*more on positive action in Chapter 14*). Therefore, now more than ever, there is a need to address EDI because it is the right thing to do to create a fair and just world where everybody can thrive.

In addition to this moral case for EDI, the business case for EDI remains strong and is frequently cited as a reason why organisations should stick with efforts and utilise resources to support the EDI agenda: that is that EDI is "good for business". For example, leaders believe that inclusive leadership empowers team members to take risks and bring their authentic selves to work while also helping organisations to innovate and capitalise on new business opportunities.[7] In addition, organisations leveraging diversity through inclusion can reap the many benefits of a diverse workforce. This includes by tapping into marginalised employees' identity-related knowledge and experiences as resources for learning how the organisation could perform better.[8]

Business case versus the moral case for inclusion

In the section above, we outline arguments for both the business case for inclusion (i.e., that diversity and inclusion is good for business) and the moral case (i.e., that increasing diversity and fostering inclusion in the workplace is the right thing to do). Georgeac and Rattan (2023)[9] explored the effect the adoption of these different approaches to arguing for EDI has on marginalised groups. In Study 1, they found that the business case was far more prevalent than the moral case among the Fortune 500. They then tested their prediction that the business case undermines marginalised groups' anticipated sense of belonging to, and subsequent interest in joining organisations, by randomly assigning participants from different identity groups to read an organisation's business case, moral case, or presented no case (a control group). They found that participants anticipated lower belonging and, in turn, less attraction to organisations using a business case versus moral case or control for LGBTQ+ professionals, female science, technology, engineering, and mathematics (STEM) jobseekers, and African American students. Their findings suggest that despite the assumed positivity of the business case for EDI, which is the most prevalent case employed by organisations, it paradoxically undermines belonging across LGBTQ+ individuals, STEM women, and African Americans, thus hindering organisations' EDI goals.

Similar research has been conducted in the context of higher education in the US in relation to efforts to expand and support racial diversity in majority-white educational institutions.[10] Similar to the business versus moral case described above, the integration of public schools and affirmative action was originally justified by moral rationales (i.e., aligned with intrinsic values and principles) versus the instrumental rationale (i.e., that diversity is an asset that facilitates organisations' ability to accomplish their routine objectives). However, scholars have criticised this instrumental rationale (or business case), as when EDI efforts are aligned with broader organisational or societal interests, these broader interests are by definition representative of the racial majority group (i.e., white American). Consequently, it is argued, these rationales tacitly prioritise the benefits of EDI for the majority group over the interests of racial minorities themselves. Research[11] found that instrumental rationales (business cases) are preferred by white but not Black Americans, that this rationale is understood as suiting white students best, and that the instrumental rationale was the most common approach to diversity in higher education. Critically, the research also evaluated the extent to which the instrumental and moral language on universities' websites were associated with graduation rates of Black and white students. Results showed that neither rationale was associated with the graduation rates of white students. However, for Black students' graduation rates, results indicated that when the universities' use of moral rationales was low, their degree of instrumental rationale use was negatively related to Black students' graduation rates but was unrelated otherwise. These data indicate that the disparities between white and Black students' graduation rates increase when universities are more instrumentally motivated, especially when they have little moral motivation as well.

Overall, studies such as these highlight the complexities that must be considered in relation to the narratives around why EDI is important. The business case tends to be prioritised so investments in EDI are commercially justifiable. However, organisations must find an approach that is broadly appealing, and yet not at the expense of marginalised individuals. Otherwise, while they might secure EDI investment, they might then be unattractive to marginalised talent, which is counterproductive. Based on the research detailed above, the importance of always highlighting the moral imperative for driving EDI is clear.

Outcomes of inclusion

While recent research, as highlighted above, has demonstrated the differing impact of the moral versus business case used by organisations to promote EDI, the academic literature has been concerned with identifying the relationship between inclusive leadership and important outcomes for individuals, teams, and organisations. As with the substantial body of leadership literature that preceded the development of inclusive leadership, scholars have long been concerned with identifying the most "effective" approach to leadership. Therefore, in this next section we briefly summarise the evidence, which clearly shows a vast range of outcomes of inclusive leadership.

Improved wellbeing

Research indicates that inclusive leadership leads to enhanced wellbeing,[12] decreased psychological distress,[13] decreased work-family conflict, and improved work-family enrichment.[14] Inclusive leadership impacts outcomes linked to wellbeing as inclusive leaders minimise the impact of negative group behaviours. These negative group behaviours can include ingroup favouritism, belittling outgroup members, and tribalism (a "them versus us" mentality).[15] The desire to belong to a group and to identify with and be connected with others is a fundamental human need, [16], a need that is so strong that people who do not feel socially connected (and therefore experience loneliness) have a 50 per cent increased risk of mortality.[17] Therefore, experiencing a sense of belonging will improve our wellbeing by satisfying a basic human need to connect with others.

Improved innovation

Employees working for inclusive leaders demonstrate improved innovation[18] and team creativity[19], as inclusive leaders create the conditions for individuals to feel safe. Therefore, those individuals are free to experiment and create, confident in the knowledge that they have a secure base in the team that they can return to[20], free from repercussion should their experimentations not work out as planned.[21]

Improved engagement

Evidence shows that inclusive leadership leads to improved work engagement,[22] enthusiasm,[23] and drive to work,[24] and to increased psychological empowerment.[25] When we feel a sense of empowerment in relation to our work, we are more likely to feel engaged and consequently perform better. Inclusive leaders enhance employees' psychological empowerment by listening to their opinions and providing them with opportunities to influence decision-making.

Improved decision-making

Individuals led by inclusive leaders experience enhanced decision-making[26] and improved cognitive function.[27] The link between improved decision-making and diversity is relatively straightforward: working with people different from you challenges you to overcome old ways of thinking, highlighting alternative perspectives that a wider range of knowledge and experience brings[28]. However, the importance of inclusion (in addition to diversity) in decision-making is highlighted by research on the impact of social exclusion on cognitive processes.[29] In a series of experiments, participants who were led to believe that they would end up alone in life (therefore were socially excluded) experienced a decline in cognitive performance in tasks linked to decision-making. These effects were specific to social exclusion, as the same effects were not observed for participants who received predictions of physical accidents or injuries. Social exclusion is experienced as a threatening, aversive event and as people strive to suppress their emotional distress, it impairs their performance in decision-making tasks. Considered together, these findings are clear that diversity with inclusive leadership offers improved decision-making.

Improved learning

Inclusive leadership leads to increased engagement in learning,[30] team learning,[31] knowledge sharing and learning from errors,[32] improved employee readiness for organisational change,[33] and career adaptability.[34] Learning is an inherently risky behaviour as it involves abandoning our old, established ways of working and experimenting with new, unfamiliar strategies. As these new ways of working are practised and developed, there will inevitably be mistakes along the way and even a temporary dip in performance before the learning is embedded. Inclusive leaders create the conditions for individuals to feel safe and therefore free to experiment with new skills, secure in the knowledge that the learning journey will be supported by their leader and other team members.

Improved performance

Organisations with inclusive leaders benefit from improved organisation[35] and task performance,[36] the ability to adapt performance to changing work conditions,[37] improved project success,[38] and increased organisational citizenship behaviour.[39]

Chapter 2 in summary

- The moral case demonstrates how prioritising EDI is the right thing to do from a fairness and justice perspective.
- Compounding the effects of the pandemic, an anti-EDI movement fuelled by political rhetoric, particularly in the US has gained traction and regressed EDI efforts.
- The business case remains strong and demonstrates clear commercial benefits for organisations to prioritise EDI.
- However, research demonstrates the differing effects the business and moral cases for EDI have on marginalised groups, with evidence indicating the importance of maintaining a focus on the moral case for EDI.
- The academic literature has explored the relationship between inclusive leadership and a variety of outcomes for individuals, teams, and organisations, including wellbeing, innovation, engagement, decision-making, learning, and performance.

Notes

1 World Economic Forum. (2023). *Global Gender Gap Report 2023*. Accessed from https://www.weforum.org/publications/global-gender-gap-report-2023/. Retrieved 24 September 2024.
2 United Nations. (2023). *The gender snapshot 2023*. Accessed from https://unstats.un.org/sdgs/gender-snapshot/2023/. Retrieved 24 September 2023.
3 United Nations. (2024). *Sustainable goals progress report*. Accessed from https://unstats.un.org/sdgs/files/report/2024/secretary-general-sdg-report-2024--EN.pdf. Retrieved 24 September 2024.
4 PwC. (2021). *Ethnicity pay gap report 2021*. Accessed from https://www.strategyand.pwc.com/uk/en/reports/ethnicity-pay-gap-report.pdf. Retrieved 24 September 2024.
5 Kochhar, R. (2023). *The enduring grip of the gender pay gap*. Accessed from https://www.pewresearch.org/social-trends/2023/03/01/the-enduring-

grip-of-the-gender-pay-gap/#:~:text=Gender%20pay%20gap%20differs%20widely%20by%20race%20and%20ethnicity,-Looking%20across%20racial&text=In%202022%2C%20Black%20women%20earned,%2C%20making%2093%25%20as%20much. Retrieved 24 September 2024.

6 Platt, L. (2021). COVID-19 and ethnic inequalities in England. *LSE Public Policy Review, 1*(4).

7 Korn Ferry. (n.d.). *The five disciplines of inclusive leaders: unleashing the power of all of us.* Accessed from https://www.kornferry.com/insights/featured-topics/diversity-equity-inclusion/5-disciplines-of-inclusive-leaders. Retrieved 13 September 2024.

8 Ely, R. J., & Thomas, D. A. (2020). Getting serious about diversity. *Harvard Business Review, 98*(6), 114–122.

9 Georgeac, O. A., & Rattan, A. (2023). The business case for diversity backfires: Detrimental effects of organizations' instrumental diversity rhetoric for underrepresented group members' sense of belonging. *Journal of Personality and Social Psychology, 124*(1), 69.

10 Starck, J. G., Sinclair, S., & Shelton, J. N. (2021). How university diversity rationales inform student preferences and outcomes. *Proceedings of the National Academy of Sciences, 118*(16), e2013833118.

11 Starck, J. G., Sinclair, S., & Shelton, J. N. (2021). How university diversity rationales inform student preferences and outcomes. *Proceedings of the National Academy of Sciences, 118*(16), e2013833118.

12 Lee, H. I., & Lu, H. (2020). Promoting knowledge sharing with effective leadership – A case study from socio-organisational perspective. *Knowledge Management Research & Practice,* 1–14.

13 Ahmed, F., Zhao, F., Faraz, N. A., & Qin, Y. J. (2021). How inclusive leadership paves way for psychological well-being of employees during trauma and crisis: A three-wave longitudinal mediation study. *Journal of Advanced Nursing, 77*(2), 819–831.

14 Luu, T. T. (2021). A tale of two countries: How do employees with disabilities respond to disability inclusive HR practices in tourism and hospitality industry? *Journal of Sustainable Tourism,* 1–31.

15 Eppich, W. J., & Schmutz, J. B. (2019). From "them" to "us": Bridging group boundaries through team inclusiveness. *Medical Education, 53*(8), 756–758.

16 Thornton, C (2016). *Group and team coaching: The secret life of groups.* New York: Routledge.

17 Holt-Lunstad, J., Smith, T. B., & Layton, J. B. (2010). Social relationships and mortality risk: A meta-analytic review. *PLoS Medicine,* 7.

18 Aboramadan, M., Dahleez, K. A., & Farao, C. (2022). Inclusive leadership and extra-role behaviors in higher education: Does organizational learning mediate the relationship? *International Journal of Educational Management, 36*(4), 397-418;

Mansoor, A., Farrukh, M., Wu, Y., & Abdul Wahab, S. (2021). Does inclusive leadership incite innovative work behavior? *Human Systems Management, 40*(1), 93–102.

19 Leroy, H., Buengeler, C., Veestraeten, M., Shemla, M., & Hoever, I. J. (2022). Fostering team creativity through team-focused inclusion: The role of leader harvesting the benefits of diversity and cultivating value-in-diversity beliefs. *Group & Organization Management, 47*(4), 798–839; Siyal, S., Xin, C., Umrani, W. A., Fatima, S., & Pal, D. (2021). How do leaders influence innovation and creativity in employees? The mediating role of intrinsic motivation. *Administration & Society, 53*(9), 1337–1361.

20 Moore, J. R., Maxey, E. C., Waite, A. M., & Wendover, J. D. (2020). Inclusive organizations: Developmental reciprocity through authentic leader-employee relationships. *Journal of Management Development, 39*(9/10), 1029–1039.

21 Edmondson, A. (1999). Psychological safety and learning behavior in work teams. *Administrative Science Quarterly, 44*(2), 350–383.

22 Bannay, D. F., Hadi, M. J., & Amanah, A. A. (2020). The impact of inclusive leadership behaviors on innovative workplace behavior with an emphasis on the mediating role of work engagement. *Problems and Perspectives in Management, 18*(3), 479; Du, J., Ma, E., & Lin, X. (2021). When diversity leads to divided teams: A multi-level moderated mediation model of team faultlines and employee engagement. *International Journal of Hospitality Management, 94*, 102818.

23 Qurrahtulain, K., Bashir, T., Hussain, I., Ahmed, S., & Nisar, A. (2022). Impact of inclusive leadership on adaptive performance with the mediation of vigor at work and moderation of internal locus of control. *Journal of Public Affairs, 22*(1), e2380.

24 Fatima, T., Majeed, M., & Zulfiqar Ali Shah, S. (2021). A moderating mediation model of the antecedents of being driven to work: The role of inclusive leaders as change agents. *Canadian Journal of Administrative Sciences/Revue Canadienne des Sciences de l'Administration, 38*(3), 257–271.

25 Khan, J., Jaafar, M., Javed, B., Mubarak, N., & Saudagar, T. (2020). Does inclusive leadership affect project success? The mediating role of perceived psychological empowerment and psychological safety. *International Journal of Managing Projects in Business, 13*(5), 1077–1096.

26 Wegge, J., Roth, C., Neubach, B., Schmidt, K. H., & Kanfer, R. (2008). Age and gender diversity as determinants of performance and health in a public organization: The role of task complexity and group size. *Journal of Applied Psychology, 93*(6), 1301.

27 Baumeister, R. F., Twenge, J. M., & Nuss, C. K. (2002). Effects of social exclusion on cognitive processes: Anticipated aloneness reduces intelligent thought. *Journal of Personality and Social Psychology, 83*(4), 817.

28 Rock, D., & Grant, H. (2016). Why diverse teams are smarter. *Harvard Business Review, 4*(4), 2–5.

29 Baumeister, R. F., Twenge, J. M., & Nuss, C. K. (2002). Effects of social exclusion on cognitive processes: Anticipated aloneness reduces intelligent thought. *Journal of Personality and Social Psychology, 83*(4), 817.

30 Hassan, S., & Jiang, Z. (2021). Facilitating learning to improve performance of law enforcement workgroups: The role of inclusive leadership behavior. *International Public Management Journal, 24*(1), 106–130.

31 Meeuwissen, S. N., Gijselaers, W. H., van Oorschot, T. D., Wolfhagen, I. H., & Oude Egbrink, M. G. (2021). enhancing team learning through leader inclusiveness: A one-year ethnographic case study of an interdisciplinary teacher team. *Teaching and Learning in Medicine*, 1–11.

32 Ye, Q., Wang, D., & Li, X. (2018). Promoting employees' learning from errors by inclusive leadership: Do positive mood and gender matter? *Baltic Journal of Management, 13*(1), 125–142.

33 Fatima, T., Majeed, M., & Zulfiqar Ali Shah, S. (2021). A moderating mediation model of the antecedents of being driven to work: The role of inclusive leaders as change agents. *Canadian Journal of Administrative Sciences/Revue Canadienne des Sciences de l'Administration, 38*(3), 257–271.

34 Shabeer, S., Nasir, N., & Rehman, S. (2020). Inclusive leadership and career adaptability: The mediating role of organization-based self-esteem and the moderating role of organizational justice. *International Journal of Leadership in Education*, 1–20.

35 Gong, L., Liu, Z., Rong, Y., & Fu, L. (2021). Inclusive leadership, ambidextrous innovation and organizational performance: The moderating role of environment uncertainty. *Leadership & Organization Development Journal, 42*(5), 783–801.

36 Xiaotao, Z., Yang, X., Diaz, I., & Yu, M. (2018). Is too much inclusive leadership a good thing? An examination of curvilinear relationship between inclusive leadership and employees' task performance. *International Journal of Manpower, 39*(7), 882–895.

37 Qurrahtulain, K., Bashir, T., Hussain, I., Ahmed, S., & Nisar, A. (2022). Impact of inclusive leadership on adaptive performance with the mediation of vigor at work and moderation of internal locus of control. *Journal of Public Affairs, 22*(1), e2380.

38 Khan, J., Jaafar, M., Javed, B., Mubarak, N., & Saudagar, T. (2020). Does inclusive leadership affect project success? The mediating role of perceived psychological empowerment and psychological safety. *International Journal of Managing Projects in Business, 13*(5), 1077–1096.

39 Aboramadan, M., Dahleez, K. A., & Farao, C. (2022). Inclusive leadership and extra-role behaviors in higher education: Does organizational learning mediate the relationship? *International Journal of Educational Management, 36*(4), 397–418.

Psychological safety and inclusion　　**3**

Psychological safety is a core construct in the context of inclusion. It can be considered an outcome of inclusion (i.e., when we are included, we feel psychologically safe) and also a predictor of inclusion (we are more likely to feel included when we are psychologically safe). Psychological safety describes perceptions of the consequences of taking interpersonal risks in a particular context such as a workplace[1] and consists of two components:

1. *Relational component.* Team members experience mutual trust and support reflecting the shared belief that team members respect and support each other's divergent needs, interests, and vulnerabilities.[2]
2. *Voice-raising component.* Team members believe that it is safe to speak up openly and challenge others without being negatively judged or socially distanced.[3]

These two aspects are intertwined and operate together to form a team's psychological safety. Only when members mutually trust and support each other will they all openly speak up without fearing adverse interpersonal consequences.[4]

Therefore, when we think about what it feels like to work in a psychologically safe environment, we can think of four aspects that characterise this experience:

1. We are able to make mistakes and take calculated risks, learning from these without penalties.
2. We can talk about difficult things, giving and receiving constructive feedback, speaking up when we do not agree.

DOI: 10.4324/9781003598022-5

3. We experience acceptance of our differences and uniqueness, including when we hold different social identities to the majority in the group. We are understood, integrated into the ingroup, and safe from prejudice and stereotypes.
4. We are able to ask for help, to support each other, and to trust and be trusted.

Limitation of the psychological safety literature

A key limitation of the psychological safety literature is that it mostly has been conducted from a dominant group's perspective. This means that the perspective of marginalised groups has not been explicitly considered and explored. Rather, it has been assumed that psychological safety looks and feels the same for everyone. Yet we know that everyone does not have the same experience at work – if this was the case, we would not need laws in place to address prejudice and discrimination!

Unfortunately, many marginalised groups are often judged unfairly based on stereotypes and bias, which can influence how we view behaviours that relate to psychological safety. For example, Black women are often subjected to the negative stereotype of being perceived as "aggressive" when they speak up, compared to white women, who might be seen as "passionate". Therefore, even when marginalised groups do feel safe and speak up, they may then be penalised for engaging in the exact behaviours that are valued in a psychologically safe environment.

In addition to challenges around how we view a person when they speak up, another premise of psychological safety is that it allows individuals to believe that they can bring their "true selves" to work,[5] without fear of being judged as inferior or incompetent. However, being your "true self" might mean very different things for different identities. For example, in the case of LGBTQ+ individuals, the experience of psychological safety could encompass being able to publicly express themselves with regard to their sexual orientation and/or gender identity.[6] This expression of identity would inevitably be more challenging for individuals working in heteronormative spaces compared to heterosexual individuals working in those spaces, whose expression of identity would likely conform more closely to the identities of others around them.

Therefore, if we do not take into account the differing experiences of marginalised groups in the context of psychological safety, we are at risk of applying principles that overlook how power dynamics, stereotypes, and stereotype threats influence behaviour, such as bringing one's true self to work and speaking up. Meaning that what feels safe or possible for one person may not for another. These nuances must be considered to ensure psychological safety is truly inclusive.

We propose that when we consider how leaders create a psychologically safe environment, it is important to focus on four critical skills that we believe to be fundamental in enabling psychological safety: emotional agility, social intelligence, feedback, and growth mindset. We provide an overview of each of these skills in the context of psychological safety next.

Emotional agility

When we feel triggered for any reason, particularly when we are stressed or when tired, we tend to struggle to self-regulate. This is often when the worst version of ourselves might show up, consequently disrupting relationships and trust and hindering psychological safety for everyone. For example, when someone presents an opposing view in a meeting, we might shut them down, rather than hearing them out. Inclusive leaders strive to avoid reacting in haste or suppressing their emotions. Instead, they are able to recognise their emotions, pause and stay with the discomfort before responding. In Chapter 21, we discuss emotional agility in more detail, emphasising that emotional agility involves embracing and being flexible with emotions, rather than, for example, suppressing or fixating on a perceived threat.

Creating this safe space for each other, where we can pause and stay with our emotions before responding, is an important habit to develop so that we avoid situations where the recipient of a triggered behaviour might feel psychologically unsafe and therefore react negatively – creating a vicious circle. The key here is not necessarily to expect that the trigger will not occur, instead it is to learn how to practise acceptance and regulate ourselves when we are triggered. Acceptance in this context is the willingness to experience thoughts, feelings, and physiological sensations, without allowing them to drive our actions or trying to control them.[7]

A practical way of implementing this is, for example, when we receive an email with feedback that we feel defensive about, we leave some time and space to reflect on our triggered emotions before we respond. Similarly, in a conversation, if we receive negative feedback, rather than react immediately, we can briefly pause and take a breath, and respond with a question, maybe something like: "Can you share a little more about what led you to that conclusion?"

Social intelligence

As you will notice throughout this book, a key principle of inclusive leadership is recognising that different people need different things: we are all unique, therefore a "one size fits all" approach does not work! Therefore it is critical to be able to read and manage social interactions as well as individual behaviours to establish if a person or group are feeling psychologically safe. For example, a person who is shy might need a different treatment to feel safe to speak up compared to someone who is outspoken. The same outcome (speaking up) is achieved, but different treatment is needed to get there. Developing our social intelligence can support us in creating psychological safety by enabling us to tune into the different treatment that different people need.

Throughout every aspect of our lives we interact with different social groups, for example people of different ages or cultural identities. Being able to acknowledge and understand people's different backgrounds is a key way to connect with them. Social intelligence includes social awareness (which describes our ability to listen actively and experience empathy) (*more on empathy in Chapter 12*) and how effective we are when actually interacting with others (i.e., our ability to influence and show that we care).

Social awareness is sensing another's inner state, feelings, and thoughts, and being able to perceive complicated social situations, including the ability to sense another person's feelings, through non-verbal signals or body language, which is referred to as primal empathy.[8] Body language can be very powerful in driving or hindering psychological safety. Of course, body language will vary across cultures, and this also needs to be taken into consideration. Leaders need to tune into what the other person is saying physically and not just verbally, as in many cases when people do not feel psychologically safe they will not voice their concerns. This is especially important because, to experience the positive impact of psychological safety on outcomes such as innovation, we must create an environment where there is high intellectual friction (to encourage creative abrasion and constructive dissent) but low social friction.[9] Equally, it is important to recognise that individuals may have varying abilities of social intelligence and differing ways of interpreting social cues. Therefore, it is important to create clear guidelines for communication, offer regular feedback, and provide tailored support. Some neurodivergent individuals, for example, may benefit from additional support or structured strategies to help navigate social dynamics, as they may experience social cues differently.

A practical way to practise your social intelligence is to spend time observing other people's body language in meetings and reflect on what they might be thinking and feeling. In addition, you can tune into body language and integrate the non-verbal intelligence into the verbal discussion. For example, "I can sense you hesitated when I said ABC, is that a fair reading?"

Feedback skills

At its core, giving feedback is about speaking up. Giving negative feedback means talking about difficult things and therefore it is deeply connected to psychological safety. The radical candour framework[10] is one that can help us to understand how to give constructive feedback. This framework focusses on our behaviour when we are giving feedback and proposes that when we give feedback, for it to be most impactful we must care personally and we must challenge directly. The framework distinguishes four types of feedback behaviour:

- Radical candour that is kind and helpful is far-reaching, thorough and truthful; it is when we care personally and challenge directly.
- Obnoxious aggression happens when we challenge directly, but do not care personally. Obnoxious aggression can also be called brutal honesty. It is criticism or feedback that is not delivered kindly.
- Ruinous empathy is what happens when you want to spare someone's short-term feelings, so we do not tell them something they need to know. It is when we care personally, but fail to challenge directly. It is praise that is not specific enough to help the person understand what was good, or criticism that is sugar-coated and unclear, or simply silence. Ruinous empathy may feel nice or safe, but it is ultimately unhelpful and even damaging.
- Manipulative insincerity looks like backstabbing, political, or passive-aggressive behaviour. This is when we neither care personally nor challenge directly, and it often involves praise that is insincere, flattery to a person's face, and harsh criticism behind their back.

A practical way to demonstrate radical candour is by providing clear, honest, and specific feedback that helps the receiver of the feedback with a steer on how to improve. For example, instead of "This report is boring", we might say "To engage the reader, can you provide some more specific examples to illustrate these points and bring the content to life".

Growth mindset

Growth mindset describes the belief that ability is malleable and with the right level of effort and resources, we can all learn and improve.[11] An integral part of this process is getting things wrong along the way and taking risks. Mistakes and negative outcomes are how we generate the critical learning that is required for even better results. Psychological safety needs to be present for this to happen, as when we work in a psychologically safe environment, we are able to make mistakes and take calculated risks, learning from these without penalties.

However, in leadership, the pressure is often to achieve results with minimal resources and time, which can be problematic for creating the space to learn from mistakes and therefore nurture a growth mindset. Low psychological safety often manifests itself in fear of failure. Therefore, leaders must recognise this pressure and prioritise normalising mistakes as an integral part of the learning cycle to make this process as safe as possible, ensuring that people do not experience shame when things go wrong and potentially withdraw from learning altogether. Therefore, if mistakes occur, leaders can replace reproach with curiosity. Instead of blaming the employee, leaders can work with the individual to identify what caused the mistake and celebrate the learning from the experience that also informs the future. Employees also observe how their leaders deal with their own mistakes and whether they openly admit to these or try to cover them up, therefore leaders are role models for learning from mistakes. If a leader is not willing or able to be open about accepting when they have made a mistake and visibly explore and learn from this, it is highly unlikely that this will be possible for the rest of their team.

Adopting a growth mindset encourages us to view negative outcomes and challenging situations as a step closer to greater outcomes in the long term. Focusing on what can be learned from negative outcomes and how they can leverage these learnings to achieve even greater results can help mistakes to be embraced and normalised. A practical tip to help foster a growth mindset is instead of asking "What went wrong and what went right?" we can switch to "What have I learned and what will I do differently now that I have this knowledge?".

Psychological safety and marginalised groups

Earlier, we highlighted that to create a psychologically safe environment we must focus on equality of psychological safety outcomes with equity of treatment: different people need different treatment to experience psychological safety. This is especially important when we are leading a diverse team.

Marginalised groups are most at risk of experiencing low psychological safety and this is because they are often penalised more harshly when they make mistakes,[12] can find it harder to speak up when they do not agree,[13] are less likely to experience acceptance for their uniqueness and therefore be authentic at work,[14] and it can be much more difficult to ask for help and be vulnerable given that they are often judged to much higher standards.

In addition to understanding that different people will need different inputs to experience psychological safety, it is helpful to consider power dynamics within different ecosystems to understand what might compromise psychological safety. A good way to examine power dynamics is by mapping out ingroup and outgroup unwritten rules. In the context of psychological safety, when we are part of the outgroup, our power to speak up is weakened, our feedback is seen as less valued and relevant, we are afraid of taking risks or communicating our mistakes because of the penalties we might face when compared to the ingroup, and, in general, there is an issue around trust. To address this, leaders can consider:

- What are the unwritten rules and stereotypes that exist within your team or department and how might these rules and stereotypes influence individuals' rights or ability to speak up?
- Who are these rules and stereotypes servicing?
- What might influence the ability of group members from different social identities to abide by these unwritten rules?
- What is the purpose of these rules and stereotypes?
- What does a more helpful purpose look like?
- How can we bring in people who are in the outgroup to break the psychological safety/ingroup reinforcement cycle?

Chapter 3 in summary

- Psychological safety describes perceptions of the consequences of taking interpersonal risks in a particular context such as a workplace.
- Psychological safety happens when members mutually trust and support each other – they will openly speak up without fearing adverse interpersonal consequences.
- The psychological safety literature has been built on the experiences of dominant groups, therefore we must recognise that the experience of psychological safety will likely be different for marginalised groups.
- We can practise four skills to nurture psychological safety:
  o Practise emotional intelligence by pausing when emotionally triggered and accept the experience without reaction.
  o Learn strategies to better understand non-verbal cues, recognise emotional states, or interpret social contexts using tailored support or targeted training if necessary.
  o Care personally and challenge directly when providing feedback.
  o Normalise mistakes as a critical part of the learning process.

Notes

1 Edmondson, A. (1999). Psychological safety and learning behavior in work teams. *Administrative Science Quarterly, 44*(2), 350–383.
2 Edmondson, A. (1999). Psychological safety and learning behavior in work teams. *Administrative Science Quarterly, 44*(2), 350–383.
3 Detert, J. R., & Edmondson, A. C. (2011). Implicit voice theories: Taken-for-granted rules of self-censorship at work. Academy of *Management Journal, 54*(3), 461–488.
4 Edmondson, A. C. (2003). *Managing the Risk of Learning: Psychological Safety in Work Teams* (pp. 255–275). Cambridge, MA: Division of Research, Harvard Business School.
5 Kožo, A., Hodžić, I., & Bičo Ćar, M. (2022). Job insecurity and psychological safety in the workplace: Evidence from Bosnia and Herzegovina. In I. Karabegović, A. Kovačević, & S. Mandžuka (Eds.), *International Conference New Technologies, Development and Applications* (pp. 981–990). Cham, Switzerland: Springer.
6 Silva, L. H. D., Ferreira, B. M. A., Passos, A. P. P. D., & Schmitt, T. (2024). Effects of psychological safety and marginalization on the search for LGBTQIAPN+ leadership positions. *Brazilian Business Review, 21*(6), e20221446.

7   Bond, F. W. (2004). The role of acceptance and job control in mental health, job satisfaction, and work performance. Journal of Applied Psychology, 88(6), 1057–1067.

8   Goleman, D. (2007). *Social intelligence.* New York: Random House.

9   Clark, T. R. (2020). *The 4 stages of psychological safety: Defining the path to inclusion and innovation.* Oakland, CA: Berrett-Koehler Publishers.

10 Scott, K. (2019). *Radical candor: fully revised & updated edition: be a kick-ass boss without losing your humanity.* New York: St. Martin's Press.

11 Dweck, C. S. (2013). *Mindset: The psychology of success.* New York: Random House.

12 Heilman, M. E. (2012). Gender stereotypes and workplace bias. *Research in organizational Behavior, 32,* 113–135; Wingfield, A. H. (2010). Are some emotions marked "whites only"? Racialized feeling rules in professional workplaces. *Social Problems, 57*(2), 251–268.

13 Cooper, R., Mosseri, S., Vromen, A., Baird, M., Hill, E., & Probyn, E. (2021). Gender matters: A multilevel analysis of gender and voice at work. *British Journal of Management, 32*(3), 725–743; Rank, J. (2009). Challenging the status quo: Diversity, employee voice and proactive behaviour. In M. F. Özbilgin (Ed.), *Equality, diversity and inclusion at work: A research companion* (pp. 195–215). Cheltenham, UK: Edward Elgar.

14 Green, D. C., Holloway, I. W., Pickering, C. E., Tan, D., Tzen, M., Goldbach, J. T., & Castro, C. A. (2021). Group perceptions of acceptance of racial/ethnic, sexual and gender minorities in the United States military. *Military Behavioral Health, 9*(2), 139–150.

Part Two
The inclusive leader system

We developed the inclusive leader system to provide a framework to help leaders and organisations understand what it takes to practise inclusive leadership. The Inclusive Leader System consists of three interlinked components that impact one another, enhancing or undermining inclusive leadership capability. Part Two of this book explores each of these components: leader wellbeing, drivers of inclusive leadership, and inclusive leadership behaviours.

DOI: 10.4324/9781003598022-6

Section One

Leader wellbeing

We know that wellbeing and inclusion are interdependent: inclusion enhances wellbeing, yet we struggle to behave in an inclusive way when our wellbeing is low. For example, if we are juggling an extremely heavy workload with a tight deadline, we are more likely to exclude others from decision-making as we try to minimise using additional time and energy that we do not have. Similarly, if we are tired due to insufficient breaks from work, we are more likely to operate under autopilot as we conserve energy. The implication is that our autopilot is able to use less energy because it operates with biased reactions and therefore will exclude or resist anything that is not familiar and different. As a result, if we ignore our wellbeing, our ability to be inclusive will be compromised – consequently, leaders should prioritise their wellbeing.

To help us understand how we can ensure that low wellbeing does not become a barrier to inclusive leadership, we must consider and measure the multiple aspects of our wellbeing while at work. We use a comprehensive model of wellbeing that explores five aspects of workplace wellbeing: professional (Chapter 4), relational (Chapter 5), emotional (Chapter 6), cognitive (Chapter 7), and physical (Chapter 8). Each aspect covers a specific independent element of wellbeing, although all elements are also interdependent: it is unusual to experience very low wellbeing in one area while the others are unaffected. It is also important to note that in this section we focus on wellbeing at work as the workplace is the focus of this book. In reality, a holistic approach to understanding wellbeing can be helpful, as our wellbeing in our home life will impact our wellbeing at work and vice versa.

DOI: 10.4324/9781003598022-7

Finally we must recognise the different challenges marginalised groups might face with regard to their wellbeing at work, due to the emotional labour of navigating systemic discrimination, stereotype threats, microaggressions, and implicit biases. These experiences disproportionately drain mental and emotional resources, exacerbating stress and perpetuating inequities in workplace wellbeing. As we saw in Chapter 2, an outcome of inclusion is enhanced wellbeing. It therefore follows that for marginalised employees who may experience exclusion at work, their wellbeing will likely be negatively impacted by this experience. It is deeply unjust that those most affected by systemic inequities are often expected to find their own ways to cope, when in fact the responsibility lies with institutions to dismantle the conditions that cause harm in the first place. Therefore, if you are a leader from a marginalised group, we invite you to approach these chapters with self-compassion and critical reflection in relation to the system, consider what feels possible for you in your current context, what is fair to expect of yourself, and what may not be applicable given the systemic barriers you face.

This section explores each of these five aspects of wellbeing, including defining each component, explaining how it links to inclusion, and providing recommendations for how each aspect of wellbeing can be enhanced.

Professional wellbeing   **4**

Professional wellbeing is an overarching term that describes aspects of job-related motivation. We can consider motivation to be the reason why we act or behave in a certain way. We can likely all appreciate the difference in how we feel when we are motivated versus when we are not. A classic example from outside of the work context is whether we feel motivated to exercise or not. Often the experience (or absence) of the feeling of motivation will predict our behaviour (either we exercise or we do not). Motivation relates to wellbeing because it generally feels better when we feel motivated versus when we do not. When we feel motivated, we tend to feel more energised, focused, and purposeful, which, overall, supports our wellbeing.

When we consider professional wellbeing, we focus on intrinsic motivators. We can break this down into three specific needs that all humans experience. When these needs are met at work and we believe that the work that we do represents an important part of who we are, we will feel more motivated, experience work as rewarding and positive,[1] and consequently experience higher professional wellbeing. The three needs are:

- *Aspiration or ambition* is our hope or desire to achieve something. We experience aspiration when we seek to extend ourselves in ways that are personally significant, often via pursuing challenging goals. Low aspiration is reflected in apathy and acceptance of the status quo, no matter how unsatisfactory.[2]
- *Confidence or belief* in our own ability to achieve something or successfully behave in a particular way. When our self-belief and self-efficacy are high, we tend to set ourselves more challenging goals, therefore our self-belief can also influence our aspiration and ambition.[3]

DOI: 10.4324/9781003598022-8

- *Autonomy or the level of control* we have in deciding on the work that we do and how we complete this work. Autonomy is the degree to which we have the power and freedom to make decisions, following our own opinions and actions.[4]

What does professional wellbeing have to do with practising inclusive leadership?

When motivation is low, leaders may disengage, struggle to inspire others, and default to the status quo rather than pushing for systemic change. Furthermore, inclusive leadership is an active rather than passive style of leadership and consequently, if the leader is in a state of apathy, they are unlikely to be motivated, experience the required resilience, or be driven to work inclusively. This is why inclusive leaders must also take responsibility to protect their own professional wellbeing as part of the journey towards working more inclusively. As with all aspects of wellbeing, this is an ongoing, continual process, particularly pertinent as when inclusive leaders work to change the system, they will likely experience adversity, their autonomy around decision-making and change might be restricted, and consequently their motivation might drop, with a subsequent negative impact on professional wellbeing.

To illustrate the link between professional wellbeing and inclusion, we can imagine what it feels like when our professional wellbeing is low while trying to practise inclusive leadership. For example, imagine the following scenarios:

- You have no aspiration to achieve anything new, different, or challenging.
- You feel a sense of apathy, a lack of interest, no enthusiasm or concern when you think about your work.
- You have no drive to change things at work, even when they are unpleasant, boring, or unfair.
- You doubt your own ability to achieve your goals and objectives at work, assuming you are likely to fail or perform inadequately.
- You easily feel depleted with challenges and setbacks, lacking resilience to persist against resistance.
- You have no control over the work you do, decisions are made for you all the time, you only follow the directions of others, and you must complete each task in a way that is dictated by others.

Case example

I have been trying to do the right thing, but I feel like I'm going against the world. As a white, middle-aged woman, it is already challenging to keep holding myself accountable to be more inclusive when I don't have the lived experience to strengthen my awareness around racialised experiences. I often need to work proactively on my awareness to recognise whose perspective I am not considering and who I am leaving behind.

Then, when I finally manage to address this gap and, in the process, raise expectations – as people expect you to put things right when you listen to them – I find myself alone. My peers and boss, to be perfectly honest, are just not interested. I experience guilt because I am now aware of the unfairness faced by some individuals, and they understandably expect me to take action. However, I feel powerless to make a significant change!

For example, I nominated someone for promotion during our last talent review meeting. This person is not from my team but has been consistently extraordinary in supporting my team. However, I was outvoted. It is obvious that their line manager has his own favourites. The evidence he presented for the nomination of an alternative candidate, who was the one who ended up being promoted, was mainly based on a project he gave to this person who he likes personally, so you can see affinity bias at play. I introduced a calibration technique where we asked ourselves why we should promote and not promote each candidate. The reason they gave for not endorsing my nominee was that she struggled to follow directions sometimes. Yet seconds later, they described the same behaviour as positive for the other nominee! They said he was confident and could challenge the status quo when needed. The double standards were so infuriating. When I challenged the leadership team, they all agreed, probably because they knew I was a nominated sponsor for EDI, but they still went ahead and voted against my recommendation. Keeping my motivation up is the hardest part about being an EDI sponsor.

What can you do to enhance professional wellbeing?

While our professional wellbeing is likely to be affected by outside constraints such as our line manager, the culture, structures, and processes within our organisation, we all have the power to take steps to protect our professional wellbeing. Below we share our recommendations for how to enhance professional wellbeing. We break this down into the three aspects of professional wellbeing: aspiration, ambition and motivation; confidence and self-belief; and autonomy.

Aspiration, ambition and motivation

As an inclusive leader, you need to pay attention to your intrinsic motivators, which define your professional aspiration, ambition, and drive to do your job – and do it inclusively. Furthermore, it is not unusual for inclusive leaders to face resistance when advocating for others, challenging systemic prejudice while calling out privileges. Therefore, linking your aspirations and ambitions to your values is a great way to boost your motivation and resilience to keep growing when faced with adversity. Some questions to help you explore how to improve your aspiration, ambition and motivation at work are:

- What do you value and why?
- What is your long-term goal? What is your dream goal? How is this goal important to you on a personal level?
- What excites you the most about your job? What excites you the most about being an inclusive leader?
- How does your work help you to achieve your values?
- What is one bold step you are willing to take to achieve your dream goal?
- Imagine that you succeed in achieving your ambition. What does that look like for you? How would this impact your life and the lives of those around you?
- Why is inclusive leadership important to you? What is the meaning of being an inclusive leader?
- What impact have you already had as an inclusive leader? How does it make you feel?

Confidence and self-belief

Confidence and self-belief are critical for all of us to feel motivated about our work. It is also related to our sense of self-worth. When we do not believe in ourselves and abilities, we will not only struggle to do our jobs well but we will also struggle to drive the changes an inclusive leader needs within the systems they operate. Inclusive leaders must draw from self-confidence to advocate for marginalised groups, often risking being unpopular when calling out privileges and making those privileges visible to themselves and others. However, self-confidence is not static, and resilience is required to overcome hardships, setbacks, and even personal attacks when advocating for others. It is okay to have a bad day and experience low confidence. This is about more than perfection and always having all the answers. This is about having appropriate resources and techniques to help inclusive leaders put themselves in the best possible scenario to succeed, and bouncing back when this is not possible. Some questions to help you explore how to improve your confidence and self-belief at work are:

- What are your three key strengths? How did they help you to succeed in the past?
- What past achievements are you most proud of? What will you look back on with pride in the future?
- What do your peers and colleagues really value about you at work?
- When did you last overcome a difficult situation? What did you do that led to the positive outcome?
- What circumstances or events trigger you to doubt your confidence? Why do you think this is?
- What are some possible resources that can help you to build your confidence? Who can support you?
- What can help you to view challenges as a learning opportunity?
- If you focus on progression and not perfection, what is possible right now and how might this impact your ultimate goal?

Autonomy

Autonomy meets a fundamental psychological safety need for self determination which is to feel that we are in control of our own lives, and, therefore, we can direct our efforts to what is important to us. Poor autonomy can represent a threat as we rely on others to make the right decision, directly impacting our wellbeing. In some organisations, autonomy is withdrawn from individuals by limiting their access to resources, limiting their choices, and/or micromanaging how they deliver their outcomes. This also leads to poor accountability, poor performance and innovation, impairs personal growth, and increases the sense of helplessness.

Clear goals and freedom in execution are critical to empower inclusive leaders to advocate and drive systemic change when considering diverse needs. This discretionary power does not mean that inclusive leaders would operate outside principles of fairness and transparency. This means that they need to contract with their key stakeholders around the level of autonomy within their roles as an integral part of their job description. This also includes agreeing on how they will communicate their decisions transparently, while testing against fairness. Some questions to help you explore how to improve your autonomy at work are:

- In which areas do you want greater autonomy? What would having greater autonomy enable you to achieve at work?
- What challenges do you have that would be easier for you to solve if you had more independence?
- What areas have you got control over at work? Consider large and small tasks, ways of working, and decision-making.
- What autonomy do you need to practice inclusive leadership and advocate for others?
- What is one small step you can take to increase the level of autonomy that you have in how you are working? What do you need to do to achieve this?
- How might your increased autonomy benefit your key stakeholders, including your line manager and your organisation?
- What concerns might your stakeholders have related to your increased autonomy and how might you address these concerns?
- What measurements of success might you use to enable stakeholders to feel confident with your increased autonomy?

Chapter 4 in summary

- Professional wellbeing describes aspects of job-related intrinsic motivation including aspiration and ambition, confidence or belief in our own abilities, and the level of control we have in how we complete our work.
- When these needs of aspiration, self-belief, and autonomy are met, we are more likely to feel motivated and have positive professional wellbeing.
- Professional wellbeing is critical to inclusion, as the absence of professional wellbeing can lead to a sense of apathy and lack of drive at work. Given that inclusive leadership is an active style of leadership, inclusive leaders must be proactive in prioritising diversity and creating inclusive systems.

- Inclusive leaders are often faced with adversity and resistance when advocating for others and encouraging systemic changes, which can negatively impact their motivation to be inclusive. Resources, support, and recovery play important roles in enabling inclusive leaders to remain motivated and resilient.

Notes

1 Deci, E. L., & Ryan, R. M. (1985). *Intrinsic motivation and self-determination in human behavior*. Berlin: Springer Science & Business Media.
2 Van Horn, J. E., Taris, T. W., Schaufeli, W. B., & Schreurs, P. J. (2004). The structure of occupational well-being: A study among Dutch teachers. *Journal of Occupational and Organizational Psychology, 77*(3), 365–375.
3 Bandura, A. (1977). *Social learning theory*. Upper Saddle River, NJ: Prentice Hall.
4 Van Horn, J. E., Taris, T. W., Schaufeli, W. B., & Schreurs, P. J. (2004). The structure of occupational well-being: A study among Dutch teachers. *Journal of Occupational and Organizational Psychology, 77*(3), 365–375.

Relational wellbeing

5

Our need to connect with others is as fundamental as our need for food and water, with research demonstrating that the experience of social pain (such as rejection and loneliness) it feels as real as physical pain[1] and that people who do not feel socially connected (and therefore who experience loneliness) have a 50 per cent increased risk of mortality[2]. Therefore, it is perhaps not surprising that when we consider our wellbeing at work, we must also consider our relationships with others at work: our relational wellbeing.

Relational wellbeing describes how individuals feel towards the people they work with and how they function within social groups at work. We can experience low relational wellbeing if our needs are unfulfilled in relation to our work relationships. When we think about relational wellbeing, we can break this down further and consider:

- Do we feel we belong at work?
- Do we feel valued and appreciated at work?
- Do we feel high levels of trust with the people we work with?

If the answer is "yes" to these questions, then it is likely that our needs to connect with others are being met while at work, therefore we are likely to experience positive relational wellbeing.

What does relational wellbeing have to do with practising inclusive leadership?

Rather than focusing on whether you as the leader are creating an environment that enables the people around you to experience high levels of trust,

DOI: 10.4324/9781003598022-9

belonging, and to feel close to the people they work with, instead, we are considering whether you as the leader are experiencing this. It is important not to forget that leaders are humans too. Leaders have the very same needs to connect with others and this can be even more critical given how lonely work can be for leaders, especially for inclusive leaders who are driving systemic change.

Furthermore relational wellbeing can be challenging for inclusive leaders because reforming systems often requires disrupting entrenched power dynamics, challenging biases, and holding people accountable – actions that can create resistance, strain relationships, and lead to isolation. Leaders may face pushback from colleagues who feel uncomfortable with change or defensive about their role in inequities. To protect their relational wellbeing, inclusive leaders need to build strong networks of support, practise self-compassion, set boundaries to prevent burnout or exhaustion, and cultivate alliances with those who share their vision.

To illustrate the link between relational wellbeing and inclusive leadership, we can imagine what it feels like when our relational wellbeing is low while trying to practise inclusive leadership. For example, imagine the following scenarios:

- You do not feel valued or appreciated for the work you are doing, particularly from your manager and/or the senior leadership in the organisation.
- You do not feel that others trust you to do your job well.
- You do not feel as though you belong at work, you often feel on the outside or periphery compared to others.
- You do not feel close to or connected with others, particularly your peers or those more senior than you.

Case example

Performative allyship* is a real issue at work. The chief executive officer (CEO) and executive team often say all the right things on paper, but profit speaks louder when it comes to making decisions that consider diverse needs. We have a diversity plan and clear diversity and inclusion key performance indicators (KPIs); however, when I refer to them, my input is initially acknowledged but ultimately ignored. I have even noticed that I have been excluded from some meetings. It is more challenging for the executive team to ignore EDI issues when I am present, so it is much easier for them not to invite me in the first place. As an organisation we have made empty promises to our employees and clients, and our external EDI strategy appears to be just for show. Why can't they be honest and realistic about what they can actually commit to?

A close work colleague even told me that I should tone it down and focus on the tasks I am paid for instead of the EDI strategy. I thought that the EDI work was part of the role that I am paid for! While my CEO praises my work to my face, behind my back, they seem to be sabotaging my access to influence decisions. I'm feeling more and more isolated at work. This is dragging me down, and I'm seriously considering moving to a different job. It's hard to promote inclusivity when you are not included yourself!

Performative allyship: positive support on the surface, usually aimed at reputational and social gains, as opposed to meaningful action and genuinely caring for a cause.

What can you do to enhance relational wellbeing?

While we often have little control over the people that we work with, there are steps that we can all take to enhance our relational wellbeing at work. We can focus our efforts on three elements that drive relational wellbeing: sense of belonging, feeling valued, and experiencing trust.

Sense of belonging

Practising inclusive leadership can sometimes challenge our own sense of belonging, as not everyone will share the same social values – which can make it difficult to connect with these people and groups. Therefore, it is not unusual to feel alone and isolated as you work towards reforming systems for inclusion. On the other hand, the quality of relationships you form with others, once you start to focus on their belonging and valuing diversity and uniqueness, can be significantly strengthened, bringing you a stronger sense of belonging as well as bringing it to those around you. Therefore, it is important for leaders to pay attention to the quality of their relationships at work to maintain their relational wellbeing.

This process includes identifying and maximising relationships where you feel most connected, while appreciating that micro-connections (i.e., brief moments of socially connecting with others in a way where you feel accepted, valued, and that you can share parts of your identity) can have a compound effect on your sense of belonging. Some questions to help you explore your own sense of belonging at work are:

- Who in your organisation do you feel most connected with, and why?
- How would you describe the quality of relationships with your work colleagues?
- What are the opportunities to strengthen the existing relationships?
- Who are you comfortable with sharing your thoughts?
- What are typical informal interactions you have at work? Who do you interact with and why?
- Are there parts of yourself that you hold back at work and why? When and with whom might you experience fully being yourself at work?
- How well do you know the people that you work with? What opportunities for micro-connections might you be missing? This can include your line manager, your peers, your direct reports, and your wider stakeholder group.
- What is one small step you can take to get to know someone a little better? For example, can you arrange a one-to-one chat, volunteer for a new project, or join a work social group or event?

Feeling valued

There are two key aspects to consider when it comes to feeling valued for inclusive leaders. The first is creating a positive cycle of mutual respect and recognition. Expressing appreciation for others can greatly enhance our own sense of value and self-worth within a team. This practice fosters social bonding, perspective-taking, and trust. The second aspect involves making your contributions visible and in service for others. People tend to value things that serve them, especially when they connect the service to something they care about. When this link is unclear, we may even take valuable contributions for granted until we lose them. Inclusive leaders should consider their value to others and how visible they are; and also how well they recognise the value of others. Some questions to help you explore feeling valued at work are:

- What does feeling valued mean to you?
- Are there any aspects of your contribution that you wish were acknowledged more?

- Create a list of everyone you work closely with and for each person list at least three of their strengths with a specific example of when you have observed that strength in action.
- How often do you share your appreciation or positive feedback with your colleagues? For example, you may wish to add some thanks or positive feedback in an email or share publicly in a meeting. Remember that feedback is most meaningful when it is specific. If we share our appreciation for others and demonstrate how we value them, they will often feel encouraged to reciprocate these positive behaviours.

Experiencing trust

Trust is connected to safety and therefore is a critical experience to maintain wellbeing. When we trust and feel trusted we experience less stress and social anxiety, and greater psychological safety, empathy between individuals, and cohesion with groups. Trust is often based on perceptions of capability, integrity, and benevolence.[3] For example:

- How capable do others think you are, e.g., how can you demonstrate your effectiveness in your role?
- How do others see your commitment to integrity, e.g., how can you demonstrate that you are committed to doing the right thing by others?
- How do others see your inclination for benevolence, e.g., how can you demonstrate that you care about the people that you work with?

Equally, trusting everyone or being trusted by everyone might not be realistic, as different people might need different things to experience trust. For example, having a trusting or untrusting personality might relate to individual traits as opposed to the experience at hand. Either way, reflecting on the meaning of trust as well as trust-building behaviours is important to fostering more trusting experiences. Some questions to help you explore experiencing trust at work are:

- What does trust mean to you? Has this definition changed over time?
- Can you recall a situation where trust was high? What contributed to this high level of trust? What were the trust-building moments?
- What are some signs that there is trust in a relationship or team?
- How much trust do you feel with the people that you work with?
- How do you typically show others that they can trust you?
- How do you typically show others that you trust them?

- If trust has been broken in the past, what can you do to repair it?
- What does communicating openly and with trust look like in difficult situations?
- When do you find it hard to stick with your promises and commitments? How do you re-contract to ensure trust is not broken?
- How do you respond when others let you down?
- What specific behaviours and habits would you set for yourself to enhance your experiences with trust? What resources do you need to implement these behaviours and/or habits?

Chapter 5 in summary

- Relational wellbeing describes how individuals feel towards the people they work with and how they function within social groups at work.
- Our relational wellbeing can include whether we feel valued and appreciated at work, feel high levels of trust with the people we work with, and feel as though we belong at work.
- As a leader, when our relational wellbeing is low, we may find that our resilience to work inclusively is reduced. Leaders have the very same needs to connect with others and this can be even more critical given how lonely work can be for leaders, especially for inclusive leaders who are driving systemic change.
- There are practical steps inclusive leaders can take to improve their sense of belonging, feeling valued, and trusted, despite the environment and challenges they might face.

Notes

1 Lieberman, M. D. (2013). *Social: Why our brains are wired to connect*. New York: Broadway Books.
2 Holt-Lunstad, J., Smith, T. B., & Layton, J. B. (2010). Social relationships and mortality risk: A meta-analytic review. *PLoS Medicine*, 1–20.
3 Mayer, R. C., Davis, J. H., & Schoorman, F. D. (1995). An integrative model of organizational trust. *Academy of Management Review, 20*(3), 709–734.

Emotional wellbeing   6

Emotional wellbeing at work describes an individual's mood at work, which is influenced by how satisfied and committed they feel about work. Emotional wellbeing ebbs and flows, reflecting an individual's emotional status at any one time.[1] Moods represent general positive or negative feelings whereas emotions are discrete constructs (e.g., anger, joy, hate, jealousy, love), usually directed towards a specific target or cause.[2] If we notice that we are generally in a bad mood at work and/or experiencing negative emotions frequently while at work, we are likely to be experiencing low emotional wellbeing at work. As with many areas of wellbeing (and inclusion generally), our emotional wellbeing is often interlinked with other aspects of wellbeing. For example, it is difficult to experience a positive mood if we are physically exhausted. Furthermore, in the context of employment, job satisfaction and organisational commitment will have a direct impact on our emotions and overall mood, particularly if we consider the amount of time we spend at work.

Job satisfaction can fluctuate and reflects overall feelings about work, or it might be considered a composite of satisfaction about more specific aspects of work and how well our needs are met. For example, emotional needs (e.g., feeling secure and psychologically safe, being recognised, having a sense of purpose, feeling connected with others, etc.) and practical needs (e.g., how satisfied we are with our pay, the support received from our line manager, our workload, our commute, our working hours, etc.). If we take the composite approach to understanding job satisfaction, even if we are dissatisfied with some aspects of our job (i.e., our pay), we might still experience overall feelings of satisfaction if we feel satisfied with other aspects of our job (i.e., the people we work with, the impact of our work on others, our hours of work, etc.).

DOI: 10.4324/9781003598022-10

Organisational commitment describes whether we feel that we have a positive relationship with our organisation. There are multiple aspects of organisational commitment; however, most relevant to emotional wellbeing is affective commitment,[3] which is the emotional attachment that we feel towards our organisation. Generally, people feel attached to their organisation when the goals and values of the organisation are largely consistent with their own. A sense of commitment to our organisation, generally produces more positive emotions and therefore reflects positive emotional wellbeing, whereas lower organisational commitment can produce more negative emotions (i.e., we might feel resentful or frustrated) and therefore reflects negative wellbeing.

What does emotional wellbeing have to do with practising inclusive leadership?

Inclusive leadership requires sustained effort, emotional labour, and the ability to navigate discomfort. Therefore, low emotional wellbeing compromises our ability to be an inclusive leader because it depletes the emotional resilience, empathy, and cognitive clarity needed to navigate complex challenges, hold space for difficult conversations, and drive meaningful change. Emotional labour (i.e., displaying a different emotion to the one you are experiencing, such as outwardly displaying a cheerful demeanour when you are inwardly feeling down) is particularly important for emotional wellbeing because it can be harmful in the long term.[4] However, even more importantly for inclusive leadership, is the argument that emotional labour uses up the individual's internal resources, such as motivational energy[5] (i.e., it requires a lot of energy to pretend that everything is okay when it is not!). This creates problems when we consider that individuals have a limited pool of resources to help us to effectively manage our performance.[6] Therefore, the self-regulation required to suppress our emotions can have costs in other domains, for example by reducing our capacity to focus our attention, listen fully, and engage in reflective thinking.[7]

To illustrate the link between emotional wellbeing and inclusive leadership, we can imagine what it feels like when our emotional wellbeing is low while trying to practise inclusive leadership. For example, imagine the following scenarios:

- You are dissatisfied with your job. Perhaps you are not satisfied with the nature of the work that you do, the extent to which your skills are used, the people that you work with, your pay, your hours of work, or even your commute to work.

- You do not feel emotionally committed to your organisation. You do not buy in to their purpose or espoused values and feel that your own work goals do not align with those of the organisation.
- You find that, on a day-to-day basis, you are often in a bad mood at work. You generally feel grouchy, surly, or testy, perhaps with no obvious reason why.
- You notice that you often experience negative emotions towards others at work or even towards things that you need to do. This can include feeling angry, frustrated, resentful, or even jealous of other people's accomplishments or of how they seem to be treated.
- You frequently need to hide your true emotions from others – for example, when dealing with members of your team, you need to conceal how frustrated you feel with them or dial down how angry you are when things go wrong.

Case example

I used to consider myself an inclusive leader. I was an active sponsor for multiple employee resource groups and led several EDI projects, but recently I have had no energy to even get through my own to do list because of how stressful my work is. I know that being inclusive should be part of my work, but the reality is that, as an inclusive leader, you need to have the extra mental energy to make a difference, and I do not have that now, as I am constantly stressed and distracted. It all started when I was transferred to commercial. Three things made the issue unmanageable: the pressure to meet targets, the increased travelling and events I need to attend, and always needing to be happy and agreeable around clients, even when I disagree. This is exhausting. Our client-focused culture is excellent, until you get a client who is not aligned with your own values. I often have to bite my tongue in client meetings where the client is sounding off and generally being ignorant. I find myself getting more and more wound up as the day goes on. As much as I hate it, the reality is that I am now fairly reactive when it comes to supporting EDI matters.

What can you do to enhance emotional wellbeing?

Experiencing negative emotions and being unsatisfied with parts of your work are not unusual. Most of us will experience both daily. Negative emotions are essential to nudge us to seek change, set boundaries, and keep us safe. The matter becomes problematic when the ratio between positive and negative emotions is not balanced. The broaden-and-build theory explains that building on positive emotions can help individuals expand the psychological resources that are needed to deal with negative emotions.[8] Negative emotions are inevitable and, in many cases, necessary for us to take action but, at the same time, if we do not have positive emotions, we compromise our emotional wellbeing and will not have the resources needed to support our resilience and respond to negative emotion in a way that will help and not hinder us. There are a number of specific things inclusive leaders can do to enhance their mood, job satisfaction, and organisational commitment at work.

Mood

Unchecked low mood unintentionally reinforces exclusion because we become less approachable, we listen less, we are less tolerant to deal with diverse views, and we spread negative sentiment even when we do not want to. Keeping your mood in check is not about suppressing emotions that are causing the low mood (*see Chapter 21 for more on working with our emotions*). Instead, it is about becoming aware of these emotions and seeking positive emotional experiences to balance our mood. Some questions to help you explore factors related to your mood at work are:

- How would you describe your general mood at work?
- What patterns can you observe when you experience more positive or negative moods?
- What factors can you identify that appear to trigger a low mood? For example, it can be hard for us to feel positive if we are physically exhausted due to long working hours or high levels of stress. Alternatively, we may find that certain tasks may bring our mood down.
- Once you have identified the trigger for your low mood, what is one step that you can take to address this trigger?
- What interventions can you easily build into your daily routine to help lift your mood? Examples include exercise, speaking to someone who is usually uplifting, listening to your favourite music, journaling to release

any negative emotions, meditating, writing down things you are grateful for, looking after your sleep, and spending time with nature.

- Who and what at work tends to lighten your mood and how can you spend more time with them?
- What is one emotion you would like to feel more of at work (e.g., calm, connected etc)? What step can you take to bring you closer to experiencing more of this emotion at work?

Job satisfaction and organisational commitment

Job satisfaction and organisational commitment are essential because they directly impact how leaders show up for their teams and for inclusive leaders to sustain the energy required to foster inclusive cultures. When leaders feel fulfilled and connected to their organisation's mission, they are more likely to lead with authenticity, empathy, and resilience, which are key qualities for practising inclusive leadership. Some questions to help you explore factors related to job satisfaction and organisational commitment at work are:

- How satisfied are you with your job?
- What areas are you dissatisfied with at work? What might be leading to this dissatisfaction?
- What changes can you make at work to improve the areas where you are dissatisfied?
- What small things can you change to bring more meaning to your work?
- What strengths and talents would you like to use more at work?
- How do you want to feel about your work in one year's time and what steps can you take today to begin creating this experience?
- How committed do you feel to your organisation?
- What initially attracted you to your current job?
- What do you like about working for this organisation?
- What are the benefits of working for your organisation?
- What aspects of your job align with your personal values?
- How does your current job role support your long-term career goals?

Chapter 6 in summary

- Emotional wellbeing at work describes an individual's mood and emotions at work.

- We can experience low emotional wellbeing if our needs are unmet at work. For example, we may not feel satisfied with our job or committed to our organisation.
- If a leader is very dissatisfied with their job and does not feel committed to their organisation, the likelihood is that they will struggle to access the discretionary effort needed to engage in a proactive leadership approach such as inclusive leadership.
- The need to mask negative emotions frequently can also use up valuable resources, depleting an individual's capacity in other areas – for example, their ability to pay attention and listen actively.
- The balance between positive and negative emotions is important to keep our emotional wellbeing healthy.
- Negative emotions play an important role in nudging us to take action to address unmet needs. Positive emotions give us the psychological resources required to address negative emotions constructively.

Notes

1 Larsen, R. J., & Prizmic, Z. (2008). Regulation of emotional well-being. *The science of subjective well-being*, 258-89.

2 Woods, S. A., & West, M. A. (2020). *The psychology of work and organizations*. Andover, UK: Cengage Learning, EMEA.

3 Meyer, J. P., & Allen, N. J. (1991). A three-component model conceptualization of organizational commitment. *Human Resource Management Review, 1*, 61–89.

4 Hochschild, A. R. (1983). *The managed heart: Commercialization of human feeling*. Berkeley, CA: University of California Press.

5 Brotheridge, C. M., & Lee, R. T. (2002). Testing a conservation of resources model of the dynamics of emotional labor. *Journal of Occupational Health Psychology, 7*(1), 57–67.

6 Grandey, A. A., & Gabriel, A. S. (2015). Emotional labor at a crossroads: Where do we go from here? *Annual Review of Organizational Psychology and Organizational Behavior, 2*(1), 323–349.

7 Muraven, M., & Baumeister, R. F. (2000). Self-regulation and depletion of limited resources: Does self-control resemble a muscle? *Psychology Bulletin, 126*(2), 247–259.

8 Fredrickson, B. L. (2004). The broaden-and-build theory of positive emotions. *Philosophical Transactions of the Royal Society of London. Series B: Biological Sciences, 359*(1449), 1367–1377.

Cognitive wellbeing 7

At work, cognitive wellbeing describes an individual's mental functioning, which includes how well we maintain focus, alertness and mental stamina, learn new things, process information, make decisions, and solve problems. An important consideration when addressing cognitive wellbeing is to understand the difference between cognitive *capacity* and cognitive *energy*. Although these concepts are related, they refer to distinct ways in which the brain processes and sustains mental activity. Cognitive capacity refers to the brain's ability to process, store, and manage information, for example, when making decisions. Cognitive energy relates to our mental stamina and the resources needed to process information in the first place. Cognitive capacity is more stable and influences us in the long term.[1] Cognitive energy relates to the mental resources we need for a specific task. Cognitive energy fluctuates depending on our motivation to engage in a task as well as being influenced by sleep, nutrition, and stress.

We can experience low cognitive wellbeing if our mental resources are stretched to full capacity. For example, it can be difficult to concentrate or learn new information if we are highly stressed, distracted, tired, or in a low emotional state. Equally, cognitive wellbeing can decline for various reasons, although often stereotypically associated with age, the degree and nature of the decline will vary widely among individuals. Furthermore, even if we are physically and emotionally well, if we have overloaded our cognitive capacity, such as when we are learning a large amount of new information at once, eventually our ability to take on anything else will be compromised.

DOI: 10.4324/9781003598022-11

Stress is particularly problematic for our cognitive wellbeing. It is important to note that stress does not always have a negative impact on us: research suggests that moderate, short-term stress actually improves cognitive processing and is therefore a highly adaptive functional response.[2] Neuroscience can help us to understand the role that stress has to play in our cognitive wellbeing. The experience of stress results in increased activity in the amygdala which causes a number of changes in our hormonal and neural systems. Stress can be considered as one of many homeostatic mechanisms in the brain: it is the process of maintaining a constant level in brain functioning.[3] Stress is used to improve brain function temporarily but then has to be reset to bring the system back to baseline. If we do not provide ourselves with the opportunity to reset (i.e., through rest and recovery) or when the level of stress increases in either frequency or intensity to a point where we can no longer cope, then we move into distress. At this point, we lose both synapses and neurones in the hippocampus (memory) and medial prefrontal cortex (cognitive function) but experience an increase in the number of synapses in the amygdala, which is responsible for our emotional response.[4] As a result, stress produces a reduction in memory and a decrease in the flexibility and creativity of planning and an increase in our experience of negative emotions.[5]

Therefore rest and recovery are important when we consider all aspects of wellbeing; however, this is particularly the case for cognitive wellbeing. The effort-recovery model[6] suggests that when we are faced with high demands at work, it will lead to what is known as "load" reactions, which can be physiological (e.g., increased cortisol levels) and psychological (e.g., fatigue) symptoms. When we finish work, if we are not exposed to further demands, these load reactions are alleviated and consequently the symptoms decrease as recovery occurs. However, if demands continue to be present, recovery will not occur and we will return to work with our resources (such as our mental capacity and energy) still depleted. This means that load reactions can accumulate over time if recovery is not possible.[7] This is because our cognitive capabilities are not limitless. This is particularly true when we factor stress into account. However, even if we are working on a task that we find enjoyable and rewarding, our cognitive resources will eventually be depleted as well. While it is completely normal to find that our cognitive resources, such as our ability to concentrate, are low at the end of a workday, if we find that we are not able to replenish these resources through rest and recovery, we will be unable to work at our full cognitive capacity the next day and may even experience greater cognitive decline over the long term.

What does cognitive wellbeing have to do with practising inclusive leadership?

As inclusive leadership nurtures an environment where individuals are constantly exposed to new ideas, backgrounds, and perspectives, being able to process new information, remain open and curious, and solve problems is critical. Low cognitive wellbeing is particularly problematic when it comes to inclusive leadership. When our cognitive resources are depleted, we are more likely to rely on our system one thinking, rather than engage our system two thinking.[8] The problem with relying on our system one thinking (which is a fast, intuitive, and automated way of thinking) when our cognitive resources are depleted, is that it operates with bias. This becomes even more problematic when we are working in a diverse environment as we will be processing new information and different perspectives much more frequently. If our cognitive wellbeing is low, our brain will ignore what is new and instead engage our system one thinking, which relies on heuristics or mental shortcuts to enable it to respond quickly and intuitively. Although heuristics can be useful shortcuts, in diverse contexts they often introduce bias (*more on what is meant by biases and stereotypes in Chapter 14*). This is, of course, unhelpful from an inclusive leadership perspective. Inclusive leaders must work hard to switch from system one to system two thinking (which is a slower, more intentional, and reflective way of thinking), enabling them to reflect on their biases, challenge stereotypes, and process new and diverse information (*more on this as a behaviour of inclusive leadership in Chapter 20*). Inclusive leaders must therefore be aware of the negative impact poor cognitive wellbeing can have on their ability to work inclusively.

To illustrate the link between cognitive wellbeing and inclusive leadership, we can imagine what it feels like when our cognitive wellbeing is low while trying to practise inclusive leadership. For example, imagine the following scenarios:

- Your to do list is overflowing and your mind is full of everything that you need to achieve this week.
- You have been in back-to-back meetings all day, each meeting requiring you to take an active role. Your list of actions from each meeting is steadily building.
- You are worried about an upcoming important difficult conversation you need to have. You are rehearsing what needs to be said over and over in your mind, meaning that you feel distracted and are finding it difficult to focus on the task at hand.

- You are at the end of the second day of a training course. You are loving the learning, but your mind feels full to bursting.
- You are constantly being asked to make decisions by those around you. As the day progresses, you are struggling to take an open stance to understanding all of the relevant information and instead you start to make automatic, snap judgements.

Case example

I have always prided myself on being inclusive and made sure my team members were heard and their individual needs were met. However, this process takes time and mental energy, particularly when needs overlap. Recently the organisation relaunched their flexible working policy – at the same time as a key product was launched. It was a nightmare, and it was poorly implemented from a project management point of view. People were torn between multiple competing priorities, and the workload increased significantly because of the key product launch, which meant people were very stressed and under significant time pressure. Leaders need to have the time and space to deal with things like this properly and sensitively. People were so stretched that they were not open to listening to others' perspectives and so intentionally shortened the consultation process for the policy. Because of this the policy is not fit for purpose, as different people have different ideas and needs, such as what the policy means for those who wish to work from home. But I have no energy at the moment to fight this battle and figure out a resolution that meets everyone's needs. I will need to finish this product launch first then revisit the implementation of the flexible policy.

What can you do to enhance cognitive wellbeing?

There are things you can do to improve both your cognitive capacity and your cognitive energy. Cognitive capacity involves more long-term strategies around training your brain, developing healthy habits, and managing chronic conditions, including stress and being overwhelmed. Cognitive energy consists of managing the mental fuel needed to perform a cognitive task. For example, feeling drained after intense concentration means you use all your fuel, and how you refuel is with rest, relaxation, proper nutrition, and sleep. You can also tune into seasonal rhythms by noticing how changes in daylight affect your energy levels. While not everyone has the flexibility to adjust their pace at work, simply being aware of how different times of the year might influence your natural drive to be active or restful can be a gentle way to support your wellbeing. For example, in winter, when daylight hours are shorter, many people feel a natural pull to slow down. Even if our routines do not allow for major changes, small shifts in how we care for ourselves can make a meaningful difference.

Carefully planning your breaks and recovery time is key, and you can consider daily, weekly, monthly, and annual recovery. This can include small breaks during the working day. For example, taking 10 minutes every 90 minutes away from your desk will help refresh your cognitive energy. Rest is not merely about sitting still or sleeping, the key to cognitive wellbeing is to ensure that you can detach from work psychologically, therefore it is important to distinguish between active rest and passive activities such as watching TV or scrolling on your phone. Active rest involves engaging in low-duty activities (i.e., you *choose* to engage in these activities rather than you *have* to engage in them through a sense of duty and obligation, such as housework) that refresh your mind, such as physical exercise, engaging in a hobby, and socialising with friends and family.

Furthermore, we all have peaks and troughs in our mental energy, so understanding your natural peaks and troughs and using this information to plan your day will maximise your cognitive output. For example, if you are an early bird, try to save your most cognitively taxing tasks for the first part of the day (even before checking your emails) wherever possible. You will likely find that the quality of your work is much higher, and you can achieve significantly more. Schedule tasks that give you energy or require less cognitive capacity (such as routine administration tasks) for the part of the day when you notice your cognitive energy is lower.

Some questions to help you explore your cognitive capacity and energy at work are:

- How would you describe your current mental workload? Does it feel manageable or overwhelming?
- How would you rate your mental energy right now on a scale from 1 to 10? What contributes to that rating?
- What signs do you notice when you are reaching your cognitive limits?
- How do you recharge mentally after a demanding day?
- What have you done in the past to help you with your mental energy and capacity?
- Who or what helps you when you are feeling overwhelmed?

- When is your cognitive energy highest? Are you an early bird or a night owl?
- How do you manage your breaks and recovery during the day, the week, the month, and the year?
- What types of breaks work better for you to recharge your mental batteries?
- What activities make you feel mentally energised?
- If your cognitive wellbeing was improved, what would you be able to do that feels difficult now?

Chapter 7 in summary

- Cognitive wellbeing at work describes an individual's mental capacity and energy. We can experience low cognitive wellbeing if our mental resources are stretched to full capacity.
- Experiencing low cognitive energy and capacity at the end of a work-day is normal. However, if we are not able to replenish our cognitive energy and resources, our longer-term cognitive wellbeing will be compromised.
- Cognitive wellbeing is important for inclusive leadership: when our cognitive wellbeing is low, we are more likely to rely on our system one thinking, which operates with bias and stereotypes.
- Inclusive leaders must work hard to engage their system two thinking, drawing on cognitive skills such as focused concentration, active listening, and reflection.
- Breaks and recovery are key to refuelling our cognitive energy and building our cognitive capacity by enabling us to detach from work psychologically.

Notes

1 Kahneman, D. (2011). *Thinking, fast and slow*. London: Penguin Books.
2 McEwen, B. (2016) In pursuit of resilience: Stress, epigenetics, and brain plasticity. *Annals of the New York Academy of Sciences, 1373*, 56–64.
3 Riddell, P. (2022). Neuroscience of coaching: Theory, research and practice. In J. Passmore & S. Leach (Eds.), *Third wave cognitive behavioural coaching: Contextual, behavioural and neuroscience approaches for evidence based coaches*. Shoreham-by-Sea, UK: Pavilion Publishing and Media.

4 McEwen, B. (2016) In pursuit of resilience: Stress, epigenetics, and brain plasticity. *Annals of the New York Academy of Sciences, 1373,* 56–64.

5 Riddell, P. (2022). Neuroscience of coaching: Theory, research and practice. In J. Passmore & S. Leach (Eds.), *Third wave cognitive behavioural coaching: Contextual, behavioural and neuroscience approaches for evidence based coaches.* Shoreham-by-Sea, UK: Pavilion Publishing and Media.

6 Meijman, T. F., & Mulder G. (1998). Psychological aspects of workload. In P. J. D. Drenth & H. Thierry (Eds.). *Handbook of work and organizational psychology, Vol. 2: Work psychology* (pp. 5–33). Hove, UK: Psychology Press.

7 Sonnentag, S., Cheng, B. H., & Parker, S. L. (2022). Recovery from work: Advancing the field toward the future. *Annual Review of Organizational Psychology and Organizational Behavior, 9*(1), 33–60.

8 Kahneman, D. (2012). *Of 2 minds: How fast and slow thinking shape perception and choice* (Excerpt). Accessed from https://www.scientificamerican.com/article/kahneman-excerpt-thinking-fast-and-slow/. Retrieved 9 November 2024.

Physical wellbeing   8

Physical wellbeing describes the presence (or lack of) physical complaints like chronic pain and compromised sleep, which can be associated with poor working conditions, being overworked, or high levels of stress because of work. Some physical complaints can be directly traced back to our working conditions. For example, we might experience headaches or eye strain from spending too much time working at a computer, and we can experience back, leg, or hip pain from spending too much time seated at a desk without adequate movement breaks. Moreover, if stress is severe and prolonged it might lead to other health problems with the cardiovascular, immune, gastrointestinal, and endocrine systems.[1]

Another common symptom of poor physical wellbeing from work is insomnia, which might involve difficulty in falling asleep and/or disrupted sleep, often linked to work-related stress and anxiety. Often this is because, when we are highly stressed, many of us will find that we engage in what is known as repetitive thought. Repetitive thought is the process of recurrently fixating attention on a specific issue or stimulus.[2] Broadly speaking, there are two types of unconstructive repetitive thought: worry and rumination. Both of these are negatively related to quality of sleep or ability to fall asleep.[3] For example, an early study in this field indicated that individuals with insomnia were ten times more likely to attribute their sleep disturbance to cognitive factors, including worrying, planning, or difficulty controlling thoughts, than to somatic complaints, such as sweating or shifting in bed.[4]

We are usually not very effective at understanding the links between our work and our physical health. For example, we may not pay sufficient attention to our physical complaints and seldom seek to understand the root cause of psychosomatic issues. Instead, we power through or hope things will

DOI: 10.4324/9781003598022-12

improve on their own. However, it is important to identify and address the psychosomatic triggers (i.e., what is making us stressed) instead of only managing the symptoms (i.e., our lack of sleep). Otherwise, any treatment will be only palliative, and physical symptoms might develop to chronic illnesses.

What does physical wellbeing have to do with practising inclusive leadership?

Physical wellbeing can have implications for inclusive leadership which we explore next, however, it is important to note that compromised physical wellbeing isn't always a disadvantage for inclusive leadership. For example, some chronic pain sufferers can develop high empathy and inclusive awareness through their lived experience.

In terms of the link between physical wellbeing and inclusive leadership, at the start of this section on wellbeing, we mentioned that the components of wellbeing are interconnected. In Chapters 6 and 7, we have already explored how our emotional and cognitive wellbeing can impact our ability to work inclusively. Inclusive leaders rely on multiple processes like awareness, empathy, perspective-taking, decision-making, critical thinking, and creativity to understand and meet different inclusion needs, and, as the research above demonstrates, poor physical wellbeing will compromise our ability to deploy these necessary skills.

Unfortunately, it is not just the link between physical, cognitive, and emotional wellbeing that has implications for inclusion. Research has shown that when we are sleep deprived, which might happen when we are in pain or stressed, we are more likely to interpret something that is neutral as negative, which the authors attribute to the principle of "better safe than sorry".[5] According to the better-safe-than-sorry principle, it is better to decide that something is a threat when it is not, rather than to decide that it is not a threat when it actually is (because a conclusion that something is safe when it is not can lead to serious harm). This automatically shuts down any curiosity or openness needed to find out more, so that the unknown "something" becomes known to us. This has major implications for inclusion as the essence of inclusion means working with diversity, which is often something that is different or less well known to us (*more on curiosity in Chapter 9*).

In addition, research indicates the multitude of negative outcomes of poor physical wellbeing on other aspects, including our cognitive functioning and emotional state. For example, the effects of sleep deprivation on cognitive processes are well documented, with studies showing that only one night of sleep deprivation reduces performance on tasks using working memory, decision-making, task switching, and attention.[6] Sleepless nights can also lead to increased irritability and volatility[7] and prolonged sleep deprivation can lead to an increase in depressed mood, anger, frustration, tension, and anxiety.[8]

Physical wellbeing as a privilege

Another important consideration in the context of physical wellbeing is that to have positive physical wellbeing, including to live free from chronic pain, is a privilege that not everyone will have access to. Chronic pain impacts not only one's ability to be an inclusive leader but also functioning in many areas of life. The scale of the issue can be illustrated by evidence from the United Kingdom, where a meta-analysis estimated that 43 per cent of adults live with some degree of chronic pain, including 30 per cent of adults aged 18–39 years.[9] Therefore, many leaders will not only be living with chronic pain but also managing people with chronic pain. Of course, being free from chronic pain does not automatically make someone an inclusive leader. Positive wellbeing alone does not guarantee the desire or ability to be inclusive, it simply provides the biological conditions that make inclusive cognitive functioning easier. Similarly, without the necessary social values, inclusivity will not happen.

Inclusive leaders tend to hold social values that prioritise fairness and equity, and therefore they will likely understand how their own pain might impact their leadership, seeking adjustments to help manage it. If leaders work in organisations that are not designed to accommodate those managing chronic pain, it will be difficult for the leader to fully support themselves and others who need similar accommodations. Seeking workplace environments where these challenges are acknowledged and supported by the system and not only the individual is key to ensuring that both leaders and employees in chronic pain can thrive.

To illustrate the link between physical wellbeing and inclusive leadership, we can imagine what it feels like when our physical wellbeing is low while trying to practise inclusive leadership. For example, imagine the following scenarios:

- You are struggling to get to sleep at night, or you are waking up in the middle of the night, unable to get back to sleep, your head full of thoughts and worries about work.
- To keep up with workload, you are working long hours, starting early, finishing late, doing extra in the evenings and weekends. You feel both mentally and physically exhausted.

- Your daily schedule is so tight that you feel tied to your desk. You cannot remember the last time you were able to take a walk (even for 10 minutes) during the workday. Your back is complaining about the number of hours sat at your desk.
- You find that by the end of a day of staring at your computer screen, your eyes are gritty and dry, and your head is pounding.

Case example

Over the last few months I've been struggling to live up to my own expectations as a leader. I started with a nagging back and neck pain that was triggered after an intense and stressful week of travelling with work, and too much time sat in a plane and at a desk. This pain got worse over time and all the muscles in my back seemed to be rock solid with tension. Although I took some painkillers to help with the pain, even with medication, it was hard for me to sit through meetings or focus on discussions and it was also affecting my ability to get to sleep. It felt like my brain was shutting down – I was so tired and I could only think about the pain. I found myself snapping at colleagues and feeling irritable. Last week, a junior member of my team was making an important point, but I cut them off because I just wanted to finish the meeting quickly. My physical pain is impacting me and my ability to be present, to listen, and to create the supportive culture that my team deserves.

What can you do to enhance physical wellbeing?

It is important for us to become aware of and monitor our physical health. We can do this by collecting data to monitor key symptoms such as the amount and quality of sleep and any aches and pains, while identifying links with work events and our psychosomatic health. A classic example is a poor night's sleep before an important presentation. This in itself is not unusual; however, this becomes problematic when daily stressors are frequently impacting our ability to sleep well and recover from work. It is also important to identify the areas in which you have control and list the changes you can make to improve your physical health. Unfortunately, for most of us, there are many areas of our work that negatively impact our health but that we have little or no control over. For example, when our organisation experiences a large change (such as a period of redundancies), this will inevitably lead to a period of stress for those affected. However, there are always steps we can take to make improvements, and even small changes can add up to having a larger impact.

Some questions to help you explore your physical wellbeing are:

- How would you describe your current physical wellbeing?
- How would you rate the quality of your sleep?
- What physical challenges, if any, have you been experiencing lately?
- What habits in your daily routine support your physical health?
- What habits might be negatively affecting your physical health, such as your ability to rest well?
- What changes can you make to improve your bedtime routine and your sleep?
- How much physical activity do you get in a typical day?
- What type of movement do you enjoy the most?
- What barriers, if any, are keeping you from being more active? How can you address them?
- How well are you managing stress, and how is it impacting your physical health?
- Are there any relaxation or mindfulness techniques you can do to help you with your physical wellbeing?
- What is one small change you can make today to improve your physical wellbeing?
- How will you know your physical wellbeing is improved?

Chapter 8 in summary

- Physical wellbeing describes the presence (or lack of) physical complaints such as pain or compromised sleep, which can be associated with poor working conditions, being overworked, or high levels of stress.
- A common symptom of poor physical wellbeing from work is insomnia, often caused by stress and anxiety at work, which is linked to unconstructive repetitive thoughts.
- Poor physical wellbeing impacts on emotional and cognitive wellbeing, limiting multiple cognitive processes, making it harder to meet the different inclusion needs of others.
- To improve physical wellbeing, we must first become aware of and monitor how our physical health is impacted by work. We can do this by collecting data to monitor key symptoms such as amount and quality of

sleep, and of pain, while identifying links between work events and our psychosomatic health.

• There are always steps we can take to make improvements, and even small changes can add up to creating a larger impact.

Notes

1 Yaribeygi, H., Panahi, Y., Sahraei, H., Johnston, T. P., & Sahebkar, A. (2017). The impact of stress on body function: A review. *EXCLI Journal, 16*, 1057–1072.

2 Segerstrom, S. C., Stanton, A. L., Alden, L. E., & Shortridge, B. E. (2003). A multidimensional structure for repetitive thought: What's on your mind, and how, and how much? *Journal of Personality and Social Psychology, 85*(5), 909.

3 Pillai, V., & Drake, C. L. (2015). Sleep and repetitive thought: the role of rumination and worry in sleep disturbance. *Sleep and Affect*, 201–225.

4 Lichstein, K. L., & Rosenthal, T. L. (1980). Insomniacs' perceptions of cognitive versus somatic determinants of sleep disturbance. *Journal of Abnormal Psychology, 89*(1), 105.

5 Tempestaa, D., Couyoumdjianb, A., Curcioa, G., Moroni, F., Marzano, C., & Gennaro, L. D. (2010). Lack of sleep affects the evaluation of emotional stimuli. *Brain Research Bulletin, 82*(1–2), 104–108.

6 Bobić, T. T., Šečić, A., Zavoreo, I., Matijević, V., Filipović, B., Kolak, Ž., …, & Sajković, D. (2016). The impact of sleep deprivation on the brain. *Acta Clinica Croatica, 55*(3), 469–473.

7 Tempestaa, D., Couyoumdjianb, A., Curcioa, G., Moroni, F., Marzano, C., & Gennaro, L. D. (2010). Lack of sleep affects the evaluation of emotional stimuli. *Brain Research Bulletin, 82*(1–2), 104–108.

8 Tempestaa, D., Couyoumdjianb, A., Curcioa, G., Moroni, F., Marzano, C., & Gennaro, L. D. (2010). Lack of sleep affects the evaluation of emotional stimuli. *Brain Research Bulletin, 82*(1–2), 104–108.

9 Faculty of Pain Medicine. (2024). *UK pain messages 2024*. Accessed from https://fpm.ac.uk/sites/fpm/files/documents/2025-02/UK%20Pain%20Message%20infographic%202024.pdf. Retrieved 29 March 2025.

Section Two

Drivers of inclusive leadership

Human behaviour is infinitely complex. Therefore to understand fully what may influence or drive the practice of inclusive leadership, it is essential to examine important traits, background, understanding, and awareness within the leaders themselves. We call these "drivers" of inclusive leadership, and these drivers form the focus of the next six chapters (Chapters 9 to 14). We propose that the drivers of inclusive leadership are interlinked and can work together to enable or allow a leader to behave inclusively. Equally, the absence of these drivers can act as barriers, inhibiting a leader's ability to engage with others inclusively. Our drivers of inclusive leadership are mindset (curiosity, humility, courage, empathy), lived experiences, and knowledge.

Mindset

Mindset explains the mental attitude and outlook of the leader. We focus on exploring the characteristics that influence how the leader views the world and engages with others. Drawing from the principles of neuroplasticity, we propose that an inclusive mindset can be developed and nurtured rather than being fixed and innate. Although restructuring and rewiring our brains might sound impossible, we can directly change our mindset by first raising awareness of our current mindset and then proactively pursuing new habits and then nurturing new qualities around our desired mindset. The presence

DOI: 10.4324/9781003598022-13

of an inclusive mindset can enhance a leader's capability to identify and consequently mitigate biases in their thinking and behaviour for themselves and others. We identify four characteristics of an inclusive mindset: curiosity (Chapter 9), humility (Chapter 10), courage (Chapter 11), and empathy (Chapter 12).

Lived experiences

Our lived experiences (experiences over the duration of our lifetime) might influence our ability to be inclusive. This is because our lived experiences as leaders may limit our capability to be empathetic and will heavily influence the biases, stereotypes, and prejudices that we hold. We argue that lived experiences are not just personal and first-hand experiences, but also intergenerational. The knowledge, beliefs, and understanding we inherit from our family, communities, and cultural narratives shape how we see identities and systemic inequalities, even if we have not personally experienced them. Therefore, in the context of practising inclusive leadership, lived experiences refer to the knowledge and insights we gather from our interactions within various systems, including family systems, as well as the extent to which we have been exposed to perspectives and backgrounds different from our own. We explore the role of lived experiences in driving inclusive leadership in Chapter 13.

Knowledge

Our final driver of inclusive leadership is knowledge. Inclusive leaders are continuously developing sound knowledge of topics and issues relevant to inclusion, while acknowledging the risks of complacency, which can come particularly with advanced expertise. This knowledge fuels awareness and is not limited to education but also includes facts and evidence of what is happening around us in terms of diversity. Without this underpinning knowledge, we are in danger of being ignorant of our ignorance! In Chapter 14 we provide an introduction into ten diversity and inclusion topics: prejudice, bias, stereotyping, privilege, merit, power, equity, positive action, microaggression, and intersectionality.

Curiosity   9

In the context of inclusive leadership, we define curiosity as a desire to understand how others view and experience the world without judgement. It has an association with a positive attitude to lifelong learning and receptivity to the "new" even when the new is not something we like or agree with in the first instance.

The origins of curiosity can be traced back through evolutionary psychology. Acquiring information is the primary evolutionary purpose of our five senses and the need to acquire information has been a major driver of evolution for hundreds of millions of years.[1] Curiosity is an internally motivated form of information seeking: the desire to understand that which we do not. It is thought that the function of curiosity is to motivate learning by acquiring information. Therefore, humans evolved to become curious, as it was our curiosity that motivated us to acquire information, often through new experiences, and this information enabled us to survive. Research from neuroscience supports this view: when we practise curiosity, we activate the part of our brain associated with rewards, producing the "feel good" neurotransmitter dopamine.[2] Therefore, in situations of uncertainty, being curious switches our brain on to remain open and learn, while reducing our threat response of the unknown.

Research has also linked curiosity with a range of different behaviours. For example, people who are more curious often seek out novel experiences,[3] read extensively,[4] scrutinise engaging images,[5] ask a large number of unprompted questions,[6] explore how others think, feel, and behave,[7] and persist on difficult tasks.[8] Some evidence suggests that, in addition to natural individual differences in curiosity (i.e., some people are more curious than others), there are also in-person variations in curiosity (i.e., some people

DOI: 10.4324/9781003598022-14

are more curious about some things than others). Research found that it is an individual's estimate of their own prior knowledge that drives their curiosity.[9] Individuals demonstrate greater curiosity when they already have a small amount of prior knowledge compared to no knowledge at all – which makes knowledge another important aspect of being an inclusive leader. In this respect, it appears as though we need to have at least enough knowledge of something to know that it is worth exploring further, and it is our feelings of curiosity that drive the desire to learn more. Therefore, in the context of inclusive leadership, foundational knowledge related to EDI can fuel curiosity (*more on knowledge as an inclusive leader in Chapter 14*).

So, if we are wired to be curious, what gets in the way? Although we are biologically wired to be curious and have a range of evolutionary benefits (e.g., those that help us learn, adapt, and solve problems), fear can inhibit this natural drive. Fear reduces our cognitive capability into binary and simple responses, making us prioritise safety and security over exploration. This is where psychological safety becomes a necessary condition to support us in practising curiosity.

What does curiosity have to do with practising inclusive leadership?

Like many mindset characteristics, most people will find that they are naturally more curious in some contexts and less curious in others. Also, research suggests that there are different types of curious people.[10] In other words, some people may feel safer being curious in certain situations than others. For some people, their curiosity translates into seeking out wide-ranging experiences and adventure. For others, their curiosity focuses on learning, with the purpose of solving problems. And, for some, curiosity is all about understanding what makes people tick.

You might find it helpful to consider how your curiosity manifests in different situations. For example:

- When you meet someone new, how curious are you to learn more?
- When you visit somewhere new, how curious are you to learn about that place?
- When you find yourself in a new situation in a work context, how curious are you to learn versus other behaviours (such as to perform)?
- When you encounter a problem, is your default response curiosity or judgement?
- When you face uncertainty, how excited do you feel about its potential possibilities and opportunities?

These types of curiosity are important for inclusion for different reasons.

Curiosity requires that we have a desire to learn about other people, to understand what is important to them, and why they behave the way that they do, especially when people are different to us. When we are curious, we are more likely to see difference in others as an opportunity to learn as opposed to a threat. Inclusive leaders appreciate diversity and uniqueness. However, to do this, they must first be curious, ask questions, explore what makes others unique, and learn to see this difference as a benefit in itself.

Inclusive leaders are culturally intelligent. This means that they are aware and appreciative of other cultures and life experiences and adapt their behaviour accordingly (*more on cultural intelligence as an inclusive leader behaviour in Chapter 16*). Being curious about other cultures and perspectives enables inclusive leaders to acquire knowledge and understanding of the world around them, which forms the foundation of cultural intelligence.

However, perhaps the time our curiosity is truly challenged is when things go wrong, because of our natural fear and threat response. Inclusive leaders are able to use their curiosity to drive a desire to understand what happened and why, while reinforcing psychological safety, so that they can gather information before jumping to conclusions or solutions.

Case example

From childhood, my parents nurtured a deep sense of curiosity in me, encouraging me to question things and embrace failure as a valuable learning opportunity. At the dinner table, my mother often asked, "What have you failed at today?" She was a brilliant scientist – and having her as a role model was a privilege. This upbringing helped me approach setbacks with curiosity rather than stress or shame. As a father, I strive to instil the same values in my children, and I can already see the positive impact I am having on them. Surprisingly, I also get to influence my direct reports as a leader. Although some of them come from backgrounds that may lead to a more fixed mindset, it is fascinating to see how the work environment can shape our perspectives. We spend a lot of time at work, which helps!

Recently, one of my team members confided in me that they had learned to listen to different perspectives with curiosity, without becoming defensive or feeling threatened. This shift was made possible because they reframed the interaction as an opportunity to learn, rather than feeling pressured to make a decision immediately. They understood that fully grasping the situation, which involved various viewpoints, was essential before forming an opinion.

One small exercise we do before meetings has inspired this change for them. We begin by having each colleague share what they know about the topic at hand. At the end of this session, we then share something new we learned from each other. We intentionally separate this first part of the meeting (focused on learning) from the second part (focused on decision-making). This structure prevents confusion between these two distinct activities. It has proven effective since no one wants to end the learning portion without sharing that they have gained new insight.

What can you do to enhance curiosity?

We can foster our curiosity by proactively seeking out novel and unknown experiences. Trying new things and incorporating changes into our routine creates novel experiences, which can trigger questions driven by curiosity. Besides being intentional in seeking out novel and unknown experiences, we can also check our own state of safety and fear by using self-awareness and emotional regulation techniques (*more on being emotionally agile in Chapter 21*).

The following questions can help you to explore curiosity in the context of inclusive leadership:

- What conditions help you feel safe enough to be curious?
- What emotions tend to block your curiosity, and how can you navigate them?
- When you find yourself forming a judgement about something or someone (i.e., it is good or bad, right or wrong), what might a more neutral or positive perspective look like?
- When was the last time you questioned a long-held belief? What did you learn?
- What can you do to set aside your biases and viewpoints while listening openly?
- Which cultures do you hold the most stereotypes about, and what is something new you can learn about these cultures that does not reinforce these stereotypes?
- How can you introduce new experiences into your life so that your brain perceives new as a reward rather than a threat (this might be different foods, travelling to new places, or picking up a new hobby)?

- When was the last time you intentionally did something that stretched your comfort zone?
- When and how do you usually like to learn something new and what motivates you in these instances?
- In what area of life do you assume you already "know enough"? How would approaching this area as a beginner change your perspective?
- What would you attempt if you knew you could not fail?
- What is one new thing you could do today that might open up possibilities with something where you are feeling stuck?

Chapter 9 in summary

- Curiosity in the context of inclusive leadership is a desire to understand, without judgement, how others view and experience the world.
- Being curious is an evolutionary trait, however it shuts down when we experience fear and feel unsafe.
- There are different types of curious people and we can be more curious in some contexts than others.
- Curiosity helps us see what is different as an opportunity to learn as opposed to a threat. It increases the production of the "feel good" neurotransmitter dopamine and reduces our threat response.
- We can practise a curious mindset by actively seeking new experiences daily while reframing what is different as an opportunity to learn.
- Curiosity is critical for inclusion as it drives us to understand what makes others unique, enables us to learn about other cultures and perspectives, and enables us to gather information to learn from it when things go wrong.

Notes

1 Kidd, C., & Hayden, B. Y. (2015). The psychology and neuroscience of curiosity. *Neuron*, 88(3), 449–460.
2 Rock, D. (2009). *Your brain at work: Strategies for overcoming distraction, regaining focus, and working smarter all day long.* London: Harper Business.
3 Zuckerman, M. (1994). *Behavioral expressions and biosocial bases of sensation seeking.* New York: Cambridge University Press.
4 Schiefele, U. (1999). Interest and learning from text. *Scientific Studies of Reading*, 3, 257–279.
5 Silvia, P. J. (2005). What is interesting? Exploring the appraisal structure of interest. *Emotion*, 5, 89–102.

6 Peters, R. A. (1978). Effects of anxiety, curiosity, and perceived instructor threat on student verbal behavior in the college classroom. *Journal of Educational Psychology, 70,* 388–395.

7 Renner, B. (2006). Curiosity about people: The development of a social curiosity measure in adults. *Journal of Personality Assessment, 87,* 305–316.

8 Sansone, C., & Smith, J. L. (2000). Interest and self-regulation: The relation between having to and wanting to. In C. Sansone & J. M. Harackiewicz (Eds.), *Intrinsic and extrinsic motivation* (pp. 341–372). San Diego, CA: Academic.

9 Wade, S., & Kidd, C. (2019). The role of prior knowledge and curiosity in learning. *Psychonomic Bulletin & Review, 26,* 1377–1387.

10 Kashdan, T. B., Stiksma, M. C., Disabato, D. J., McKnight, P. E., Bekier, J., Kaji, J., & Lazarus, R. (2018). The five-dimensional curiosity scale: Capturing the bandwidth of curiosity and identifying four unique subgroups of curious people. *Journal of Research in Personality, 73,* 130–149.

Humility   **10**

In the context of inclusive leadership, we define humility as the ability of the leader to remain grounded, aware of their privileges, and recognise their own limitations while being open to feedback and learning from mistakes.

Humility is considered by psychologists to be a core personality dimension that can be observed across different languages and cultures.[1] Humility is also conceptualised as a strength that has been shown to support human flourishing.[2] The origins of the word "humility" can be traced back to the Latin word *humilitas*, which means "grounded" or "from the earth".[3] As such, humility is considered to be a virtuous strength as it enables individuals to have a clear, rooted-in-reality perspective of themselves.[4]

Therefore, to be humble means that we are able to view ourselves accurately. This includes an appreciation that we are not the centre of all of our relationships with others. When we are humble, we are able to be vulnerable, acknowledging our mistakes and weaknesses to ourselves and others. When we are humble, we recognise the role of privileges in being successful and also recognise and appreciate the strengths of others. Humble individuals are generally receptive to new ideas and feedback,[5] and they value diversity and uniqueness in others, appreciating the contribution this can make to innovation and problem-solving.[6]

DOI: 10.4324/9781003598022-15

Modesty, gender and cross-cultural differences

In this book, we distinguish modesty from humility. Modesty is more about outward self-presentation, usually associated with downplaying our achievements and deeds. Humility is more of an inward process and is associated with acknowledging our limitations and our strengths, without self-deprecation, and being open to learn and grow.

In the context of EDI, modesty can be problematic as, in many cases, societal expectations might set the norm for how people *should* behave with regard to modesty. From a gender point of view, for example, evidence shows how the gender "modesty norm" impacts women's progression in academic and workplace settings.[7] In general, societal norms dictate that women should behave modestly, downplaying their achievements and generally behaving in a demure, "lady-like" manner. This creates a double-bind. On the one hand, women are penalised if they do not conform with the modesty norm, as they are judged harshly for self-promotion, perhaps being seen as arrogant. However, if they do conform with the modesty norm, they will struggle to reach their full professional potential as this inevitably requires a degree of self-promotion to navigate recruitment and promotion opportunities. This penalty can be linked to patriarchal systems, as modesty is a behavioural expectation of women, encouraging them to be subservient, reinforcing gender power dynamics, and therefore reinforcing male domination.

Equally, cultural values also play an important role in the demonstration of modesty. For example, Chinese people might communicate an underestimation of their abilities to maintain harmony, which is a priority in collectivist cultures, therefore to be modest about one's own good deeds and achievements, particularly in public, is expected.[8] Conversely, in the USA, the social expectation is to minimise displays of modesty, particularly for men. Cultures (such as those of the USA) that have a history of extending their power through dominance (i.e., military, economic, and cultural) might also have an illusion of superiority that does not align with modesty.

Therefore, as inclusive leaders, it is important to hold space for modesty both as a barrier to enabling the level playing field but also as a cultural influence that plays an important role in collective harmony.

To fully understand humility, it can be helpful to consider the opposite of humility which is "hubris". Hubris occurs when a person exhibits extreme pride or dangerous overconfidence, including an overestimation of one's competence, capabilities, and accomplishments.[9] Whereas humility is considered to be grounded in reality, hubris signals a loss of awareness of reality. This often includes attributing successes solely to one's own actions rather than recognising the contribution of the team. Success can sometimes breed hubris, as individuals may become deluded about their sense of self-importance, closed off from feedback from others, overly confident, and eventually convinced that they can do no wrong.[10]

While hubris indicates an overconfidence, being humble does not mean that we are not confident or not secure in our own abilities. Instead, when we are humble, we acknowledge our strengths and weaknesses, while also seeing the strengths of others and experiencing gratitude for the contributions that others bring to the work that we do.

What does humility have to do with practising inclusive leadership?

When leaders demonstrate humility it benefits those around them in multiple ways. Research has indicated that as humble leaders listen to the ideas and feedback of those around them,[11] those who work with these leaders will speak up more frequently.[12] In addition, as humble leaders role-model feedback-seeking, research has found that those who work with humble leaders *also* engage in feedback-seeking behaviours more frequently.[13] Therefore, humility is integral to inclusive leadership as leaders who model humbleness create an environment grounded in respect and tolerance.[14]

Humility specifically plays out in relation to valuing diversity and uniqueness. Humble, inclusive leaders recognise that the differences in individuals' ways of thinking and seeing the world, influenced by their own unique lived experiences, are key to innovation and problem solving. Therefore, inclusive leaders are not trying to create clones of themselves, they do not want a team of people all working the same way. Instead, they create a flexible environment where people can work in ways that play to their diverse strengths.

Recognising the value in the contribution of others means that inclusive leaders create space for others to speak up and contribute. Combined with the leaders' own willingness to acknowledge their mistakes and weaknesses, humility means that such leaders create a psychologically safe working environment (*for more on psychological safety and inclusion see Chapter 3*).

The double standards of humility for marginalised leaders

Hopefully we have made a clear case as to why humility is a critical trait for inclusive leaders. However, unfortunately the reality is not so simple if you are a marginalised leader, as our ability to demonstrate humility in the workplace is influenced by our identity and our environment.

What happens when you demonstrate humility, acknowledging your mistakes and weaknesses, when you are a marginalised leader working in a non-inclusive environment?

The problem for marginalised leaders is that, due to the range of stereotypes, systems of oppression, and power imbalances that operate in our society, when working in a non-inclusive environment, the marginalised leader is likely to be operating from a starting point of assumed incompetence until proven otherwise. For example, research has shown that students consistently underestimate the educational credentials and academic rank of women and minority professors,[15] and a series of studies has shown that when people are asked to think of what they might consider a "star" performer, they consistently find it more difficult to see a woman in that role, known as the "think star, think men" phenomenon.[16]

We also know that girls are more likely to downplay aspects of themselves and to be modest, and female bonding often consists of admitting vulnerabilities to one another, whereas the opposite is true for male bonding.[17] However, when men are modest, we tend to assume that they must be better than they claim, yet when women are modest, we believe them[18]. On top of this, women's tendency to be modest or humble is often judged against men's tendency to be overconfident, meaning that women can come across as lacking in confidence and assertiveness.[19] Unfortunately, while the research indicates the value in humble leadership, marginalised leaders must walk a very careful tightrope of balancing humility (such as owning one's mistakes, recognising the contribution of others) without being seen as lacking in confidence or assertiveness, while still having to prove their competence to others.

What are the implications of this for humility? If we start from a position of being underrated in terms of our authority and expertise and we then downplay our own strengths and contributions, openly share our vulnerabilities, weaknesses, and mistakes, and highlight the contributions of the rest of the team in our successes, will we be viewed as humble leaders or as "less than competent" leaders? The research indicates that if you are marginalised in your organisation, the likelihood is that being "too humble" may actually be a disadvantage in your ability to be seen as a credible and competent leader.

This is why, when we coach marginalised leaders on this topic, we always take a nuanced approach. It is important to recognise the context in which the marginalised leader is operating and take this into account when considering how humble they can be. For example, when the leader is surrounded by individuals they trust and from whom they already have the respect and recognition as a leader, they may be safe to be humble and this will bring with it all the advantages from an inclusive leader perspective, as detailed above. However, if that leader is with a group where they are in the minority, perhaps the only person of their identity in that environment, it may be much riskier for them to demonstrate humility in this context.

Case example

Our CEO recently made an internal announcement that did not go down well. He was addressing our gender pay gap report, which revealed significant discrepancies in bonus payments. His initial response was a brief, generalised acknowledgment of a recently conducted equal pay audit, during which he expressed confidence that our pay policies were unbiased. However, he failed to recognise the systemic issues that underpinned the audit and overlooked additional points raised by staff, such as concerns about performance ratings.

Upon realising his misunderstanding, the CEO recorded a heartfelt video and sent it to the entire workforce. In this message, he sincerely apologised for his oversight and recognised that the data pointed to deeper problems related to gender bias within the company, including the performance rating system. He then took the initiative to hire an external firm to audit our pay and performance policies to identify gender-related systemic barriers affecting pay increases and bonus calculations. This firm also conducted focus groups with marginalised gender employees.

The CEO is now committed to transparency by providing us with monthly updates. He has also agreed to review the bonus distribution from last year's performance cycle and rectify any discrepancies by compensating individuals where appropriate. As a result, the bonus pool will be smaller this year, leading to dissatisfaction among many employees. Nevertheless, he remains steadfast in his plan and has demonstrated accountability, humbly accepting his misjudgement.

Interestingly, our engagement survey includes a question about our trust in senior leadership. Last year, following the incident, trust was incredibly low, but this year it has reached its highest score since this CEO was appointed.

What can you do to enhance humility?

The underlying approach to practising humility in leadership includes fostering self-awareness and openness to feedback and learning (while taking responsibility for mistakes) and focusing on collaboration rather than self-promotion. Humility in leadership builds on influencing others based on collaboration, trust, and empowerment as opposed to control and dominance.

Some questions that can help you to explore humility in the context of inclusive leadership include:

- Can you recall a time when a piece of feedback from your team challenged you? How did you react?
- What holds you back from seeking more feedback and how can you overcome this?
- Can you recall a time when you admitted to a mistake? How did it impact you and those around you? What emotions came up for you and how did these emotions influence your response?
- In what ways have you learnt from your colleagues at work recently?
- How do you ensure others' ideas are heard and valued?
- In your most recent success, how did your team contribute to the outcome?
- In what ways has privilege or circumstance contributed to your success? How can you recognise this while staying accountable for your actions?
- When was the last time you showed appreciation to someone? How do you typically show appreciation?
- Can you think of a situation where you prioritised your team's success before your own?

- How do you encourage others to take ownership of decisions and outcomes? How would you say you lead by example in this area?
- How might you stay open to learning from those who have less experience than you?
- What would it look like if you embraced making mistakes as an integral part of learning?

Chapter 10 in summary

- To be humble means that we view ourselves accurately, we are able to be vulnerable, are self-aware, and we acknowledge our mistakes and weaknesses to ourselves and others.
- Humility in leadership means to recognise the value in the contributions of others and therefore create space for others to speak up and contribute.
- Humility in leadership means to recognise and appreciate others' strengths and to be receptive to new ideas and feedback from all backgrounds and levels of experience.
- Humility supports inclusive leadership, as leaders recognise the importance of diversity and uniqueness in innovation and problem solving. Inclusive leaders create a flexible environment where people can work in ways that play to their diverse strengths in a collaborative way.
- However, there are important considerations for marginalised leaders and humility due to threats from stereotypes about competence. Leaders from marginalised groups might experience being seen as "too humble" as a disadvantage, challenging their ability to be seen as credible and competent. Therefore, for marginalised leaders, it is also important to consider the environment when demonstrating humility.

Notes

1 Ashton, M. C., & Lee, K. (2007). Empirical, theoretical, and practical advantages of the HEXACO model of personality structure. *Personality and Social Psychology Review, 11*, 150–166. http://dx.doi.org/10.1177/1088868306294907.

2 Peterson, C., & Seligman, M. E. P. (2004). *Character strengths and virtues: A handbook and classification.* Washington, DC: APA Press.

3 Kelemen, T. K., Matthews, S. H., Matthews, M. J., & Henry, S. E. (2023). Humble leadership: A review and synthesis of leader expressed humility. *Journal of Organizational Behavior, 44*(2), 202–224.

4 Greenberg, J. (2005). *Kant and the ethics of humility: A story of dependence, corruption, and virtue.* New York: Cambridge University Press.

5 Jeung, C. W., & Yoon, H. J. (2016). Leader humility and psychological empowerment: Investigating contingencies. *Journal of Managerial Psychology*, *31*, 1122–1136.

6 Argandona, A. (2015). Humility in management. *Journal of Business Ethics*, *132*(1), 63–71.

7 Smith, J. L., & Huntoon, M. (2013). Women's bragging rights: Overcoming modesty norms to facilitate women's self-promotion. *Psychology of Women Quarterly*, *38*(4), 447–459.

8 Genyue, F., Heyman, G. & Lee, K. (2010). Reasoning about modesty among adolescents and adults in China and the US. *Journal of Adolescence*, *34*, 599–608.

9 Murrell, A. (2018). *Effective leaders choose humility over hubris.* Accessed from https://www.forbes.com/sites/audreymurrell/2018/12/20/effective-leaders-must-choose-humility-over-hubris/. Retrieved 2 January 2025.

10 Laker, B. (2021). *Why modern executives are more susceptible to hubris than ever.* Accessed from https://sloanreview.mit.edu/article/why-modern-executives-are-more-susceptible-to-hubris-than-ever/. Retrieved 2 January 2025.

11 Owens, B. P., Johnson, M. D., & Mitchell, T. R. (2013). Expressed humility in organizations: Implications for performance, teams, and leadership. *Organization Science*, *24*, 1517–1538.

12 Shaw, K. H., & Mao, J. (2021). Leader–follower congruence in humility and follower voice: The mediating role of affective attachment. *Current Psychology*, 1–10.

13 Qian, S., Liu, Y., & Chen, Y. (2022). Leader humility as a predictor of employees' feedback-seeking behavior: The intervening role of psychological safety and job insecurity. *Current Psychology*, *41*(3), 1348–1360.

14 Murrell, A. (2018). *Effective leaders choose humility over hubris.* Accessed from https://www.forbes.com/sites/audreymurrell/2018/12/20/effective-leaders-must-choose-humility-over-hubris/. Retrieved 2 January 2025.

15 Miller, J., & Chamberlin, M. (2000). Women are teachers, men are professors: A study of student perceptions. *Teaching Sociology*, 283–298.

16 Villamor, I., & Aguinis, H. (2024). Think star, think men? Implicit star performer theories. *Journal of Organizational Behavior*, *45*(6), 783–799.

17 Sieghart, M. A. (2022). *The authority gap: Why women are still taken less seriously than men, and what we can do about it.* New York: W. W. Norton.

18 Sieghart, M. A. (2022). *The authority gap: Why women are still taken less seriously than men, and what we can do about it.* New York: W. W. Norton.

19 Chamorro-Premuzic, T. (2013). Why do so many incompetent men become leaders. *Harvard Business Review*, *22*.

Courage 11

In the context of inclusive leadership, we define courage as the act of speaking up against bias and unjust behaviour, particularly when it is uncomfortable. Courage is also admitting and correcting mistakes without defensiveness. The saying "burning your own house down with you inside" is a powerful metaphor that illustrates the courage required by leaders to reform systems to be more inclusive.

Courage is considered a virtue that enables the enactment of all other virtues.[1] All humans experience a tension between the need to remain safe and the desire to experience personal growth.[2] Courage is the energising catalyst that enables us to choose personal growth over safety needs as it enables us to move toward a goal despite the presence of fear.

> One set [of needs] clings to safety and defensiveness out of fear, tending to regress backward, hanging on to the past ... afraid to take chances, afraid to jeopardize what one already has, afraid of independence, freedom and separateness. The other set of forces impels one forward [...] toward full functioning of all ones capacities, toward confidence in the face of the external world.[3]

Workplace courage can be defined as an action for a worthy cause or a higher purpose, despite significant risks perceivable in the moment to the actor.[4] Courage allows us to act effectively under conditions of danger, risk, and fear (including the fear of isolation, abandonment, shame, and disgrace).[5]

Although often not openly discussed in the workplace, many important actions require a huge amount of courage. Changing our behaviour

DOI: 10.4324/9781003598022-16

requires courage as we step out of our comfort zone and open ourselves up to the potential for failure. Innovating requires courage as we share new and unique ideas for the critique of others. Standing up for others and speaking out requires courage as we push against the status quo. We all have the capacity to behave courageously. Once we recognise the importance of courage at work, we can take action to foster and develop this mindset.

For an act to be considered courageous it must involve a degree of risk to the actor. In the context of the workplace, this risk may involve jeopardising our economic security and professional standing, which may compromise our promotion and progression opportunities.[6] In addition to the risks a courageous act may pose to financial security and career progression, courage will also be required when engaging in actions that risk our social image, might damage our relationship with others, or challenge our social acceptance.[7] When we engage in a courageous act, we are aware of the risks to ourselves, and we persist despite these risks. This is why impulsive acts fuelled by emotion alone are usually not considered to be courageous.[8]

What does courage have to do with practising inclusive leadership?

Unfortunately there is still a great need for courage in the workplace. Approximately 30 per cent of employees have observed illegal actions in the workplace and almost 80 per cent of employees have observed abusive behaviour from a co-worker, yet only a small percentage speak up in relation to these bad behaviours.[9] In fact, there is growing evidence to indicate that witnessing uncivil, illegal actions and abusive supervision can actually lead others to perpetuate the same behaviours rather than trying to stop them.

When we consider courage in the workplace and inclusion, courage is required to address injustice, such as an unethical or oppressive act, particularly if this is perpetuated by someone in power. Courage may also be required to challenge a powerful individual – for example, when problem solving or decision-making. Courage is needed to go against the views of colleagues and friends at work by speaking out and disagreeing with the status quo, risking being ostracised by a group.[10] Courage is required to engage in acts that might mean that you damage relationships and/or damage your reputation within ingroups – for example, admitting when you have made a major or costly mistake.[11] Courage might also be required *not* to take any action – for example, refusing to engage in unethical or immoral acts despite substantial pressure to do so.

The primary link between inclusive leadership and courage is via advocating for others, including being an ally to support and voice the needs of marginalised groups. This takes courage as it will generally involve speaking up against the group and putting oneself at risk on behalf of equality and justice (*more on practising allyship in Chapter 18*). This process of speaking up against injustice or the status quo can be particularly risky if you are challenging someone more senior than yourself. However, it can also be embarrassing, call unwanted attention to yourself, or feel awkward or uncomfortable. Having difficult conversations, especially about topics such as privilege, prejudice, and discrimination is extremely challenging and uncomfortable for almost everybody! Being the person to speak up against the group goes against almost every human instinct – which is to fit in and run with the herd. It takes courage!

However, inclusive leaders recognise that leadership is a privilege and therefore leaders have a responsibility to speak up and use the legitimate power that they have been granted to ensure that the work environment is inclusive. Whether you identify with this or not, as a leader, you have power and influence and with this comes responsibility. This is especially true for leaders from dominant groups. It is everybody's responsibility to create a fair, inclusive, and just workplace and not solely the responsibility of marginalised groups, who will likely be those most frequently impacted, to speak up and challenge unfair, exclusionary, and unjust systems.

In addition to these "big" acts of courage (i.e., speaking up against an abusive, more senior member of staff), from the perspective of an inclusive leader we can also consider "smaller" acts of courage, such as trying out new, risky behaviours.

Trying new behaviours, particularly those linked to resisting oppressive behaviours such as racism, sexism, and other forms of discrimination, takes a huge amount of courage. Whenever we try something new, there is a risk that we will get it wrong, we might say the wrong thing, or we might even unintentionally offend someone. The more you learn about this topic the more you realise the risk of getting it wrong. However, inclusive leaders consistently push themselves regardless, recognising that mistakes will be made along the way and appreciating that learning from mistakes is one of the ways in which we can improve. It takes courage to do this. To take yourself to the learning edge, in public, and to stay there, day-in-day-out, takes courage.

The importance of attempting a name

An important sign of an inclusive leader is a leader who takes the time and effort to ensure that they learn how to pronounce peoples' names correctly. Our names are an important part of our identity, our culture, our personal history, and are part of what makes us uniquely us. Therefore, when others get our name wrong, this can have important implications.

For some, the habitual mispronunciation of someone's name can feel like another way in which they are "othered". It can remind them they are different, not of this place, with their names being seen as "not normal", "weird", "too hard", "too foreign" (according to an anglicised world view). This might bring with it all the associations of not belonging.

Unfortunately there is a long, dark history associated with misnaming or mispronouncing people's names and discrimination and slavery. Historically, this played out as the common practice of individuals marginalised by society being renamed against their will (often indigenous peoples, immigrants, and enslaved Africans and their descendants), including the process of frequent and deliberate mispronunciation or the forced anglicisation of the name.[12] This process of publicly renaming and shaming individuals is a form of racial subjugation and served to strip away the individual's identity and power. Unfortunately, these practices are still not relegated to the history books and there are still many cases where the onus is on the individual with the "difficult" name to make accommodations. For example, in 2009, the US conservative commentator, Mark Krikorian, stated that there "ought to be limits" on how far individuals should go in attempting to pronounce names in accordance with the individual's preference and that "[O]ne of the areas where conformity is appropriate is how your new countrymen say your name".[13] To add further insult to injury, Krikorian's comments were in relation to someone born and raised in the US.

Therefore, inclusive leaders, especially inclusive leaders who are operating in their native tongue, recognise the critical in saying people's names correctly. This means that they give time and attention to listening and learning how to say someone's name. If they read or hear the person's name and they are not sure how to correctly say it, they politely and respectfully ask the person how to pronounce their name and/or to repeat it. As soon as they are able, they might make a note of how to say the name phonetically, which can help them to learn and remember how to say the name correctly. Remember, each person has their own way of pronouncing their name so even if you think you have heard the same name before, it is important to understand how this individual pronounces their own name. If you find pronouncing names challenging due to speech barriers, language difficulties, or neurodiversity, you should communicate openly with the individual, letting them know you are committed to getting it right and keeping them informed of the steps you are taking to improve. Furthermore, unfamiliar names may involve sounds, rhythms, or tones that are not part of your native language, requiring you to practise, and possibly fail a few times, before getting it right.

What might this have to do with courage? For some, this won't be an issue. For example, if you work cross-culturally, you may have plenty of experience and confidence in learning how to pronounce names from different countries and cultures to your own. However, for those who have limited cross-cultural experience, this can feel particularly daunting. This is especially true once you understand the potential implications for exclusion with getting a name wrong, coupled with the fear of embarrassment over attempting the name and getting it wrong, then even the seemingly simple and certainly everyday act of saying someone's name can become one in which courage is required. The easier, less courageous route would be to avoid saying someone's name. However, to those who are aware that others might find it difficult to pronounce their name, the consistent avoidance of actually saying the name is as obvious as a neon flashing light stating "I don't know how to say your name"!

Watch out for double standards (for some, being courageous is held against them)

In this chapter we have advocated for the need for inclusive leaders to have courage: to be able to speak up and call out unethical, discriminatory, biased, or unjust behaviour when they see it. However, it is also important to acknowledge that, as with many aspects of life, unfortunately, courage is one area where double standards are in operation.

For example, back in Chapter 3, we described research that highlights the backlash that Black girls and women can face when they speak up, with Black women and girls who speak up being seen as argumentative, confrontational, and aggressive.[14] This double standard is unfortunately not uncommon. When people of colour have interpersonal conflicts or disagreements with white people, they are often labelled as "angry" or "hostile".[15] There are also issues for women when speaking up. When women engage in assertive behaviour such as speaking up, which is likely to require courage, they are judged much more harshly than men who engage in the same behaviour.[16] This means that marginalised groups face even greater challenges when being courageous. Not only do they need to navigate the fears and risks associated with the courageous act as detailed above, they also need to navigate the backlash or double standards that dominant groups will not face when engaging in the same courageous acts. And we all judge marginalised groups more harshly, including members of the marginalised groups themselves.[17]

Therefore we can all pause and catch our own biases when people do speak up. Notice how we are responding to that person. Do we judge them harshly? If we notice this, reflect on why we are experiencing this response. Challenge ourselves to explore whether we would have the same response if it was someone of a different social identity speaking up.

Case example

The CEO of a multinational consumer goods organisation, faced challenges related to a branding and marketing campaign that was said to be perpetuating racial stereotypes. The CEO was faced with a choice of remaining silent and weathering the storm, considering the huge investment and how much this product accounted for revenue, or rebrand. The CEO decided to rebrand. They acknowledged the problem, with a personal statement accepting the harm caused, and committed to change even if it meant losing market share in some regions. The rebrand and product reform started replacing any lines and imagery that reinforced stereotypes. They also introduced diversity quotas for leadership to ensure future decisions would not revert back to biased outcomes. The CEO needed to address internal resistance, arguing why the cost and disruption to the business was necessary. They were pressured by some regional consumers who threatened to boycott the new branded product, and there was heavy criticism from investors who accused the CEO of prioritising social issues over profits – both posed significant risks for the CEO while being accountable for potential negative outcomes. The company has since become widely recognised for its leadership in corporate responsibility.

What can you do to enhance courage?

Courage in the workplace is not only about bold actions. It is about creating the conditions to foster psychological safety, resilience, and growth. There are some key attributes that will support the leader to display and role-model courage. There are three dimensions to the practice of courage: confidence and self-belief (the first step to countering fear and the impulse to protect ourselves), connecting to a higher purpose (helps to fuel resilience), and managing fear (enables self-regulation).[18]

Furthermore, anger is an important fuel for courageous action.[19] Anger at injustice, unfairness, or violations of human rights may give a person the impetus to act courageously. Therefore, constructively embracing anger is also important for practising courage in leadership.

Some questions that can help you explore courage in the context of inclusive leadership include:

Confidence and self-belief

- What strengths and skills have you displayed in the past when you were courageous?
- What past success can you draw on to remind yourself of your courage?
- What is the worst outcome you might encounter if you take a courageous step?
- What is one positive outcome you can imagine from a situation of fear? What step can you take to move closer to it?
- What resources are available to support you in the case of a negative outcome after a courageous act?
- Who are the courageous people in your life and what can you learn from them?

Connecting to a higher purpose

- How does facing this fear align with your personal values and purpose?
- What is the bigger impact you are hoping to have by acting with courage in a given (fearful) situation?
- Who might benefit from your courage?
- How might focusing on others rather than yourself help you to move forward with courage?

- What would your future self say about the fear you are experiencing and what advice would your future self give?
- What might be the ripple effect of your courage on your life and those around you?

Managing fear

- What fears are holding you back?
- How realistic are these fears?
- What opportunities might these fears present to you?
- What would it take for fears to motivate you as opposed to triggering a safety response?
- What is the smallest risk you can take to build your courage?
- Imagine you have acted with courage in the face of your fear, what does success look like?
- What might anger be telling you about the situation and how can you constructively redirect anger to a courageous act?

Chapter 11 in summary

- Courage in the context of inclusive leadership is required to address injustice (such as an unethical or oppressive act), to speak out and disagree with the status quo, and to engage in acts that might mean that you lose the respect or esteem of others. Courage might also be required *not* to take any action, for example refusing to engage in illegal or immoral acts despite pressure to do so.
- Courage can be defined as an action for a worthy cause despite significant risks perceivable in the moment to the actor. It allows us to act under conditions of danger, risk, and fear, including the fear of isolation, abandonment, shame, and disgrace.
- Inclusive leaders need courage to practise allyship, supporting and voicing the needs of marginalised groups, speaking up against the norm and highlighting injustices, even when these are perpetuated by those in senior positions of authority.
- Inclusive leaders also frequently need to engage in new behaviours linked to sensitive topics, such as addressing racism, sexism, and other forms of discrimination, which takes courage as the leader risks making mistakes and getting things wrong.

- We can practise being courageous by building our confidence and self-efficacy, connecting to a higher purpose, and managing the fear response. Equally, anger, when managed constructively, can fuel courageous acts.

Notes

1 Scarre, G. (2010). *On courage*. New York: Routledge.
2 Goud, N. H. (2005). Courage: Its nature and development. *The Journal of Humanistic Counseling, Education and Development, 44*(1), 102–116.
3 Maslow, A. (1968). *Toward a psychology of being* (p. 46). New York: Van Nostrand Reinhold.
4 Detert, J. R., & Bruno, E. A. (2017). Workplace courage: Review, synthesis, and future agenda for a complex construct. *Academy of Management Annals, 11*(2), 593–639.
5 Goud, N. H. (2005). Courage: Its nature and development. *The Journal of Humanistic Counseling, Education and Development, 44*(1), 102–116.
6 Magee, J. C., & Galinsky, A. D. (2008). Social hierarchy: The self-reinforcing nature of power and status. *Academy of Management Annals, 2,* 351–398.
7 Howard, M. C., & Holmes, P. E. (2020). Social courage fosters both voice and silence in the workplace: A study on multidimensional voice and silence with boundary conditions. *Journal of Organizational Effectiveness: People and Performance, 7*(1), 53–73.
8 Goud, N. H. (2005). Courage: Its nature and development. *The Journal of Humanistic Counseling, Education and Development, 44*(1), 102–116.
9 Schilpzand, P., Hekman, D. R., & Mitchell, T. R. (2015). An inductively generated typology and process model of workplace courage. *Organization Science, 26*(1), 52–77.
10 Detert, J. R., & Bruno, E. A. (2017). Workplace courage: Review, synthesis, and future agenda for a complex construct. *Academy of Management Annals, 11*(2), 593–639.
11 Howard, M. C., & Holmes, P. E. (2020). Social courage fosters both voice and silence in the workplace: A study on multidimensional voice and silence with boundary conditions. *Journal of Organizational Effectiveness: People and Performance, 7*(1), 53–73.
12 Bucholtz, M. (2016). On being called out of one's name. In H. Samy Alim, John R. Rickford, & Arnetha F. Ball (Eds.), *Raciolinguistics: How language shapes our ideas about race* (pp. 273–289). New York: Oxford University Press.
13 Bucholtz, M. (2016). On being called out of one's name. In H. Samy Alim, John R. Rickford, & Arnetha F. Ball (Eds.) *Raciolinguistics: How language shapes our ideas about race* (pp. 273–289). New York: Oxford University Press.

14 Woodson, A. N. (2020). Don't let me be misunderstood: Psychological safety, Black girls' speech, and Black feminist perspectives on directness. *Journal of Educational Psychology, 112*(3), 567.

15 Nadal, K. (2023). *How the "angry minority" trope gaslights people of color.* Accessed from https://www.psychologytoday.com/gb/blog/psychology-for-the-people/202309/how-the-angry-minority-trope-gaslights-people-of-color. Retrieved 5 January 2023.

16 Sieghart, M. A. (2022). *The authority gap: Why women are still taken less seriously than men, and what we can do about it.* New York: W. W. Norton.

17 Sieghart, M. A. (2022). *The authority gap: Why women are still taken less seriously than men, and what we can do about it.* New York: W. W. Norton.

18 Goud, N. H. (2005). Courage: Its nature and development. *The Journal of Humanistic Counseling, Education and Development, 44*(1), 102–116.

19 Stemmler, G., Aue, T., & Wacker, J. (2007). Anger and fear: Separable effects of emotion and motivational direction on somatovisceral responses. *International Journal of Psychophysiology, 66*(2), 141–153.

Empathy   **12**

In the context of inclusive leadership, we define empathy as the ability to understand and share the feelings of others. It also involves validating the diverse experiences of others, particularly those from marginalised groups.

There are several dimensions to empathy including types of empathy – such as emotional empathy (sharing feelings of others) and cognitive empathy (understanding someone else's perspective). In the context of inclusion, perhaps the most important concept is empathic concern. This means bridging the gap between feeling and action. It ensures that empathy does not remain passive but instead it motivates action.[1]

Emotional empathy describes when we are able to share the emotions that are experienced or expressed by another individual. For example, when perceiving sadness in another, empathy will cause sadness in the observer.[2] Emotional empathy differs from sympathy in that when we experience sympathy we experience an emotion "for" the individual (rather than "with" the individual). For example, when we perceive sadness in another, rather than also experiencing sadness as we would with empathy, sympathy means there is often a sense of distance and we might experience feelings of concern or pity for the individual. Cognitive empathy on the other hand describes the process of understanding another's situation, or experience.[3] Cognitive empathy is often described as being able to put oneself into another person's shoes or being able to take their perspective.

DOI: 10.4324/9781003598022-17

Autism and empathy

There is a persistent narrative within Western society that autistic people lack empathy, however this is an untrue stereotype.[4] In fact, the reality is that, like neurotypical individuals, autistic individuals will vary in their empathetic experiences, ranging from some who experience low empathy to many who experience very high levels of empathy, known as hyper-empathy, which can be extremely overwhelming and distressing for the individual experiencing these emotions. Equally, both neurotypical and autistic people may experience different forms of empathy imbalance, for example, an individual may have high emotional empathy but challenges with cognitive empathy.[5]

Some autistic individuals may find it hard to pick up on the social and emotional cues that might warrant an empathic response.[6] Some autistic individuals may also find that while they experience empathy for others, they may find it challenging to communicate effectively the empathy they are experiencing to the other party, given the emphasis placed on cues such as eye contact and verbal and non-verbal expressions to acknowledge the other person's emotions.[7] This is because some autistic individuals find that they experience overstimulation and being overwhelmed when making eye contact, and they may have difficulties in understanding body language and other social cues.[8]

Another important aspect in relation to empathy and autism is to consider the motivational factors at play that influence how people approach or avoid empathy. For example, some might avoid empathy due to the pain associated with other's suffering or even the costs to help them.[9] Others might actually move towards empathy because it leads to positive social connections and enhances personal values. We all are managing our empathic responses as we navigate our emotional experience of the world. Therefore, if someone disengages from a shared emotional empathetic response, it does not automatically mean that they do not care.

The key point to note here is that no two individuals on the autistic spectrum are the same and therefore it is critical not to make assumptions or employ stereotypes when it comes to the ability of an autistic individual to be empathetic (or not).

What does empathy have to do with practising inclusive leadership?

Research tells us that there is a clear link between empathy and effective leadership, or perhaps more specifically, a lack of leader empathy is a major problem for the leader's direct reports and the organisation as a whole. For example, a large-scale study assessing 15,000 leaders and managers in 300 organisations across 20 industries and 18 countries, found that empathy was one of the most important drivers of overall leadership performance.[10] Research has also shown that employees who work for a leader who demonstrates higher levels of empathy experience significantly less burnout and chronic stress, and have higher job satisfaction and engagement.[11] Overall, an organisational culture that lacks empathy results in decreased creativity, teamwork, and performance.[12]

Therefore, empathy is an important trait for all leaders; however, it is especially important for inclusive leaders. When we communicate our empathy to others, it helps them to feel understood and validated, which, importantly, contributes to experiences of belonging – a central aspect of inclusion. Furthermore, inclusive leaders are driven by a desire for the world to be fair and equitable. As we have explored in Section One on wellbeing, inclusive leadership is a proactive style of leadership. Therefore, inclusive leaders hold strong empathic concern and want to act to remove injustice and suffering for others. When we are the recipient of an experience that we perceive to be unfair or unjust, we will often experience anger. Inclusive leaders empathise with this experience, also feeling anger at the unfair and unjust situation themselves even if they are not the recipient of the unfair or unjust behaviour. Anger, in particular, is an action emotion, it activates us to do something when we feel it. Therefore, if managed constructively, anger can be a powerful catalyst for change.

In addition to this, cognitive empathy is also critically important for inclusive leaders, as they are required to take the perspective of those different to themselves to understand their lived experience and the barriers they may face in the workplace and beyond. However, there are some important challenges when it comes to empathy and those who are different to us in the form of empathetic bias. Research has shown that people tend to experience less empathy for those they see as being in their "outgroups" compared to those who they see as being in their "ingroups".[13] Therefore, when people are different to us in any particular categorisation (such as gender, race, age, language, socioeconomic status, or culture, for example), we are more likely to view them as being in the outgroup and thus we are likely to experience less empathy for these individuals.

Part of the challenge with experiencing empathy for those in outgroups or those different to us is that we do not truly know, and can never know, what it is like to live life in their shoes and therefore we may struggle to appreciate the true magnitude of the impact of the unfairness and injustice they experience. For example, when discussing the experience of empathy for Black people, Kendall (2013) writes: "often, unless the stories are undeniably horrendous, white people don't seem to be moved" (p. 61).[14] How does it make you feel to read this statement? Is this something you have noticed? Or did it provoke a defensive reaction? How about when you read in Chapter 11 about how it can feel to have your name consistently mispronounced. What did you think and feel when you read that section? Did you experience empathy (assuming that you were not someone who is on the receiving end of this particular microaggression), or did you wonder what the big deal was?

Unfortunately, in our desensitised world, if we judge an experience to be "not too bad", we will struggle to experience empathy, to see what it might be like from the other person's perspective. Instead, we might consider that person to be a "snowflake" – someone who is overly emotional and easily offended. However, this is the essence of privilege. To be unable to see the challenges that others face because we ourselves have never had to experience them (*see Chapter 14 for more on privilege*). One of the antidotes to privilege is empathy, which is why it is such a critical trait for inclusive leaders.

Empathetic fatigue

Trying to understand and share the feelings of others is not easy, coming at an emotional and cognitive cost in terms of draining and depleting resources and energy.[15] In the context of EDI, the stress and exhaustion associated with regularly experiencing empathy are well documented and referred to as empathetic fatigue. Inclusive leaders, EDI champions, and professionals who are continuously pushing for change, often with limited resources and against immense resistance, can become burnt out and feel isolated and frustrated with the lack of progress being made.[16] It is therefore important to acknowledge the risk of empathetic fatigue when working in this space. Normalising the stress, frustration, exhaustion, and anger that can accompany being an inclusive leader is the first step in mitigating these negative emotions, such as taking steps to support and protect your own wellbeing as detailed in Section One of this book. Unfortunately, the systemic barriers that marginalised employees face are complex and multi-layered and will therefore not be dismantled overnight, meaning that inclusive leaders must be aware of and take steps to manage the fatigue that they will most likely experience at some point along the way. Prioritising wellbeing, planning recovery (emotional and cognitive), setting boundaries, and practising self-compassion (meeting your own needs) are key to prevent empathetic fatigue.

Case example

For me, since I started working with EDI, engaging senior leadership empathy towards marginalised experiences was the key to achieving the best results. This enabled senior leadership to get emotionally connected to the topic so that they advocated for EDI and prioritised resources and budgets to address EDI matters. One practical way in which we achieved this was through the use of reverse mentoring. Initially, there was some debate because of the risks associated with the deployment of reverse mentoring, hence I had never really pushed for this. This is because some individuals from marginalised communities are uncomfortable with the idea of using their personal resources to educate dominant groups on how they contribute to systemic oppression. They even felt it could be unethical to ask a Black person to mentor a white person on why racism still exists in the workplace and why it is harmful. Additionally, there are risks of exposing marginalised groups to unpleasant situations where power dynamics could influence the relationship. That said, this initiative was 100 per cent driven by our staff networks and they were willing to take the risks. We made sure all participants volunteered (mentors and mentees) to mitigate some of these risks. One executive approached me and shared, "I realised I've always believed that talent rises to the top without fully understanding how unequal the competition really is. My mentee (a Black woman in her 20s) shared some of the microaggressions she had faced in the past. Sharing the pain with her was a real wake-up call. I never truly appreciated how deeply harmful racism can be, even when it shows up in subtle ways. Once you are made aware of the situation, it is very hard to sleep at night. I need to use my power to make real changes, just talking about it is no longer enough, otherwise it feels like I am just pretending that I care when I don't."

What can you do to enhance empathy?

As with the other mindset categories, being empathetic may come more naturally to some leaders than others. And different situations might lead us to choose to engage or avoid empathy. However, we can foster and enhance our ability to be empathetic by actively listening to diverse perspectives, validating the experiences of others, and responding with care and understanding. Enhancing empathic concern (taking action) means being proactive in addressing inequities, ensuring that everyone feels seen, heard, and supported in the workplace. Lastly, drawing an inclusive-empathy map[17] helps us to reflect on our relationships with work colleagues, shining a light on potential empathetic biases (i.e., we may feel more empathy for some of our team members than others). To do this we can map (i.e., by drawing) the physical distance and interpersonal closeness between us and the rest of the team. We can consider our emotional reactions to each individual through questions like "How much distance do we perceive between ourselves and this individual?". We can also move beyond rational analysis and ask "What colour represents our thoughts about the relationship?" and explain the choice.

Some questions that can help you to explore empathy in the context of inclusive leadership include:

- How can you actively seek out opportunities to engage with people who have different perspectives or backgrounds?
- Can you see any patterns within your existing friendship groups? What assumptions do you hold about your current social circle, and how could expanding your friendships deepen your understanding of others?
- How can reflection and journalling about your daily interactions help you identify patterns in your emotional responses and what insights can you gain to improve your empathy?
- When do you engage or avoid empathetic responses?
- Which situations do you experience empathic concern (the need to act)?
- Which communication techniques, language, or questions can you adopt to make your interactions more empathetic and ensure the other person feels validated, heard, and understood?
- When did you last ask others how they are feeling or experiencing a situation? How often do you do this?
- How can you use the inclusive-empathy map to assess your relationships with team members and identify areas where you could strengthen your emotional connection and empathy?
- When engaging with others, how can you step into their shoes to better understand their emotions and viewpoints, and how might this change your response?
- How can you create an environment where your team members feel safe to share their emotions without fear of judgement or backlash?
- What strategies can you use to ensure that your digital communications (such as email) foster empathy, understanding, and connection?
- How do you currently prioritise your emotional and cognitive wellbeing to prevent empathetic fatigue?

- What self-compassion practices could you introduce into your routine to replenish your emotional resources?
- How can you create a balanced approach to maintaining empathy while taking care of your own needs?

Chapter 12 in summary

- Emotional empathy describes when we are able to share the emotions that are experienced or expressed by another individual. Emotional empathy enables us to experience the activating emotion of anger when we witness unfairness or injustice, energising and engaging us to take action, to be a catalyst for change.
- Cognitive empathy describes the process of understanding another's feelings, situation, or experience: being able to put ourselves into another person's shoes or being able to take their perspective. Cognitive empathy gives us the awareness, through taking another's perspective, that there is something that we need to take action because an injustice or unfairness exists.
- Empathic concern is the bridge between sharing emotions and understanding another's perspective, to taking action to relieve the suffering of others. Empathic concern is critical for inclusive leadership as it drives action.
- Empathy is experienced and shared in different ways depending on our motivations to engage or avoid empathy in each interaction. Empathetic responses will vary from person to person. It is important to be aware that there are unhelpful stereotypes associated with autistic individuals and empathy that are not evidence-based.
- Inclusive leaders can enhance empathetic responses by using a range of strategies to practise empathy. Equally, it is important to consider recovery strategies to reduce the risk of empathy fatigue.

Notes

1 Zaki, J. (2019). *The war for kindness: Building empathy in a fractured world*. New York: Crown Publishing Group.
2 Cuff, B. M., Brown, S. J., Taylor, L., & Howat, D. J. (2016). Empathy: A review of the concept. *Emotion Review, 8*(2), 144–153.
3 Makoelle, T. M. (2019). Teacher empathy: A prerequisite for an inclusive classroom. *Encyclopaedia of Teacher Education, 11*(2), 27–39.

4 Gindi, J., & Pascu, A. (2023). *Autistic & Smashing It*. United Kingdom: B-Insight Publishing.

5 Kimber, L., Verrier, D., & Connolly, S. (2024). Autistic people's experience of empathy and the autistic empathy deficit narrative. *Autism in Adulthood, 6*(3), 321–330.

6 Kimber, L., Verrier, D., & Connolly, S. (2024). Autistic people's experience of empathy and the autistic empathy deficit narrative. *Autism in Adulthood, 6*(3), 321–330.

7 Nakamura, Y. T., Milner, T., & Milner, J. (2022). Inclusive-empathy in leadership. *The Journal of Applied Behavioral Science, 58*(1), 161–163. https://doi.org/10.1177/0021886320982022.

8 Gindi, J., & Pascu, A. (2023). *Autistic & Smashing It*. United Kingdom: B-Insight Publishing.

9 Zaki, J. (2014). Empathy: A motivated account. *Psychological Bulletin, 140*(6), 1608–1647. https://doi.org/10.1037/A0037679.

10 Development Dimensions International. (2014). *Is empathy boss? The science behind soft skills—What really drives performance?* Retrieved from https://www.ddiworld.com/hirezleadership/is-empathy-boss. Accessed 18 January 2025.

11 Maslach, C. (2017). Finding solutions to the problem of burnout. *Consulting Psychology Journal: Practice and Research, 69*, 143–152.

12 Nowack, K., & Zak, P. (2020). Empathy enhancing antidotes for interpersonally toxic leaders. *Consulting Psychology Journal: Practice and Research, 72*(2), 119.

13 Vaughn, D. A., Savjani, R. R. S., Cohen, M. S., & Eagleman, D. M. (2018). Empathic neural responses predict group allegiance. *Frontiers in Human Neuroscience, 12*, 302.

14 Kendall, F. (2012). *Understanding white privilege: Creating pathways to authentic relationships across race*. New York: Routledge.

15 Nowack, K., & Zak, P. (2020). Empathy enhancing antidotes for interpersonally toxic leaders. *Consulting Psychology Journal: Practice and Research, 72*(2), 119.

16 Rae, A. (2023). *DEI fatigue: Resistance or opportunity? Unpacking this moment and navigating the path forward*. Retrieved from https://www.forbes.com/sites/aparnarae/2023/08/17/dei-fatigue-resistance-or-opportunity-unpacking-this-moment-and-navigating-the-path-forward/. Accessed 18 January 2025.

17 Nakamura, Y. T., Milner, T., & Milner, J. (2022). Inclusive-empathy in leadership. *The Journal of Applied Behavioral Science, 58*(1), 161–163. https://doi.org/10.1177/0021886320982022.

Lived experience   13

Our lived experiences (experiences over the duration of our lifetime) might influence our ability to be inclusive. In the context of diversity, lived experience is often referred to as the personal, first-hand knowledge and understanding that individuals gain from navigating the world through the lenses of their identities and backgrounds. However, we argue that lived experiences are not just personal and first-hand experiences, but also intergenerational. The knowledge, beliefs, and understanding we inherit from our families, communities, and cultural narratives, shape how we see identities, biases, systemic inequalities, and stereotypes – even if we have not personally experienced them. Therefore, in the context of practising inclusive leadership, lived experiences refer to the knowledge and insights we gather from our interactions within various systems, including family systems, as well as the extent to which we have been exposed to perspectives and backgrounds different from our own. For example, often, if we have had little direct contact with people different from ourselves, these narratives will rely more heavily on stereotypes that we have learned from others, including the media (*more on this in Chapter 14*). When considering lived experiences, we should reflect on narratives that we have created ourselves as well as those which we have inherited from our family and others around us.

In the context of practising inclusive leadership, it is essential to acknowledge the importance of understanding lived experiences of marginalisation, systems of oppression, and appreciating how our own lived experiences drive our ability to be empathetic, have broader perspectives, and recognise structural inequalities, which are all critical to inclusive leaders.

DOI: 10.4324/9781003598022-18

What does lived experience have to do with practising inclusive leadership?

Diverse lived experiences offer unique perspectives that can inform appropriate policy response and better address structural inequalities. Our lived experiences as leaders may limit our capability to be empathetic and will heavily influence the biases, stereotypes, and prejudices that we hold. As we discussed in Chapter 12 ("Empathy"), research has shown that we tend to experience less empathy for those who we see as being in our "outgroups" and more empathy for those who we see as being in our "ingroups".[1] Therefore, by expanding our networks to be diverse and developing relationships that move from "us and them" to "you and I", we can, through the act of empathy, connect deeply with those whose experiences differ significantly from our own.

If we do not have first-hand experience, being exposed to other cultures and perspectives can support us in identifying our knowledge gaps and can help to counteract our stereotypes and assumptions. It also helps us to become more aware of systemic inequalities and the privileges we hold. This exposure helps to challenge how we think about the "correct" way of doing things, by raising awareness of perspectives and ways of living different from our own. It enables us to see that others' needs are not necessarily the same as ours and, conversely, to appreciate ways in which even people quite different from us can also share similarities. This awareness can help us to work in ways that are more creative and innovative, appreciating that solutions to problems can be reached via unknown and varied paths.

"I have a Black/gay/neurodiverse friend/partner/child, therefore I cannot be racist/homophobic/ableist"

Have you ever heard this statement? There is an interesting phenomenon where some individuals believe that, because they have a Black/gay/neurodiverse (add any identity characteristic here) friend/partner/child, this automatically makes them inclusive. While having a very close relationship with someone who is different from you in identities subject to systemic oppression will undoubtedly mean that you do have some awareness of their lived experience, this will not automatically mean that you will fully understand all the unique and complex challenges everyone of that identity faces. In fact, many of us unknowingly display microaggressions towards the people we care about (*more on microaggressions in Chapter 14*).

Let's pause for a moment and consider this in the context of gender. Heteronormative couples have a partner of the opposite gender; however, this does not automatically mean that the men in these couples have a full and complete understanding of the barriers women face at work. In fact, many women are not aware of the full complexity of the barriers women face and even they are susceptible to engaging in many of the unconsciously biased behaviours that work against women themselves![2] Therefore, it would seem naïve to imagine that, because someone has a number of friends who are a different ethnicity to them, for example, they will fully understand and appreciate not only their friends' lived experiences, but the lived experiences of others of this ethnicity. In particular, if we consider the dynamics of intersectionality, people who share one characteristic will almost certainly have very different experiences.

Inclusive leaders recognise that even when we do have extensive knowledge, awareness, and understanding, we must never assume. Instead, we are always learning, and we can never fully understand the challenges another might face that are unique to them. This includes recognising that even if we have the lived experiences from one system of oppression, we cannot automatically assume we understand all forms of oppression.

There are several ways we can broaden our perspective: for example, by diversifying our networks and friendship groups and being willing to engage, learn about, and improve our awareness of perspectives that are different from our own. Travel, if possible, is one of many ways to broaden our lived experieces. For example, engaging with local culture and people, can help to shine a spotlight on our own cultural habits and support our ability to understand those of others.[3] Research from neuroscience has shown that when a person's brain is exposed to novel and complex environments, such as through travel, it forms new neural connections as it categorises the new and unusual stimuli, boosting cognitive health,[4] which in turn expands that person's perspective.

Case example

I grew up in a working-class family in a relatively deprived rural town in the United Kingdom, with virtually no racial diversity. Although we travelled occasionally, this was exclusively to tourist destinations catering for British holidaymakers. I did not have the opportunity to study abroad or experience cultural diversity during my upbringing. My parents never talked about diversity or social justice, so it never felt like a problem. I cannot exactly pinpoint what sparked my interest in social justice but, for as long as I can remember, I felt very strongly about the unfairness and injustice I could see in the world around me – to the point that I started disagreeing with my parents and my own siblings. I realised that, growing up, we never discussed different lived experiences, and I certainly was never exposed to different lived experiences. As an adult, I now have the power to shape my lived experiences, including actively seeking exposure to diversity. More importantly, I recognise my responsibility to challenge and influence the narratives and stereotypes I've held, by practising deep listening and continuous learning. I make a conscious effort to surround myself with people who are different from me, both at work and in my personal life. I also regularly consult with others to ensure I am not unintentionally leaving anyone behind or making assumptions. This inclusive approach often requires more time and resources than the conventional way of doing things, but it has profoundly enriched both my professional and personal life.

I don't always get it right, and I am fully aware that there are perspectives or experiences I might overlook. However, I value these moments as opportunities to grow. I am often surprised by new insights from colleagues that I could not see on my own. When I reflect on leaders who do not make an effort to prioritise inclusion, I cannot help but wonder how many decisions they make that fail to consider the diversity of perspectives and experiences around them.

What can you do to enhance lived experience?

While our lived experiences up until the present are fixed, the *narrative* we tell ourselves about our experiences (and even the experiences we have inherited from our family) are not. Crucially, responses to lived experiences can vary greatly and therefore, in themselves, they do not predict inclusive behaviours: two individuals with very similar lived experiences may exhibit very different inclusionary (or exclusionary) behaviours. Therefore, most importantly, inclusive leaders seek to understand how their lived experiences and the lived experiences of others, differ through the use of focused reflective practice and by ensuring they are surrounded by diverse representation.

Guided reflective writing or working with a coach (if possible) can also be beneficial, and bring awareness of our invisible privileges and marginalised experiences. Equally, it is important to reframe where necessary the narratives we tell ourselves in relation to our family experiences, particularly if these narratives are influenced by stereotypes.

You can start this reflective process by considering the following questions:

- Growing up, what did you learn about characteristics including but not limited to gender / race / sexuality / disability / age?
- What exposure did you have to systems of oppression related to these characteristics?
- What parts of your leadership style have been shaped by your lived experience?
- How do your personal experiences influence the way you understand the challenges others face?
- What assumption might you be making about those individuals whose experiences are different from yours?
- How well do you understand the lived experiences of people you lead? How do you know this?
- When was the last time you sought out perspectives from someone with a background very different from yours? What did you learn?
- What were you able to take for granted (privilege that you have experienced)? How might your privileges limit your understanding of other people's realities?
- What opportunities can you create to immerse yourself in experiences different from yours?

Furthermore, we can always change the course of our lived experiences in the present and future. For example, inclusive leaders seek new experiences to enrich their appreciation for diversity. This can include expanding their social networks to purposefully reach out and embrace different and unfamiliar people and cultures.

Inclusive leaders also seek to be open to and understand the lived experiences of others, accepting that we all have our own narratives and stories that shape who we are. Inclusive leaders appreciate the importance of this openness and awareness, to avoid misjudging or overlooking an individual's intentions and needs, and to enable them to take the perspective of others. A great place to start in being open to and understanding the lived experiences of others is to use open questions to stay curious and learn more. For example, you might ask:

- I'd love to learn more about what leads you to feel that way. Would you be happy to share this with me?
- That's really interesting and very different from how I interpreted this situation. Can you tell me more to help me to understand your point of view?

- Can you tell me, from your perspective, how you feel about this situation?
- What parts of your lived experience do you feel are most overlooked by others?
- What challenges have you faced that others, including me, might not immediately understand?
- What strengths have you developed as a result of your lived experiences?
- What advice would you give to someone trying to understand people with similar experiences to yours?

Chapter 13 in summary

- Lived experiences refer to the knowledge and insights we gather from our interactions within various systems, including family systems, as well as the extent to which we have been exposed to perspectives and backgrounds different from our own.
- We argue that lived experiences are not just personal and first-hand experiences, but also intergenerational.
- Our lived experiences as leaders may limit our capability to be empathetic and will heavily influence the biases, stereotypes, and prejudices that we hold.
- However, exposure to different lived experiences can support us to address this gap. Therefore, it is important for inclusive leaders to keep seeking new experiences and at the same time to surround themselves with diverse representation that will help them identify when they might overlook other perspectives and exclude others.

Notes

1 Vaughn, D. A., Savjani, R. R. S., Cohen, M. S., & Eagleman, D. M. (2018). Empathic neural responses predict group allegiance. *Frontiers in Human Neuroscience, 12,* 302.

2 Sieghart, M. A. (2022). *The authority gap: Why women are still taken less seriously than men, and what we can do about it.* New York: W. W. Norton.

3 Shaw, K. (2016). *Travel broadens the mind, but can it alter the brain?* Accessed from https://www.theguardian.com/education/2016/jan/18/travel-broadens-the-mind-but-can-it-alter-the-brain. Retrieved 19 January 2025.

4 Shaw, K. (2016). *Travel broadens the mind, but can it alter the brain?* Accessed from https://www.theguardian.com/education/2016/jan/18/travel-broadens-the-mind-but-can-it-alter-the-brain. Retrieved 19 January 2025.

Knowledge   **14**

Our final driver of inclusive leadership is knowledge and while knowledge alone may not change behaviour, it is a critical step. It acts as an open door, inviting us towards new ways of doing things. We have the choice to either ignore it or step through.

Inclusive leaders continuously develop sound knowledge of topics and issues relevant to inclusion, while acknowledging the risks of complacency that can come, particularly with advanced expertise. This is especially important in the context of inclusive leadership, as our knowledge and understanding of EDI topics is constantly evolving. This knowledge is not limited to education – it also includes evidence of what is happening around us regarding our impact on others and our understanding of the different lived experiences of others. Without this underpinning knowledge, we are in danger of being ignorant of our ignorance.

Developing knowledge in the field of inclusion can be triggering, and it takes time for us to truly embody new insights. It requires courage to stay with the discomfort some of these concepts might cause, but it is a key part of the learning journey. Leaders, in particular, must be prepared to face these challenges head-on, as it is through this discomfort that growth and understanding can be achieved.

We identified ten key knowledge areas, which we briefly explore in this chapter: prejudice, bias, stereotyping, privilege, merit, power, equity, positive action, microaggression, and intersectionality.

DOI: 10.4324/9781003598022-19

Prejudice

Prejudice is a learned, negative attitude and feeling towards someone based on the identity group to which they belong.[1] This pre-judgement tends to be hostile and is not based on facts. Outcomes of prejudice include exclusion, discrimination, avoidance, abuse, violence, and even genocide.

In addition, benevolent prejudice, similar to benevolent sexism, where women are seen as the sex that is more delicate and in need of protection, may appear positive compared to more overtly negative forms of prejudice, but it is still a form of bias that can lead to harmful outcomes. For example, benevolent sexism reinforces gender role stereotypes, portraying women as weak, dependent, and less capable, while depicting men as strong and competent. Similarly, benevolent ableism, such as instinctively jumping in to help a physically disabled person without asking, can undermine autonomy and reinforce assumptions that disabled people are helpless or incapable of independence.

Addressing prejudice through education and awareness raising is a key priorities of inclusive leaders. Equally, inclusive leaders are active bystanders and they role-model a culture of dignity and respect by taking action against prejudice.

Bias

Bias involves the use of mental shortcuts that enable us to make fast decisions and react quickly.[2] Bias is a natural part of human decision-making, as it is not possible to engage in deliberate thinking all of the time. Kahneman (2011)[3] identified two models of thinking – system one and system two thinking. The system one thinking is our default mode of thinking. It is fast and intuitive, allowing us to operate with minimal effort, but it can lead to more biased reactions. The system two thinking is generally less biased because it allows more deliberate and reflective thinking. Generally, our brains prefer system one as we use less energy and it is faster – consequently we underuse system two thinking.

Therefore, if we are not consciously including others, this means that by relying on our system one thinking (which is mostly biased), we are excluding them by default. There are several types of biases and, as more studies are conducted, the list of biases continues to expand – for example, proximity bias (favouring individuals who are closer to us), confirmation bias (seeking out information to confirm what we believe is right), or familiarity bias (preferring what is familiar to us). These biases are barriers to inclusion and can give rise to other biases, such as racial and gender biases. Biases are often implicit as we may be unaware of their influence on our thoughts and behaviours.

You may have noticed we use the term "implicit bias" rather than "unconscious bias" because "unconscious" technically refers to being asleep or not awake, which can be misleading. We suggest that "implicit bias" is more accurate from a neuroscience perspective. It refers to automatic, learned associations in the brain that influence our judgements without deliberate awareness, but can still be measured and changed.

Inclusive leaders understand that everyone has biases, including themselves. They identify their biases by seeking feedback, reflecting on their own thoughts, and by creating methods to help them disrupt biased thinking. For example, listing assumptions about a meeting topic before attending the meeting. Additionally, inclusive leaders know that the best way to address biases is to proactively seek out information that challenges their preconceived ideas. *We explore the importance of disrupting biases as well as the most common workplace biases in Chapter 20.*

Stereotyping

Stereotypes are formed from a very early age and are reinforced over time. We start developing stereotypes from childhood and can usually list several attributes about a person or group when probed to do so. Stereotypes are not based on facts and they are not accurate. Instead, they are overgeneralised and simplified notions of people and things we use to make sense of the world. Stereotypes are usually associated with a group and can be based on, but are not limited to, ethnicity, age, gender, and sexual orientation. Therefore, stereotypes usually lead to prejudice and discrimination.[4]

Stereotypes do not only impact our ability to experience the world more meaningfully and accurately but also harm the groups we wrongly attribute them to. For example, research has shown that even the risk of confirming a negative stereotype about one's group is enough to impede performance.[5] Hence, it is not unusual to avoid questions about protected characteristics in application forms to avoid activating negative stereotypes. Showcasing successful individuals from marginalised groups can reduce the negative impact of stereotypes.[6] These role models are known as "social vaccines" because they assist individuals from similar groups in inoculating against or strengthening their self-concept, countering the stereotypes.

Inclusive leaders appreciate that stereotypes can disadvantage groups and provide a distorted mental framework that leads to biased behaviour.

They challenge their own assumptions and those of others and seek objective information before making decisions. Additionally, they recognise the importance of counteracting stereotypes and take every opportunity to challenge and change them through education. They also take extra steps to highlight the successes of their team members and peers from marginalised groups because they understand the importance of showcasing successful individuals from marginalised groups. *We further explore stereotypes in Chapter 20.*

Privilege

Have you ever heard of the privilege walk?

As privilege tends to be taken for granted and is invisible to those who have it, many people use this activity to help individuals understand social privileges and social disadvantages and how they affect our lives. With this exercise, participants are asked to form a straight line, leaving space in front and behind. Then, statements are read out detailing privileges and disadvantages, asking participants to take a step forward if they have a privilege and a step back if they have experienced a disadvantage. Privilege and disadvantage statements might include: "Take a step forward if two parents raised you" or "Take a step backward if you're uncomfortable holding your partner's hand in public".

Although this exercise became popular for raising awareness within dominant groups, it is also an excellent example of how we systematically exclude the needs of marginalised groups and prioritise the needs of dominant groups, even when teaching the meaning of privilege. Consideration is rarely given to whether marginalised groups *want* to expose themselves as part of this exercise or that they may potentially experience shame and embarrassment in service of the learning for the privileged group.

Privilege is the unearned advantage received due to our membership of a certain identity group (e.g., white, male, heterosexual, etc.). Privilege is not absolute, instead it is relative. It exists in relation to others in a given context, where we might experience privilege in certain areas and disadvantage in others. For example, white privilege is the daily systemic and institutionalised advantage that people of colour do not experience.[7] Racism is not only an individual act, it is also present, invisibly, in societal systems. Therefore, to understand privilege we must acknowledge that it is the *absence* of worries and distress that marginalised groups experience daily.

Privilege checklist

Below is a checklist that you can use to self-check the privileges you have experienced. This list is by no means exhaustive, but it demonstrates the breadth of privileges we can experience. What else can you add to the list? What other privileges have you experienced in your life?

- [ ] I can access my place of work easily.
- [ ] I can access a toilet at my place of work easily.
- [ ] I do not need to worry about adjustments to do my job as my work is designed to my needs.
- [ ] I am comfortable having my camera on in Zoom meetings.
- [ ] I feel comfortable holding hands with my romantic partner in public.
- [ ] I feel safe using public toilets.
- [ ] I do not need to worry about hate crimes and my physical safety when in public.
- [ ] I am comfortable walking home when it is dark.
- [ ] I am comfortable walking alone at night without worrying about being stopped by the police.
- [ ] I can celebrate a promotion without having my peers suspecting that I got the job because of my gender or race.
- [ ] I can easily find bandages that match the colour of my skin.
- [ ] I do not need to worry about explaining to my children about racism and how they need to protect themselves from it.
- [ ] I am comfortable socialising in a crowded bar without worrying about unwanted touching or groping.
- [ ] There are people who look like me making decisions at the most senior level in my organisation.
- [ ] I do not need to worry about coming across as bossy at work.
- [ ] I am able to work past my contractual hours if I choose, I have someone to look after my children at home.
- [ ] I had a quiet place to complete my homework while I was at school.
- [ ] I was able to attend university.

The reality of privilege is that we cannot give it back, even if we do not want it. However, while we cannot choose to *not* have the privileges we have been granted, we can choose *how* we use them.[8] Therefore, inclusive leaders are aware of and regularly consider their own privileges and those of dominant groups, including the vast and varied way privilege benefits those who hold it. They understand the challenges faced by those who have not benefitted from those privileges and proactively identify ways in which the cumulative advantages associated with privilege are minimised in service of levelling the playing field.

Merit

How often have you heard the saying "the best person should get the job"? But what makes someone "the best person for the job"? What access to resources did your perfect candidate have in the past to make them the person they are today?

These are typical questions inclusive leaders reflect on when thinking about merit. Merit relates to our sense of worthiness and whether we deserve praise or reward. However, no matter how hard they work, people will consistently achieve more or achieve less depending on their privileges or on the prejudices they face. Due to the prevalence of systemic discrimination, most people worldwide will work incredibly hard to survive, not thrive. Although merit might seem fair, it can perpetuate inequality by rewarding those with access to privileges, such as education or exposure to pivotal experiences or stretch assignments which support career advancement.[9] This reality check can be painful because it might feel like we are discrediting our hard work, our sense of worthiness, and whether or not we deserve a reward or praise. Effort and achievement still matter when assessed fairly, however the concpet of meritrocracy is flawed in unequal sytems.

Inclusive leaders can better contextualise their decisions around performance management and recruitment if they understand the implications of merit. For example, someone might come across as a hard worker if they work long hours, and this might be seen as merit for promotion. However, many employees will not have the option to work long hours – for example, if they have caring responsibilities outside of work. Therefore, inclusive leaders will appreciate that a long-hours culture will exclude many from career opportunities as well as negatively affecting everyone's wellbeing. Inclusive leaders focus on the journey as much as on the final destination. They appreciate that if we only look at someone's past performance or experience, we will never accurately understand their capability and potential. They consider systemic prejudice and, with a growth mindset, they are equally interested in learning about efforts and contexts as well as results.

Inclusive leaders are proud of their achievements, but at the same time, they do not judge the worthiness of others solely based on accomplishments and credentials. They appreciate that meritocracy does not work when you have an unlevel playing field in all systems of society. They are humble when sharing their successes and recognise their privileges as much as their achievements.

Power

We refer to power in the context of EDI as social structures that attribute rights, recognition, and resources and thus give some individuals or groups an advantage and even control over others. We explore power from two different perspectives: social justice and leader power.

From a social justice perspective, inequalities originate from social structures based on an uneven distribution of power and a lack of recognition of different group identities.

A key framework for understanding power in society is critical theory, an approach that examines how social, historical, and ideological forces shape and constrain culture. Critical theory seeks to uncover the ways in which systemic structures, such as capitalism, patriarchy, and racism, sustain unjust power dynamics.[10] It has laid the foundation for several important contributions, including critical consciousness (the process of recognising and challenging oppression), critical race theory (which examines how racism is embedded in legal and social systems), and broader calls for decolonisation (the process of dismantling colonial power structures and their lasting impacts).

For inclusive leaders, understanding critical theory is crucial because it provides a lens to recognise how power operates in organisations and society. It helps leaders move beyond surface-level diversity efforts to address the deeper, historical systemic barriers that maintain inequality. By engaging with these ideas, leaders can develop the awareness and agency needed to challenge exclusionary practices, foster truly equitable workplaces, and ensure that inclusion efforts do not unintentionally reinforce these existing hierarchies.

Furthermore, when power is unevenly distributed, there will be dominance and oppression.[11] By not addressing the uneven distribution of power and instead trying to suppress or ignore social group differences, we fail to consider the unique lived experiences of marginalised groups. This is relevant, as some argue that highlighting differences between groups reinforces stereotypes. Hence some organisations focus solely on inclusion (and not diversity). However, we can only truly pursue inclusion once we dismantle these systems of oppression, otherwise we risk dismissing unique needs, barriers, and experiences, which must be addressed to make systems fair for everyone and not just those who created them.

Leader power is also necessary to explore, as all leaders are legitimate power-holders and can choose how to use this power. Leaders hold power to make decisions that impact others, giving them influence and gravitas, and those decisions will influence the team's social dynamics and the broader organisation. Therefore, effective leaders are highly concerned about the moral exercise of power.[12] Informed by considering both the social justice perspective and leader power, inclusive leaders recognise that, to be inclusive, they cannot treat everyone equally and they will actively distribute power and resources to marginalised groups. They will appreciate that leadership is a privilege and exercise their power morally and responsibly.

Equity

Different to equality, equity means that different people will need different opportunities in order to have the same outcomes as the rest. Equity recognises structural barriers and historical disadvantages in terms of systemic inequalities.[13] An example might be offering women-only programmes to accelerate women in leadership roles as, historically, women have had fewer opportunities than men to advance in their career.

Inclusive leaders will take an equitable approach towards allocating resources and development opportunities to their employees. They will appreciate that we cannot treat everyone the same because of systemic barriers. They will focus on equitable treatment for equality of outcomes.

Positive action

Positive action, affirmative action, and positive discrimination are often used interchangeably, however they have quite different meanings.

Positive action focuses on removing barriers or accelerating the development of marginalised groups so they can compete for vacancies fairly. It is a term used in the European Union and the United Kingdom. On the other hand, affirmative action, mostly used in the United States, gives priority to marginalised groups in hiring and admissions, typically using quotas. Affirmative action was supported by research that examined over 45,000 students and the benefits of affirmative action for these students and society, demonstrating the importance of race-conscious admissions in higher education.[14] For most social reformers, affirmative action is necessary to correct historical injustices and address inequalities. However, in June 2023, the US Supreme Court ruled to stop the use of race as a factor in college admissions, and ended race-based affirmative action policies at most universities across the country.

One way to imagine positive action is like slowing down the competition for privileged groups while accelerating progress for marginalised groups, so that eventually everyone starts from the same place. Affirmative action, on the other hand, is like still having the competition but reserving a place on the podium for someone from a marginalised group.

Positive discrimination refers to preferential treatment of individuals from marginalised groups, even when they are not the most qualified person for the job. Positive discrimination is illegal in the UK and many other countries except in certain limited circumstances. Instead, positive action is more widely adopted.

Inclusive leaders need to familiarise themselves with the relevant legal framework designed to promote a level playing field. Without positive and affirmative action where applicable, it is inevitable that we will keep perpetuating the problem, as, if we strive to treat everybody the "same", by default this means we are treating everybody as though they are white males.[15]

There are some practical steps that leaders can pay attention to when thinking about positive action. This includes educating the broader team on the importance of these interventions to enable a level playing field, remove the myth and stigma around positive action, and be able to explain the difference between positive discrimination and positive action. Furthermore, when allocating workload, development opportunities, and sponsorship, inclusive leaders should consider the potential of marginalised groups, not the past performance of dominant groups. Many people believe that the most qualified person should be hired for a job, but what defines the most qualified person? Typically, the answer refers to having access to opportunities, development, and resources. As an inclusive leader, it is crucial to prioritise fair access in the present and compensate for historical disparities to prevent perpetuating inequalities.

Microaggression

Microaggressions are everyday words, actions, or situations that harm and insult marginalised groups, even if not intended.[16] They make members of marginalised groups feel that they are not as good, that they are bad, or that they do not belong. An example of a microaggression is a white person saying to a Black person "You're so eloquent" as though it is not expected.

Historical social structures have had a significant impact on our beliefs and the language we use, leading to all sorts of discrimination. Therefore, it is crucial to be mindful of the language we use and the beliefs we hold. For instance, when we say, "Anyone can succeed in this society if they work hard enough", we may be disregarding the obstacles and biases faced by marginalised groups to succeed while also unfairly associating them with laziness or incapability. While each individual microaggression may not seem like a "big deal", microaggressions can be viewed like a small cut that is never allowed to heal, each day (maybe multiple times a day) the cut is reopened as individuals experience a continual barrage of microaggressions in all walks of life, creating a cumulative negative impact on their wellbeing, belonging, sense of identity, and self-worth.

Inclusive leaders understand that their words can have an impact, even if they did not mean to cause offence. They recognise that what is inoffensive to one person may be offensive to another and they are open to learning from these differences. For example, saying "Your name is so exotic!" may be meant as a compliment, but it can also imply that the person does not belong, that their name is foreign and unusual. When inclusive leaders realise that they have upset someone, they pause, reflect, and address their mistake calmly. They take it as an opportunity to apologise, learn, and find a better way to express themselves. They do not become defensive or try to justify their actions; instead, they acknowledge their limitations and seek to understand the situation, to grow from it in a calm manner. If they observe a microaggression, they interject, supporting the learning process, setting boundaries, and offering extra support to the person experiencing the microaggression.

Intersectionality

The term intersectionality was first used by Crenshaw in her paper "Demarginalising the Intersection of Race and Sex" (1989).[17] This paper played a critical role in legal studies and informed many other scholars in considering the compounding impact of discrimination when numerous identity dimensions are influenced by systemic inequality and power structures (i.e., when racism and sexism intersect). This leads to unique forms of discrimination that most legal systems are not designed to address. The gender pay gap, through the lens of gender and race is a great example, showing that women of colour face wider pay gaps when compared to white women and men. These disparities also change depending on the demographics of each country. For example, in North America, Hispanic women experience discrimination associated with immigration status as well as skin colour.[18]

Inclusive leaders will appreciate that intersectional groups experience barriers to inclusion differently and more harshly, and interventions might not address their unique challenges. For example, inclusive leaders also move away from focusing on the identity, such as race, and instead focus on racism. In practice, this will influence how data needs to be collected and analysed. For example, simply analysing engagement surveys by demographics does not fully capture the experiences of marginalised groups. Instead, it is necessary to specifically measure factors such as racism, ageism, sexism, ableism, and other forms of discrimination. Hence, the legal system recognises that individuals from marginalised groups are at greater risk of bullying, harassment, and discrimination. The greater the cumulative effect of marginalised characteristics, the greater the risk. Inclusive leaders will be vigilant in ensuring psychological safety for these groups while proactively tailoring action to meet their unique needs.

What can you do to enhance your knowledge?

Inclusive leaders proactively create time and space to continue learning about EDI. They understand that they cannot be complacent and that the risk of exclusion, prejudice, systems of oppression, and discrimination will always exist unless power is balanced. Therefore, they are constantly learning from historically marginalised groups about their lived experiences and following best practices of inclusion and belonging targeted to support them. This includes attending training, watching talks online, listening to podcasts, and reading (the references listed in this chapter's notes are a great starting point). It is important to set aside time to revisit and refresh your knowledge of EDI regularly, as this is an evolving topic that requires continual learning.

Additional recommendations include:

- Attend any diversity and inclusion courses available to you at work.
- Research topics that might benefit you and your team to learn. For example, suppose you have a new starter from a different ethnicity than most of the team. In that case, you can research their culture, typical microaggressions that this specific group might experience, and any particular arrangements you might need to make so they can feel included.
- Ask the individuals within the team about their lived experiences, cultural sensitivities, and needs.
- When reading the news or social media content concerning EDI, explore various perspectives, taking a critical view, before forming your opinion. EDI is a topic often used for political wars, so misinformation is common.
- Follow experts or groups online to keep yourself updated.
- Keep up with employment legislation by signing up for newsletters from employment law firms.

Chapter 14 in summary

- Knowledge is critical in becoming an inclusive leader.
- Developing knowledge in the field of inclusion can be challenging and takes courage, as it may bring up feelings of guilt, shame, and defensiveness.
- Knowledge comes not only from books and science but also from learning from people with different lived experiences than our own.
- We explored ten different areas of knowledge important for inclusive leadership:
  - Prejudice, which is a learned, hostile attitude with negative feelings towards someone just because they belong to a group.
  - Biases are the mental shortcuts that allow us to make decisions quickly without taking the time for proper thought and consideration.
  - Stereotypes are overgeneralised and simplified notions of people and things that we use to make sense of the world.
  - Privilege is the unearned advantage received due to our membership of a certain identity group.
  - Merit can perpetuate inequality by rewarding those who had access to privilege.
  - Power is the social structure that attributes rights, recognition, and resources to give some individuals or groups an advantage and even control over others.
  - Equity is the different treatment required to enable equal outcomes.
  - Positive action focuses on removing barriers or accelerating the development of marginalised groups so they can compete fairly.
  - Microaggressions are everyday words, actions, or situations that harm and insult marginalised groups, even if not intended.
  - Intersectionality describes the compounding impact of discrimination when multiple characteristics are subject to prejudice.
- We can proactively improve our knowledge by attending training, reading, watching talks online, and listening to podcasts.

Notes

1 Allport, G. W. (1979). *The nature of prejudice* (25th Anniversary edition). Boston, MA: Addison-Wesley.
2 Tversky, A., & Kahneman, D. (1974). Judgment under uncertainty: Heuristics and biases. *Science, 185*(4157), 1124–1131.
3 Kahneman, D. (2011). Thinking, fast and slow. New York: Farrar, Straus and Giroux.

4 Allport, G. W. (1979). *The nature of prejudice* (25th Anniversary edition). Boston, MA: Addison-Wesley.

5 Steele, C. M., & Aronson, J. (1995). Stereotype threat and the intellectual test performance of African Americans. *Journal of Personality and Social Psychology, 69*(5), 797–811.

6 Dasgupta, N. (2011). Ingroup experts and peers as social vaccines who inoculate the self-concept: The stereotype inoculation model. *Psychological Inquiry, 22*(4), 231–246.

7 McIntosh, P. (2020). *On privilege, fraudulence, and teaching learning. Selected essays 1981–2019.* New York: Routledge.

8 Kendall, F. E. (2013). *Understanding white privilege: Creating pathways to authentic relationships across race.* New York: Routledge.

9 Young, M. (2017). *The rise of the meritocracy* (2nd edition). Routledge.

10 McArthur, J. (2021). Critical theory in a decolonial age. *Educational Philosophy and Theory, 54*(10), 1681–1692. https://doi.org/10.1080/00131857.2021.1934670.

11 Young, M. I., & Aleen, D. S. (2011). *Justice and the politics of difference.* Princeton, NJ: Princeton University Press.

12 McClelland, D. C. (1975). *Power: The inner experience.* New York: Irvington Publishers (distributed by Halsted Press).

13 Young, M. I., & Aleen, D. S. (2011). *Justice and the politics of difference.* Princeton, NJ: Princeton University Press.

14 Bowen, W., & Bok, D. (1998). *The shape of the river: Long-term consequences of considering race in college and university admissions* (The Williams G. Bowen Series, Twentieth Anniversary edition). Princeton, NJ: Princeton University Press.

15 Kendall, F. E. (2013). *Understanding white privilege: Creating pathways to authentic relationships across race.* New York: Routledge.

16 Sue, D. W. (2010). *Microaggressions in everyday life: Race, gender and sexual orientation.* Hoboken, NJ: Wiley.

17 Crenshaw, K. (2013; first published 1989). Demarginalizing the intersection of race and sex: A Black feminist critique of antidiscrimination doctrine, feminist theory and antiracist politics. In K. Maschke (Ed.), *Feminist legal theories* (pp. 23–51). New York: Routledge.

18 International Labour Organisation. (2020). Global wage report 2020–2021: Wages and minimum wages in the time of COVID-19. https://www.ilo.org/publications/flagship-reports/global-wage-report-2020-21-wages-and-minimum-wages-time-covid-19.

Section Three

Inclusive leadership behaviours

The final element of the Inclusive Leader System is inclusive leadership behaviours. These describe our actions or the things that we do. Often, our behaviours are outside of our awareness and are driven by our autopilot, due to the brain's dependency on automatic processing (to reduce mental load) and unconscious patterns (to enable quick responses). However, they are extremely important, as our behaviours are often what have the greatest impact on those around us. To reset behaviours, we need to consciously shift our intentions and habits. These new behaviours can then be nurtured to become our new habits, with leaders paying attention to their motivations to change. Once we connect to our motivation, we can identify triggers of certain behaviours, disrupt those triggers and the consequent patterns of behaviour, and replace the old behaviours with new ones. Organisations can also encourage and support these behaviours by embedding them in leadership competency frameworks, talent assessment criteria, and learning and development curriculums.

We identify seven inclusive leadership behaviours, which we explore in the next seven chapters.

Bringing people together (Chapter 15). Inclusive leaders are collaborative, they remove obstacles to enable others to work collaboratively, and they support feelings of belonging across identities and cultures.

Being culturally intelligent (Chapter 16). Inclusive leaders are aware and appreciative of other cultures and life experiences, and they adapt their

DOI: 10.4324/9781003598022-20

behaviour accordingly. They behave in a non-judgemental way, particularly when they are feeling uncomfortable.

Focusing on fairness and equity (Chapter 17). Inclusive leaders ensure that everyone has a fair opportunity. They prioritise distributing power, ensuring equitable treatment, listening attentively, and focusing on employee needs.

Practising allyship (Chapter 18). Inclusive leaders understand that leadership is a privilege that should be used to support and voice the needs of marginalised groups and to reform systems by dismantling inequity, unfairness, and discrimination.

Promoting uniqueness (Chapter 19). Inclusive leaders have a concern for others' interests, they consider differences among team members, they facilitate, motivate, and appreciate individual contributions, and they value distinctiveness.

Disrupting biases (Chapter 20). Inclusive leaders recognise that leading inclusively is fluid and not static and therefore engage in regular reflective learning to continually identify, disrupt, and mitigate biases.

Being emotionally agile (Chapter 21). Inclusive leaders are able to identify, express and, where appropriate, regulate their own emotions, particularly when working in unknown or unfamiliar contexts, and they are able to tolerate ambiguity. They have a high awareness of their own and others' emotions and are able to adapt their behaviour accordingly.

Bringing people together 15

As outlined in Chapter 1, inclusive leaders enable others to feel as though they belong. This means that inclusive leaders engage a range of competencies to bring people together to enable belonging to occur, including:

- *Being collaborative.* Inclusive leaders know that two heads are better than one – and three heads are better than two – particularly when they offer different perspectives. Therefore, they are constantly co-creating, consulting, and encouraging others to do the same.
- *Removing obstacles to enable others to work collaboratively.* Inclusive leaders appreciate that working collaboratively does not always happen automatically. There can be multiple obstacles that can hinder collaboration, whether due to physical distance (such as processes or location) or psychological and social differences (such as different personality types or backgrounds).
- *Supporting feelings of belonging across identities and cultures.* Inclusive leaders recognise the importance of a sense of connection to others, an environment, or context, alongside being recognised as a respected and valued contributor. Inclusive leaders also recognise that different identities and cultures might need different things to enable them to experience belonging as a diverse group.

Inclusive leaders recognise that, when we consider the behaviour of bringing people together, we are focusing on the actions the leader takes to enable this to happen. Across a work context there are multiple situations where leaders are required to bring people together (i.e., to encourage

DOI: 10.4324/9781003598022-21

collaboration, to remove obstacles to collaboration, to support feelings of belonging across identities and cultures). In this chapter, we focus on two key work contexts that illustrate the importance of bringing people together for inclusion: chairing meetings and when managing outgroups.

Chairing meetings

Meetings are a critical scenario where exclusion occurs. What makes meetings even more critical is their frequency and their public nature (if an individual or individuals are excluded during a meeting, it is witnessed by everyone in the meeting). This means that people's experiences in meetings dictate how included or not they feel and what is seen as acceptable behaviour in terms of exclusion, even if it is implicit.

Exclusion can manifest itself in multiple ways in meetings. Even before the meeting has started, we can consider who has been invited to the meeting as an opportunity for inclusion. The experience of being left out, whether intentional or not, has a deep impact on our self-esteem ("Am I so unimportant that I do not need to be there or am I so easily forgotten?") and our sense of autonomy ("I have no control over what happens to my team").

Case example: Being left out of a meeting and feeling devalued

An important meeting that I should have been involved with (critical decisions were made relating to my department that I would normally have been consulted on) went ahead without me. I only became aware of this after the decisions had been acted on and it was too late for changes to be made. I was left feeling angry, confused, frustrated, and, of course, excluded. Why hadn't I been invited to the meeting? Was my opinion of what happened in my department so irrelevant? Had I just been forgotten? This experience remained with me and placed a rupture in the working relationship between myself and the colleague who had chaired the meeting. I found it difficult to let it go and move on.

Within a meeting, exclusion can happen with regard to who feels safe and able to speak during the meeting and also whether they are listened to and their contribution is valued when they speak. In Chapter 3 we explored the concept of psychological safety and outlined how, when psychological safety is present, people will feel able to speak up, even when their message is difficult or challenging. During a meeting, there are multiple factors that can influence how safe an individual feels, whether they feel able to speak up, and that their contribution will be valued:

- People may find it difficult to find space to speak up, especially if the meeting is dominated by louder, more senior, or extraverted individuals who may have a preference for "thinking aloud". This can make it challenging to find a pause in the flow of conversation to make a contribution.
- Marginalised groups may find it harder to speak up as they are more at risk of being judged harshly when they do disagree. They will also find it harder to be listened to, especially if they are an "only" in the room (i.e., the only person from that identity in the room).
- People who are more introverted or are reflective thinkers may find it harder to speak up, as they may not feel comfortable sharing their views in a public forum and/or they may not feel ready to share their thoughts until those thoughts are fully formulated.
- The tone of the meeting can influence how likely it is for someone to speak up, including the respect (or lack of respect) shown to individuals who disagree. Has the leader invited opposing views or have they made it clear that they are expecting others to agree during the meeting?
- Meetings without a clear agenda and expectations can cause confusion, especially for some neurodivergent individuals, meaning that they find it difficult to understand the purpose and goals of the meeting. This can create an environment of uncertainty, which is uncomfortable for people who prefer routine and predictability, thus making it challenging for them to speak up and contribute.
- Practical constraints can also influence experiences of inclusion in a meeting. This is especially true for hybrid meetings. If some people are in a meeting room together and some are online, how easily are the online participants able to contribute? Can they fully see and hear what is happening in the meeting room, including reading the social cues from participants' body language? Are they fully involved or are they ignored or on the periphery of the discussion?
- Unwritten rules can impact meeting dynamics, influencing what is valued or dismissed. They are not always obvious, making them difficult to be spotted in action.

- Outgroup dynamics show up frequently in meetings, as they are how we humans categorise ourselves in social situations. However, outgroups lead to some participants feeling less engaged, isolated, left behind, dismissed, and misunderstood. Outgroups are so critical to consider when bringing people together that we explore them in more detail next.

Managing outgroups

When people work together, they will naturally form ingroups and outgroups – this is a normal consequence of being a social creature.[1] When we are a member of an ingroup, we hold positive views of others within our ingroup, and we tend to give them preferential treatment, the benefit of the doubt, considering them to be part of our "tribe". It feels good and easy to spend time with part of the ingroup. Anyone not in this ingroup is in the outgroup. Outgroups are viewed more negatively: they receive inferior treatment compared to ingroup members, they are less likely to be given the benefit of the doubt, and, instead, their behaviour is judged more harshly. We generally form ingroups with people who we work more closely with and people who are similar to us. This of course generates problems when we consider diversity. It is harder to form an ingroup with a diverse group of individuals with differing social identities. It is much easier to form an ingroup with people that share our social identity and contexts. Therefore, individuals from marginalised groups are at a much higher risk of being pushed into the outgroup.

While members of the ingroup will experience a strong sense of belonging, members of the outgroup will feel isolated, ignored, snubbed, or brushed off, even when interactions between ingroups and outgroups is respectful. Therefore, being a member of the outgroup has a negative impact on well-being as well as serious negative consequences on an individual's career. Research has consistently demonstrated the positive impact of social capital on career progression.[2] Social capital describes the individual's potential resources derived from their social connections and network.[3] We are more likely to experience strong social connections with other members of our ingroup and weaker social connections with members of the outgroup; consequently being a member of the outgroup will lead to weaker social connections, less social capital, and fewer career progression benefits. Outgroup members will also find it more challenging for their voices to be heard by the rest of the team and their contributions to be taken seriously. They are more likely to be overlooked for critical experiences and, when things go wrong, they are more likely to be judged harshly or blamed for the mistake.

Case example: Experiencing group dynamics as a member of an outgroup

I know I will never be promoted. In fact, my job is secure only because I am delivering my numbers at the moment. Last year I had a bad month in sales and my line manager was on my case constantly – and disproportionately if I compare myself with other members of the team who had not just one bad month but a whole year. In sales, you must go out for drinks on Fridays and like golfing; otherwise, you are not part of the club. I even tried in the past, but the price to pay was too high. My boy waits for me to put him to bed every Friday. I cannot do bedtime any other day because I get home too late, and he has school the next morning. Plus, I wouldn't say I like golfing. I like going to the theatre, but I don't share this with the team because they will make fun of me. It is also very frustrating. Meetings are a great example: I am always behind or left out altogether from discussions because they start the meeting on the golf course or Friday night. The situation is not ideal, but work suits me for the moment – however, I know I need to leave if I want to progress in my career.

What can inclusive leaders do?

Group dynamics play a crucial role in workplace collaboration, yet they can also create barriers to belonging when ingroups and outgroups form. Meetings, a fundamental part of many roles, often become spaces where these dynamics manifest themselves, reinforcing exclusion rather than fostering connection. To counteract this, inclusive leaders must take an active role in recognising and dismantling exclusionary group dynamics. This starts with self-awareness, reflecting on how they might unintentionally contribute to ingroup formation and acknowledging the unwritten rules shaping their team's culture. Meetings, in particular, offer an opportunity to disrupt outgroup disadvantages by ensuring all voices are heard, setting clear expectations for participation, and balancing informal relationship-building opportunities so they do not become barriers to career progression.

Below are some practical recommendations to bring people together in meetings and address the impact of the formation of ingroups and outgroups.

Chairing meetings

- Consider who you are inviting (and who you are not inviting) to the meeting, and ask yourself who you might be forgetting. Inclusive leaders do not necessarily include everyone in all meetings all of the time, however they do communicate with openness and transparency the reasons why people have or have not been invited.
- Ensure that you communicate clearly the purpose of the meeting, the agenda, and the desired outcome prior to the meeting, and reiterate this at the start of the meeting. Where complex issues are to be discussed, consider sharing pre-reading to enable participants to get prepared and start thinking about the issue prior to the meeting. Contract with participants to stay on track with the agenda and to park discussions if necessary for another time.
- Pay attention to the timing of meetings. Avoid early mornings and late finishes that might automatically exclude those who have parental or caring responsibilities. Also consider and respect public holidays from different cultural calendars.
- Hybrid meetings are very challenging to manage inclusively. Either invest in suitable technology to ensure that all participants in the physical room are clearly visible and audible to all the online participants or opt for a fully online meeting. If you are chairing a hybrid meeting, ensure that you consistently bring in contributions from participants in the room and online. Allocate another participant in the room to monitor the chat and to bring this into the meeting as appropriate.
- Prior to the start of the meeting, take a moment to reflect on and "park" any biases or emotions you might be aware of that might influence how you show up in the meeting. An example of this would be: "I know that I can become frustrated when the team gets focused on the minor details, however I will park this frustration and respect their need to learn more about what we are doing".
- Contract at the start of every meeting to create conditions for safety and set the ground rules for the meeting. For example, agree the objectives of the meeting and emphasise how important it is that every voice is heard and that colleagues are entitled to have and share different opinions.
- Ask permission to hold members of the meeting accountable to the contract, following through on this if you notice that the contract is not being followed, for example, if colleagues are interrupted.
- When conducting online meetings, contract with the group about the use of cameras. Having cameras on helps with social connection, however it is critical to be respectful of individual needs. For example, some

people, especially neurodivergent participants, may not feel comfortable having cameras on. Understanding individual preferences before the meeting can help avoid putting individuals on the spot in a public forum.

- Also with online meetings, contract around the use of chat. Chat can be a useful tool to enable individuals who feel more comfortable writing rather than verbalising their views. However, excessive use of chat can be distracting for participants and can also lead to the formation of ingroups (i.e., who is active in the chat conversation versus who is not).

- Actively evaluate and include marginalised and/or quiet colleagues. This means encouraging colleagues who speak the least to participate more, while minimising over-participation from colleagues who tend to speak up the most. However, importantly, ensure you engage with less-participative employees first to avoid putting them on the spot. It is important to explain why visibility is crucial for their career growth and social capital and offer adjustments if needed to make participation safe.

- Appreciate that the best ideas are the outcome of combined diverse views and therefore it is fundamental to explore all ideas as best ideas. Actively nudge opposing views to address conformity bias (i.e., agreeing with others rather than exercising our own independent judgement). For example, you might say "It's really important that we consider all views of this decision, I'd love to hear from some people who have a different view on this".

- As the leader, share your view last. The implicit power that leaders hold in the room will influence how others respond. Asking for others to contribute first and truly listening to what they have to say before they share and/or respond will help to minimise this implicit power influencing the group.

- For meetings that involve discussion of an important or complex decision, allow time following the meeting for more reflective thinkers to contribute afterwards. It is important to appreciate that not everyone will be ready to respond immediately during the meeting, and so it is good to provide an opportunity to capture those individuals' views.

Managing outgroups

- Recognise that outgroups are inevitable and ingroups are usually formed by affinity. This should be discussed openly with the team, exploring unwritten rules created by ingroups, including the stigmas driving these rules and the invisible penalties when the rules are not followed.

- Seek to understand other reasons for the formation of outgroups by remaining curious, avoiding assumptions, and talking in confidence with all parties concerned to explore how they have been impacted.
- Have strong awareness skills and anticipate when outgroups start to form, acting accordingly to secure reintegration. For example, you can create opportunities for all team members to get to know one another on a one-to-one basis outside pressurised and business critical interactions. Equally, you might purposely mix ingroups and outgroups to deliver a project.
- Actively counteract stigmas associated with outgroups. For example, in a male-dominated environment, mothers might face the stigma of being less committed, therefore by actively allocating high-profile projects to mothers within the team, you are by default counteracting this stigma.
- Reflect on your own ingroup activities and change course where needed. For example, take action if you notice you are always speaking to the same people about their weekends (because they have similar interests).
- Appreciate that colleagues do not need to go out together outside work to form ingroups and be subject to increased proximity bias – it might happen within work settings as well. For example, ingroups can be influenced by who we are choosing to have lunch with, spend a coffee break with, and sit beside in a meeting. Therefore, inclusive leaders promote equal social interactions – for example, include remote workers in virtual informal bonding activities such as virtual coffee catch-ups.
- Appreciate the spillover of the formation of ingroups between work and non-work domains and how these manifest favouritism at work in terms of promotion, allocation of work, performance management, and pay review. To counter this, as an inclusive leader you can create objective frameworks and processes for moderation to mitigate favouritism and bias in decision-making.

Chapter 15 in summary

- Inclusive leaders need certain competencies to bring people together, including collaboration, being able to remove obstacles to collaboration, and supporting feelings of belonging across identities and cultures.
- The frequency and public nature of meetings make them critical for experiences of inclusion. Furthermore, in meetings social dynamics tend to be heightened, enhancing exclusion.

- The nature of ingroup and outgroup formation has a direct negative impact on bringing people together. However, this is a natural part of how humans connect to one another. Although leaders cannot stop ingroup and outgroup formation completely, they can minimise the negative impact on outgroups while reintegrating them into the team.

Notes

1 Tajfel, H., Billig, M. G., & Bundy, R. P. (1971). Social categorization and inter-group behavior. *European Journal of Social Psychology, 1*, 149–178.
2 Dobrev, S. D., & Merluzzi, J. (2018). Stayers versus movers: Social capital and early career imprinting among young professionals. *Journal of Organizational Behavior, 39*(1), 67–81.
3 Williams, D. (2006). On and off the net: Scales for social capital in an online era. *Journal of Computer-Mediated Communication, 11*(2), 593–628.

Being culturally intelligent 16

Inclusive leadership is about valuing diversity and a key aspect of what makes us diverse is our cultural differences and backgrounds. When we consider cultural differences, we are referring to the ideas, customs, and social behaviour of a society. These differences have an impact on how we see the world and interact with others.

Cultural intelligence is the capability to function effectively in intercultural contexts.[1] Cultural intelligence relies on a high level of conscious awareness of cultural differences during interactions[2] and relates to the way individuals plan their behaviour before interacting with culturally diverse co-workers, the way they monitor their own assumptions during multicultural interactions, and, then, the way they make mental adjustments if expectations differ from their experiences.[3] Another aspect of cultural intelligence is a high level of motivation to interact with individuals from different cultures, meaning that they are more likely to seek out opportunities to interact with members from different cultures and persist when cross-cultural interactions become challenging – for example, due to cultural misunderstandings.[4] There are multiple studies that demonstrate that cultural intelligence relates positively to both cultural adjustment (i.e., the ability to adjust to working within another culture) and observer-rated performance.[5]

Individuals high in cultural intelligence recognise that no culture is superior to another, just different.[6] They are able to observe patterns in behaviour from individuals from the same culture, using this information to inform and adapt their own behaviour. Equally, they are able to hold these observations lightly, refraining from generalising or making broad assumptions about behaviour for whole cultures. They use their curiosity and ability to actively listen, asking questions to find out about the individual in front of

DOI: 10.4324/9781003598022-22

them. This makes individuals with high cultural intelligence very adaptive. Rather than expecting others to conform to their own cultural norms, they are able to be flexible, adjusting the way they work to the other person. For example, they may adapt their communication style to be more or to be less directive depending on the other person's preference for communicating. By adapting our behaviour in this way, we are creating an environment where our team members are able to retain what makes them unique, in recognition of the positive contribution this diversity will bring through the sharing of different perspectives, supporting creativity, innovation, and problem solving.

Our personality traits can support our ability to be culturally intelligent. For example, openness to experience is a critical predictor for success in multicultural interactions. In diverse environments, we will encounter and often work closely with individuals from different cultures. This is especially true given the connectedness of today's world and the global nature of many organisations. This makes openness to cultural differences especially critical. According to the "Five Factor Model of Personality", someone who is high in openness to experience prefers novelty over routine and is more liberal and curious.[7] Furthermore, when we are open, it enables us to connect with a fellow human without passing judgement. This non-judgemental attitude means that we remain impartial to the information we receive, which is particularly important when observing cultures different to ours (not better or worse, just different). However, maintaining a non-judgemental attitude is notoriously difficult, as passing judgement on whether a situation or an individual is likely to cause us harm is an inbuilt, evolutionary mechanism that keeps us safe, which is why it is difficult to switch it on and off.[8] Inclusive leaders understand that we overuse judgement, which takes us out of the present moment. When we judge we become disconnected from reality and rather than responding to what is actually happening, we respond to a perception or interpretation. Therefore, we must constantly challenge ourselves when a judgement is triggered, resetting our mindset from being judgemental to being curious about what is present.

Finally, open individuals are also tolerant. Tolerance is the attitude of accepting and respecting differences including those we may dislike or disagree with while committing to continuously developing our understanding and appreciation of diversity.[9] This is particularly vital for inclusive leaders, as they will inevitably encounter perspectives or beliefs that challenge their own. Take religion, for example. Inclusive leaders respect and support individuals in openly practising their faith as an essential part of their identity, however they may experience a tension when a religion is perceived to be at odds with inclusion – for example, by prioritising heteronormativity. The same can happen when the leader is influenced by more liberal cultures and is interacting with more conservative cultures. An inclusive leader's role is not to eliminate these differences but to create an environment where diverse beliefs can coexist with mutual respect and tolerance.

Inclusive leaders recognise the significance of cultural intelligence in fostering inclusion during all interactions. In this chapter, we focus on two key work contexts that illustrate the importance of being culturally intelligent: dealing with conflict and interacting informally with others.

Dealing with conflict

Conflict in the workplace is not unusual. When people are working under pressure, on work that they care about or that has an influence on outcomes important to them (such as how their own and/or their team's performance is viewed), it is not surprising that conflict can arise. It is not always obvious when conflict at work is culturally driven.[10] However, it is unfortunately a frequent cause of conflict at work. This is generally because of a range of cultural differences that influence how we approach multiple aspects of our work, such as:

- Cultural differences may dictate how people prefer to communicate including expressing opposing views or giving feedback. For example, a high-context culture makes greater use of contextual elements in communication, such as body language, the status of an individual, and the tone of voice. In high-context cultures rules are not explicitly stated. By contrast, a low-context culture makes greater use of written or spoken communication and rules are usually explicitly stated.[11] Therefore, some may perceive a very direct communication style, often associated with a low-context culture, as rude, abrupt, and cold, whereas others may perceive a less direct communication style, often associated with a high-context culture, as unclear, confusing, and hard to interpret. This can make it harder for cross-cultural teams to communicate with and understand each other.
- People from different cultures may have different views on hierarchy and authority, which might influence their willingness to challenge authority openly or to seek permission in decision-making.
- Some cultures are more open to taking risks when making decisions and see this as an integral part of innovation, whereas other cultures may prioritise stability and minimise risk and uncertainty.
- There can be cultural differences in approaches to time and the importance of schedules, with some adopting a more flexible approach versus others who might strictly adhere to deadlines.

- There are also cultural variations in work-life balance, which will likely impact the amount of time spent at work (which may be seen as an indicator of dedication to their career in some cultures).
- Different cultures may hold different priorities. For example, more individualistic cultures may emphasise personal achievement, autonomy, and competition, whereas more collectivist cultures may prioritise group harmony, loyalty, and consensus in decision-making.
- There can be different attitudes towards conflict itself. Some cultures may view conflict as a necessary part of decision-making, whereas others may avoid disagreement, preferring to maintain harmony.

Inclusive leaders have high levels of cultural intelligence, and they therefore appreciate that many conflicts might emerge from misunderstandings and cultural expectations. When conflict does arise, inclusive leaders play an active role in supporting those involved to understand and appreciate the different perspectives, emotional needs, and cultural expectations. As we explored in Chapter 12, inclusive leaders are great perspective-takers and encourage their colleagues to do the same. In times of conflict, they act as mediators when needed, helping colleagues to pause, refrain from judgement, stay curious, open lines of communication by asking questions to understand each other's needs, and find mutually satisfactory solutions.

Case example: Experiencing cultural differences at work

Leading an international team requires not only technical expertise but also a deep understanding of cultural dynamics. As the leader of a global project team based in Helsinki, I was responsible for overseeing two engineers, one in Germany and the other in Japan, whose collaboration was crucial to the project's success. During our first project review meeting, I noticed a stark contrast in communication styles. My German engineer expressed strong frustration, openly listing everything that was wrong with the project. Meanwhile, my Japanese engineer became visibly uncomfortable and later confided in me that they found the meetings too aggressive, which made them reluctant to share their ideas. Having previously worked in Japan, I was aware of the cultural emphasis on harmony and indirect communication. Though we had initially discussed cultural differences and agreed on ways of working at the start of the project, the increasing pressure seemed to override those agreements, and the project was indeed compromised.

Interacting informally with colleagues

Cultural bias is one of the strongest forms of familiarity biases because of the shared communication norms, social expectations, deep-rooted conditioning, and increased sense of belonging. We will implicitly favour interacting with people who are culturally similar to us, and these informal interactions present great implications for inclusive leadership. For example, have you heard of the saying "the real business of business happens on the golf course"? Even for those not familiar with this saying, it is likely that the sentiment itself will not be a surprise. The idea that important business decisions that happen during informal interactions away from the office (such as on the golf course or in the bar) have long been accepted as a common barrier for career progression for marginalised individuals.

This is because the amount of time we spend informally with others influences the amount of social capital we build with them. Social capital describes an individual's potential resources from social connections, including through the strength of relationships and social support.[12] High levels of social capital have a range of benefits (such as access to information, opportunities, and resources), which can lead to power, influence, improved working conditions, and career promotion[13].

Inclusive leaders recognise the importance of informal interactions for building social capital and the impact this has on career progression. They also recognise that our natural tendency is to be attracted to interacting with people similar to us culturally (familiarity bias) and favour those who are physically close to us (proximity bias). This, of course, can perpetuate systemic barriers. If we only interact informally with people like us, we form stronger bonds and build greater social capital with those individuals and hence, when opportunities arise at work that may support career progression, we are more likely to think first of those individuals who we know best and have the strongest bonds with: people like us. This can lead to marginalised groups being penalised by being excluded from informal networks.

However, informal interactions are not just limited to playing golf or going for a drink after work. We can also consider what we call "micro informal interactions" that will occur for all of us, multiple times each day. These micro interactions are often impacted by our physical workplace (i.e., the office layout, multi-site working, working from home, etc.) and can include:

- Who you sit next to in a meeting.
- Who your desk is positioned near (and if you hot-desk, whether you sit next to the same people or person each day).

- Who you tend to grab a coffee with.
- Who you might get lunch with.
- The people you have meetings with more frequently, even online, which will likely influence the amount of small talk that takes place each day.

Inclusive leaders work diligently to recognise and mitigate both familiarity and proximity biases by observing patterns and trends in their own behaviour and reactions. They use every opportunity to learn, grow, and challenge their own assumptions and stereotypes by turning up curiosity and turning down judgement. Consequently, they seek out opportunities to interact informally with people who are culturally different to them, even when they do not need to for work reasons.

Case example: Uncovering and challenging one's own cultural biases

In a male-dominated workplace like this one, I am mindful of the importance of fostering a culture where everyone feels valued. When a new project manager joined our team wearing a hijab, I was curious to get to know her and made an effort to sit beside her. Over time, we developed a strong connection, often having lunch together and sharing perspectives on work and life. Through our conversations, I realised that I had unconsciously made assumptions about her experience and identity, assuming she might struggle in this environment without ever asking. I recognised that I had approached our initial interactions with an unspoken belief that she might need support rather than simply appreciating her as a colleague and peer. My assumptions were shaped by a stereotype, that women wearing a hijab need protection in Westernised spaces and that they may lack confidence. But I could not have been more wrong. This experience deepened my understanding of how well-intended actions can be shaped by implicit biases and stereotypes, and it reinforced the importance of listening first and seeing people as individuals rather than through the lens of stereotypes.

What can inclusive leaders do?

Becoming more culturally intelligent requires us to immerse ourselves in diverse cultural experiences with a mindset of curiosity, humility, and reflection while constantly checking our assumptions. This is not only about learning the theory about different cultures, but also about engaging in first-hand experiences while challenging assumptions and expanding our perspective. Inclusive leaders cultivate both their own cultural awareness and that of their teams to foster a genuinely inclusive workplace. As they deepen this awareness, they remain mindful of avoiding developing stereotypes, recognising that each person has a unique identity shaped by culture in different ways. When engaging in cultural encounters, whether witnessing or experiencing them, they approach each individual with curiosity, holding their cultural awareness lightly rather than rigidly. They use their heightened awareness to expand possibilities but ensure they validate assumptions through meaningful dialogue and respect. They invest quality time in getting to know each team member individually. When they identify a cultural knowledge gap, they proactively seek to learn more and engage in open conversations to understand what cultural inclusion means to each person in the workplace. They then follow up with the broader team to implement inclusive changes that reflect these insights, ensuring a more supportive and culturally responsive environment.

Below are some practical recommendations on how to deploy cultural intelligence when dealing with conflict and when interacting informally with others.

Dealing with conflict

- Approach the conflict situation with curiosity rather than with assumptions or judgement. Acknowledge that cultural differences can shape perspectives, communication styles, and conflict resolution preferences.
- Pay attention to cultural expressions in daily interactions such as how people greet one another, make jokes, or express disagreement – this may help you to identify potential reasons for conflict should they arise.
- Consider how different colleagues approach hierarchy, collaboration, and decision-making based on their cultural differences and whether this may be a source of conflict.
- Spend time learning about others – their cultures, motives, and needs. This will help you to develop cultural awareness and appreciate the intentions *behind* different actions in times of conflict.
- When a judgemental thought comes to mind (likes or dislikes, good or bad, right or wrong), pause and check your biases, emotional needs, and fears. Stay open and curious with the facts and try to rationalise what is driving you to feel the way you do.

- Create and contract for a safe environment to enable dialogue, where individuals are able to deal with issues by themselves, but equally let them know that they can call on support if needed. Prioritise the repair of relationships rather than a focus on agreement only. Be attentive to signs of relationship ruptures and take action to support repair where appropriate.
- Adopt a conflict resolution practice that is culturally responsive. For example, before mediating, inclusive leaders consider how different cultural backgrounds shape expectations around addressing conflict. This might include direct confrontation or approaches focused on harmony.
- Follow up conflict resolution in a culturally responsive way. In some cultures, a written agreement might be expected, while in others, an informal gesture (shaking hands or going out for a meal) is more meaningful. Therefore, include and encourage others to embrace different expectations without judgement.

Informal interaction

- Create opportunities to spend time with people who are culturally different to you. Focus on learning about them while maintaining curiosity not judgement. Reflect on how this experience has changed or reinforced your worldview or belief system.
- Regularly reflect on how your own culture has shaped your behaviours, values, and ideas of what is wrong and what is right and the choices you make when choosing who you want to spend time with informally.
- Find the right balance between allocating time and energy with people who are different and who are similar. Explore thoughts and emotions that are making you feel uncomfortable.
- Embrace cultural discomfort, reflect on personal biases, and ask how this challenges your perspective? What can you learn from this interaction?
- Organise voluntary culturally themed events, such as lunches and celebrations where others are able to share their cultural traditions and experiences.
- Engage with culturally underrepresented colleagues and encourage connections with the wider team to provide support and to share experiences.
- Do not assume people want to talk about their culture. Always approach the situation with curiosity and check in to see if they are happy to share.

Chapter 16 in summary

- Cultural intelligence is the capability to function effectively in intercultural contexts.
- Inclusive leaders actively engage in first-hand cultural experiences to deepen their cultural awareness. At the same time, they remain mindful of avoiding developing stereotypes and approach each individual with genuine curiosity rather than making assumptions based on their cultural background.
- Inclusive leaders have high levels of cultural intelligence, and they therefore appreciate that conflicts may emerge from misunderstandings due to cultural differences. When conflict does arise, inclusive leaders play an active role in supporting those involved to understand and appreciate the different perspectives, emotional needs, and cultural expectations.
- Inclusive leaders recognise the value of informal interactions in building social capital. They are aware of the risks that cultural familiarity bias poses in reinforcing systemic oppression by shaping who they choose to engage with. As a result, they actively seek out informal interactions with people who are culturally different from themselves.

Notes

1 Earley, P. C., & Ang, S. (2003). *Cultural intelligence: Individual interactions across cultures*. Redwood City, CA: Stanford University Press.

2 Rockstuhl, T., & Ng, K. Y. (2008). The effects of cultural intelligence on interpersonal trust in multicultural teams. In S. Ang & L. Van Dyne (Eds.), *Handbook of cultural intelligence: Theory, measurement, and applications* (pp. 206–220). New York: M. E. Sharpe.

3 Ang, S., Van Dyne, L., Koh, C., Ng, K. Y., Templer, K. J., Tay, C., et al. (2007). Cultural intelligence: Its measurement and effects on cultural judgment and decision making, cultural adaptation and task performance. *Management and Organization Review, 3*(3), 335–371.

4 Ng, K. Y., Van Dyne, L. & Ang, S. (2009). From experience to experiential learning: Cultural intelligence as a learning capability for global leader development. *Academy of Management Learning & Education, 8*(4), 511–526.

5 Ang, S., Van Dyne, L., & Rockstuhl, T. (2015). Cultural intelligence: Origins, conceptualization, evolution, and methodological diversity. In C. Y. Chiu, M. Gelfand, & Y. Y. Hong (Eds.), *Advances in culture and psychology* (Vol. 1, pp. 273–323). New York: Oxford University Press.

6 Marr, B. (2022). *Cultural intelligence (CQ) is an important predictor of success. Here's how to boost your CQ.* Accessed from https://www.forbes.com/sites/bernardmarr/2022/09/05/cultural-intelligence-cq-is-an-important-predictor-of-success-heres-how-to-boost-your-cq/. Retrieved 29 January 2025.

7 McCrae, R. R., & Costa, P. T., Jr. (2003). Personality in adulthood: A five-factor theory perspective (2nd edition). New York: Guilford Press.

8 Jones, R. J. (2021). *Coaching with research in mind.* Abingdon: Routledge.

9 Rachmad, Y. E. (2019). *Progressive tolerance theory.* Self-published.

10 Dansereau, V. (2022). *What to do about cross cultural conflict in the workplace.* Accessed from https://pollackpeacebuilding.com/blog/what-to-do-about-cross-cultural-conflict-in-the-workplace/. Retrieved 29 January 2025.

11 Hall, E. T. (1976). *Beyond culture.* New York: Anchor Books.

12 Williams, D. (2006). On and off the net: Scales for social capital in an online era. *Journal of Computer-Mediated Communication, 11*(2), 593–628.

13 Dobrev, S. D., & Merluzzi, J. (2018). Stayers versus movers: Social capital and early career imprinting among young professionals. *Journal of Organizational Behavior, 39*(1), 67–81.

Focusing on fairness and equity 17

Values are the things that are important to us. When we value fairness and equity we believe in the importance of just treatment without discrimination. A belief in the importance of fairness and equity is critical in inclusive leadership. However, the belief alone is not enough to predict behaviour. Inclusive leaders focus on how their behaviour proactively dismantles systems of oppression, distributing power, ensuring equitable treatment, and levelling the playing field. Only then can equality of outcomes, fair competition, and merit really be possible.

One of the greatest challenges with regard to fairness and equity is that systems of unfairness and inequity are often hidden or not obvious, even to those who are negatively impacted by these systems. The illusion of a fair, equitable, meritocratic society is so deeply ingrained into how we are taught to see the world, that it can be difficult to spot the multiple, subtle, complex systems of oppression that still exist. Furthermore, when we compare today's society to historical conditions, it is clear that a lot of progress has been made.

In the post-Second World War, with the human rights revolution, we started to see the influence of civil rights and feminist movements in many Western democracies. This included the progressive introduction of legislation addressing racial and gender discrimination. In the United Kingdom, these laws include the Equality Act 2010, and before that the Equal Pay Act 1970, Sex Discrimination Act 1975, Race Relations Act 1976, and Disability Discrimination Act 1995, meaning that discrimination is illegal and conditions have improved. You only need to speak to a parent or grandparent about what was normal or typical behaviour at work 15, 20, or 30+ years ago, to bring this to life. Therefore, at face value, particularly for privileged groups,

DOI: 10.4324/9781003598022-23

it can be easy to believe that the hard work has been done and that we are living in a meritocratic world where the best person gets the job and is rewarded accordingly.

However, this self-made narrative, where merit is the primary driver of success, ignores structural disadvantages that have been built into the foundations of all our systems, including education, health, employment, politics, and family systems. This disconnect leads us to overestimate our progress, underestimate deep-rooted barriers, and reinforce systems of oppression.

Unfortunately, data collected from workplaces in the here-and-now show us how much progress still needs to be made. For example, research from 2023[1] reports that almost two-thirds (62 per cent) of women aged between 25 and 34 have experienced sexual harassment, bullying, or verbal abuse at work. Let's pause and reflect on this a moment. A woman who was 25 in 2023, who we assume started work at the age of 18 (or 21 if they went to university), will have started work in 2016 (or 2018), meaning that *since 2016 to now*, 62 per cent of women have experienced sexual harassment, bullying, or verbal abuse at work, highlighting how, unfortunately, sexual harassment at work is still an issue right now.

It is not just sexual harassment either. Data show us that gender and ethnicity pay gaps still exist. Women earn on average 7 per cent less than men in the UK, with a larger gap for employees aged 40 years and over and among high earners.[2] In terms of the ethnicity pay gap, statistics from 2022 show that Black, African, Caribbean, and Black British employees earned on average 6 per cent less than white employees, a gap that has been consistent since 2012.[3]

So why are issues of unfairness and inequity still such a problem?

Systemic oppression describes the historical and organised patterns of mistreatment that exist in our societies. This is because, historically, systems were created to benefit a few, via dominance and exploitation. While legislative reform has helped to address some of these unfair historical practices, providing clarity on what is and is not acceptable behaviour in the eyes of the law, the complexity of inequality and oppression mean that legislation alone is insufficient. In the work context, inequality is not lodged in positions, occupations, or even jobs but in the relationships between positions within organisations. Inequalities are similarly not lodged in people, races, or genders but in the relationships between people and between status categories. It is the relations between people and positions that generate the power, status, and selves that appear to be traits of individuals and jobs.[4]

This means that each and every one of us is responsible, in one way or another, for perpetuating systems of oppression. The way that we relate to one another reinforces a cycle of inequality on a daily basis, something that, for the majority of the time, we are completely unaware of it. This complexity makes systems of oppression a particularly "wicked" problem – a problem with many interdependent factors that make it seem impossible to solve. Below is a range of work-related barriers that reinforce systems of oppression. As you read through these, consider the part that you play in some of these points, particularly in terms of how you relate to others.

The burden of unpaid work

When women shoulder the burden of unpaid work (for example, childcare or caring for elderly relatives, and housework), it reduces the amount of time and energy (physical, emotional, and cognitive) they have available to expend on paid work and compete fairly with their male counterparts. In heterosexual households, women perform 76 per cent of all unpaid care work worldwide, accounting for three-quarters of the total hours dedicated to this type of work.[5] On average, women spend 4 hours and 25 minutes per day, compared with 1 hour and 23 minutes for men, in unpaid care work. In no country does the distribution of unpaid care work between men and women come close to being equal. Gender equality starts at home. Until our households have a shared burden of unpaid work, inequality for the genders will persist in the workplace.

Long hours culture

We live in times where the expectation is that we can always be contacted, day or night. However, what if you are not willing or able to be contacted by work out of hours? How would you be viewed? Would your commitment be questioned? Would you miss out on crucial opportunities? Equally, have you ever considered that being able to work long hours is a privilege? Even though it may not feel like it, being able to always be available is a privilege that not everyone has access to. Some people cannot be always available even if they wanted to be – for example, due to caring responsibilities, neurodiversity, or disability. This is problematic as the underlying assumption is that those who work longer hours and are always available for work are more committed to their work and will perform better. In fact, research shows that the opposite to be true. For example, people working a four-day week are generally more productive than people working a five-day week.[6] This difference is likely due to the fact that the long hours culture is more performative than productive, and is usually prevalent among full-time working men.[7] The long hours culture perpetuates inequalities and harms productivity and mental health at work. Furthermore, this culture leads to a stigma of flexible working practices.

The stigma associated with flexible and part-time working

People tend to view the commitment and dedication of those who work part-time or require flexible working as less than the commitment and dedication of those who work full-time, and therefore they are less likely to be given access to the same career opportunities as full-time employees. This largely impacts women, who are more likely to work part-time to accommodate family demands, and people with disabilities. In addition to addressing the stigma attached to flexible and part-time working, it is also important to acknowledge that some marginalised groups do not have equal access to the opportunity to adopt flexible working. For example, post-COVID 19, when homeworking was normalised, some marginalised groups did not benefit from this shift. Data show that Black men, particularly Black fathers, had low levels of homeworking, alongside Chinese and "Other Asian" workers (both men and women), particularly migrant workers from these ethnicities.[8] There is a range of possible explanations for the difference in access to working from home. For example, managers may have (unconscious) biases against Black or migrant workers, leading to a lack of trust in the ability of such workers to work from home in a productive way. It is also possible that there is a compounding effect, as minority ethnic workers, particularly migrant workers, are already at a disadvantage when it comes to career progression due to multiple layers of discrimination and oppression. Therefore, some workers may feel unable to engage in work from home, even when it is permitted by the organisation, for fear that it will have a further negative impact on their career progression due to the associated flexible working stigma.

The experience gap

People are generally promoted based on their experience. However, how do they get that experience in the first place? As leaders, we are responsible for allocating work and making decisions on who we allocate work to, consequently influencing the experience those individuals will gain, which in turn impacts the trajectory of their career (*more on allocating work below*). However, leaders often display ingroup favouritism. This bias makes leaders more likely to allocate high-visibility projects, for example, to people who share similar backgrounds, characteristics, and interests with themselves. In a male-dominated environment this can be observed by the "old boys club" effect, which not only limits opportunities for women and marginalised groups, but also further enhances the access and advantages of those who are already favoured.

Mentoring and sponsorship

Mentoring and sponsorship are crucial in shaping career trajectories, however they can dismantle or inadvertently reinforce barriers to career progression. Can you identify someone who has mentored you at some point in your career (either formally or informally)? How would you describe them? Were they like you? Mentoring and sponsorship can be influenced by a compounding cocktail of biases. For example, we might select mentees based on similarity bias (favour those who share a similar background), go the extra mile for the mentee based on affinity bias (favour those who we feel interpersonally connected with), and keep the mentee in the forefront of our minds advocating for them because of proximity biases (favour those who we spend time with). This creates a recurring gap where those who are marginalised in the workplace do not benefit from the same levels of mentoring and sponsorship as those from dominant groups.

Think star, think man

Who do you imagine when you imagine a "star performer"? According to research, the likelihood is that you imagined a man.[9] In fact, research consistently shows that marginalised groups are not automatically viewed as leaders and their authority and expertise, even when in a legitimate position of authority, are more likely to be questioned.[10] For example, the Reykjavík Index for Leadership shows that many people still do not feel comfortable with a woman as CEO, ranging from 40 per cent of respondents for the US, 42 per cent for the UK, 49 per cent for France, 52 per cent for Italy, and 64 per cent for India and Japan.[11] The type of person we imagine in leadership roles and therefore the implicit norms and assumptions we hold about leadership and gender, are heavily influenced by our stereotypes, which in turn are reinforced by who we see most frequently in senior roles. This means that when we are considering applicants for a leadership role and we are trying to identify that star performer, anyone who does not match this prototype (i.e., anyone from a marginalised group), has to work much harder for their potential to be seen. Therefore, it is critical that we have diverse representation in the most senior roles to start to counteract this "Think star, think man" leadership stereotype.

Restricted access to informal networks

Have you ever got a job through a recommendation or helped someone you know get a job? If you did, you are not alone. Research has shown that finding at least one job (and often more) through a racially homogeneous personal network is an extremely frequent occurrence[12] and a key contributor to the glass-ceiling effect for women is restricted access to social networks.[13] The glass-ceiling is a metaphor used to represent an invisible barrier that prevents a given demographic from rising beyond a certain level in a hierarchy. The impact of the glass-ceiling will be more pronounced according to the layers of intersecting systems of oppression one experiences – for example when racism, sexism, and ageism intersect, the prejudice experienced will be even more pronounced. Similar to sponsorship and mentoring, this denied access will be fuelled by biases, but with an additional implication: organisations have less influence on how these networks are formed and the influence of these networks on decision-making. The saying, "It's not what you know, it's who you know" exists for a reason. It's commonly accepted that our network can help to contribute to our success; however, when our networks are not diverse, then they will continue to perpetuate inequality.

Damned if you do and damned if you don't

We have explored a range of double-binds and stereotype threats in this book so far (for example, the modesty versus self-promotion double-bind for women covered in Chapter 10). Our societal expectations and norms dictate what we see as "acceptable" behaviour based on the roles we play in any given system. These roles and the associated norms are influenced by our position in the system, the "social order". For example, white supremacy and patriarchal systems hold the ideology that white men are inherently superior to other genders and racial backgrounds and should therefore dominate society. Whilst many of us reject the notion of these "social orders", when we try to dismantle these structures, we can be penalised (as we engage in behaviour not seen as acceptable for our role within the system), yet if we do not, we remain oppressed. This means that marginalised groups have to walk an extremely narrow tightrope of navigating behaviour that society views as acceptable for their identity group while *also* exhibiting the opposite behaviour so that they might succeed in breaking through systems of oppression, including at work.

The hidden rules of success

Organisational culture is the set of shared, taken for granted, implicit assumptions that members of that organisation hold and that determines how the members perceive, think about, and react to their environment.[14] In fact, we can also consider culture from the perspectives of different professions, where whole professions have their own set of shared, implicit assumptions that guide behaviour. The challenge with this is that, from the outside, it can be very difficult to know what these assumptions or rules for success are, or even that they exist at all: you don't know what you don't know. An example of this is university rankings. Whether it is the Russell Group in the UK or the Ivy League in the US, where you go to university can have implications for whether you are likely to get shortlisted for an interview.[15] However, if you are the first person in your family to go to university or the first person in your family to work in a profession where this is common practice, would you know? If you do not know all of the rules of the "game", how is it possible to compete fairly? In many cases, marginalised groups waste their limited resources and use enormous amounts of emotional labour trying to understand these hidden rules and this is even before they start addressing the multi-layers of prejudice they will face in getting through the door.

Inclusive leaders have a deep understanding of how our society and organisations perpetuate systems of oppression and inequalities through these barriers, and they work towards dismantling these systems in every way they can. This means that they not only value fairness and equity, they also proactively focus on the action that needs to be taken to ensure workplaces are fair and equitable. In this chapter, we focus on two key work contexts that illustrate the importance of focusing on fairness and equity: allocating work and managing pay rises.

Allocating work

We have already touched on the importance of exposure to experiences at work that stretch individuals' skills and demonstrate their capability. It is these experiences that fill out a person's CV and make them eligible (or not) to apply for a job. The experiences are what give them the examples to demonstrate their competence and capability. But what if the same people are allocated the best work – the work that enables them to demonstrate what they are capable of? It is perhaps not surprising that it will be those people who are considered first for promotion and those people who can most easily evidence their capability – they have plenty of experiences to draw upon as examples!

As leaders we are constantly needing to balance the pressure placed on us to produce results and get things done against our responsibility as leaders to develop others and nurture talent. When we have a high-stakes project, it may feel like the sensible or safe choice to allocate the task to the person who we see as our best performer or those that we spend the most time with (proximity bias). However, generally, who we see as the best performer is the person we have previously allocated the most important work to and incidentally, these are often the people we spend the most time with. This creates a cycle where only certain people are accessing the critical experiences, demonstrating their capability, and then being allocated important opportunities to shine. We cannot demonstrate our performance and gain experience without being given the opportunity. If we are not given the opportunity because we have never demonstrated our capability, we are indeed stuck in that vicious cycle where we are denied access to the very opportunities needed to demonstrate our capability in the first place.

Therefore inclusive leaders appreciate that experience and past performance might be the result of privileged opportunities as opposed to potential. This means that, when allocating work, inclusive leaders focus on the future while evaluating traits, strengths, and motivation to predict performance. To do this, inclusive leaders have to ensure that they know each member of their team well and that they fully understand what makes each team member unique, enabling the leader to form an accurate picture of each member's potential.

A final "watch out" when allocating work is bias linked to benevolence (i.e., attempting to be helpful), where ableist and sexist benevolence positions women and disabled individuals as fragile and promotes chivalrous behaviour towards them. While often the intentions behind chivalrous behaviour are good, it can lead to an individual's capabilities being underestimated in an attempt to be "helpful" and instead reinforces inequalities and stereotypes. For example, a woman may not be asked to take on additional responsibilities at work because the leader is aware that she is juggling many demands at home. Or a disabled person might not be involved in a high-stakes client project, as it is assumed they might struggle with the associated travel. As with most instances we have covered in this book, the most important action we can take is *not* to make assumptions. Instead, inclusive leaders need to be aware of the potential bias and stereotypes that can lead them to want to try to be helpful and to mitigate these by having open conversations about allocation of work with their team.

Case example: Challenging my own work allocation practices

I led a high-profile project for a major client. The project had tight deadlines and high stakes, making it tempting to default to the "safe" choice and assign critical work to the usual top performers. However, as a Black woman, I recognised early in my career how unfair work allocation had held me back, particularly for high-visibility projects. I made a conscious decision to ensure that others did not have to experience the same barriers I faced. Rather than relying on familiarity or assumptions, I developed a certain approach to allocating work. This means constantly pausing before making a decision and asking myself: "Who is the hidden talent I haven't yet seen at play?". I also track work distribution to maintain long-term equity. I welcome feedback from my peers, including around my decisions on work allocation, but, when challenged, I often find that their concerns stem from biases related to race, gender, or other systemic factors. Maybe my own lived experience has helped me recognise this pattern more easily. One moment of deep learning came when I caught myself making a decision influenced by ableism. A senior client meeting required a high level of adaptability and responsiveness. Under pressure, I instinctively leaned towards assigning the presentation to a team member known for their gravitas, presence, and verbal fluency. However, in doing so, I unconsciously overlooked another highly skilled team member, an analyst with a speech disability. The bias wasn't about capability, it was about my own assumptions of what "strong client presence" looked like, particularly my association between verbal fluency and quick thinking.

Managing pay rises

When managing pay rises there are two critical implications that inclusive leaders need to pay attention to: pay gaps and merit-based pay policies.

Despite equal pay for equal work being a legal requirement in many countries, it remains only a baseline measure for explicit discrimination. The pay gap is the measure needed to consider structural inequalities that are embedded into work systems. Achieving true pay equity requires addressing structural inequalities, not just ensuring compliance with a single equal pay law. Pay gap is a broad term that measures the average difference in pay across groups, and it continues to persist. There is no single explanation for the persistence of pay gaps and, indeed, why progress in closing the gender pay gap, for example, has stalled in general. This is despite the fact that, generally, women in Western countries often start their careers at pay parity with men and that women today are more likely than men to have graduated from university. Some of the explanations for the gender pay gap include:[16]

- Mothers aged between 25 and 44 are less likely to be employed and are more likely to work fewer hours when they are employed compared with women of the same age who do not have children. However, this is not the only explanation for the gender pay gap and evidence suggests that this reduction in earnings is modest overall or short-lived for many.
- Fathers, on the other hand, are more likely to be employed and, when they are employed, they are more likely to work more hours than men without children at home, which consequently contributes to widening the gender pay gap.
- Women are still underrepresented in leadership and in science, technology, engineering, and mathematics (STEM) occupations, and they are overrepresented in education, healthcare, personal care, and service occupations, which, on average, are lower paying occupations. Therefore, distribution of the genders across occupations remains a driver of the pay gap.

Understanding the root causes of pay gaps is crucial for inclusive leaders because it allows them to address the structural and systemic issues that contribute to these disparities, rather than simply addressing the symptoms. This understanding cannot be limited to one system of oppression, such as sexism. We must consider how other forms, like racism, ableism, and ageism, intersect and compound to influence pay. Therefore, managing pay is not only about addressing an individual's pay, but it is also about overhauling the systems and practices that cause inequity in the first place. Only by addressing these systems and practices can lasting improvements in pay, representation, and opportunity be achieved.

In addition to pay gaps, we must also consider merit-based pay policies. In Chapter 14, we discussed the concept of merit and how difficult it is to use merit as a means of driving fairness when there are systemic inequalities and an unlevel playing field. Merit only benefits fairness between members from the same group. For example, merit might bring a sense of fair competition when we compare a white single breadwinner man with another white single breadwinner man. Furthermore, merit-based practices assume that promotion decisions are free from bias, which is unrealistic and creates a false sense of fairness; this assumption leads to complacency in addressing structural inequalities. Despite these limitations, merit-based pay remains the standard practice in most organisations.

Case example: Facing the myth of meritocracy as an HR professional

For years, as an HR director, I was a firm believer in merit-based pay policies, convinced that they were the best way to drive healthy competition and reward high performance. I even implemented forced distribution curves, ensuring that only a select few received top ratings while others fell into lower performance categories. For me, this approach was fair as prolonged poor performance meant that others had to work harder, which I saw as an unfair burden on top performers. My policies aimed to incentivise excellence while addressing underperformance swiftly. My perspective began to shift when I started working more closely with EDI. Through exposure to data, lived experiences, and broader research, I realised that merit was not an objective measure but an illusion because of systemic inequalities. I came to understand that structures of inequality take root long before people enter the workforce, and they continue to be reinforced through unconscious bias, limited access to development, and disparities in opportunity. My long-held belief in a purely meritocratic system began to unravel as I recognised how I had failed to account for these contextual barriers.

What can inclusive leaders do?

Fundamentally when employees see that their contributions are not recognised fairly and that hurdles with structural inequalities are not addressed, they do not feel valued and they do not experience a true sense of belonging within their teams. Therefore, inclusive leaders play a critical role in supporting practices such as equal pay audits, transparent work assignments, pay transparency policies, and in supporting initiatives that account for structural inequalities. Furthermore, when performance is not rewarded solely by traditional merit-based metrics but also by considering the context of each individual, employees are more likely to see themselves as an integral part of the team.

Below are some practical recommendations on how to focus on fairness and equity while allocating work and managing pay rises.

Allocating work

- Carefully assess your immediate and long-term needs in terms of delivering work and supporting your colleagues to develop and grow. Make sure you create opportunities for your colleagues to thrive by playing to their strengths and their potential as well as their availability.
- Create "nudges" to pause and reflect on allocation of work patterns: this is a powerful way to mitigate proximity biases. For example, identify who are the colleagues that you allocate work to the most. Challenge the assumptions you are making about them and the other members of the team. Then, list all possible benefits and implications for the present and the future if you were to adopt a more inclusive approach to work allocation.
- Create skills and experience requirement lists and criteria for tasks and validate your assumptions with others to drive objectivity.
- Ensure that you know all your team well, and that you fully understand what makes each team member unique. This will enable you to form an accurate picture of their strengths and potential.
- Consider proactively allocating promising work to individuals from marginalised groups to accelerate their development and enable a level playing field. Inclusive leaders know that work practices need to be equitable (not equal), otherwise privilege and prejudice are systematically perpetuated. They assess each individual's characteristics, potential, and context before allocating work.
- Consider the risk of allocating work to the same people in relation to the development of team performance. For example, if you have only a few high performers in your team there is a greater risk for your own performance if they leave. Write down the possible mitigation actions for each implication.

- Appreciate that enabling a level playing field may well require more advanced planning to allocate specific work to colleagues who might need to accelerate their development to compete fairly when a promotion opportunity arises. This means taking longer to complete the work and providing extra support to enable the learning and growth.

Managing pay rises

- Acknowledge structural inequalities while evaluating merit-based pay, looking at intersectional barriers, privilege, and access to opportunities to perform in the first place.
- Adopt a hybrid system of performance metrics and equity adjustments to enable the calibration of decisions. This may include adjusting performance metrics when structural inequalities exist – for example, when internal data show that one group had more access to opportunities than another group.
- Always consider performance ratings in the context of access and allocation of opportunities. Inclusive leaders will always calibrate pay by comparing all elements impacting on performance as opposed to focusing on targets alone.
- Continuously collect performance and pay data to detect trends or patterns that might indicate bias and use these data to adjust policies as necessary. Remember to consider intersectional data to assess the impact of intersectional inequalities.
- Ensure you have a strong understanding of the difference between equal pay and pay gaps. Do not assume that you do not have an equal pay issue: instead, conduct proper job evaluation and analyse pay using comparators and market indicators.
- Avoid perpetuating pay gaps when recruiting: never ask for previous salary as a reference for pay decisions. Focus on job evaluation and market value for each role.
- Familiarise yourself with the existing pay gaps in your organisation and fully adopt any actions and targets aimed at closing these gaps. If nothing is in place, start by measuring your own team's salary data and take corrective measures where needed.
- Use your leadership position and influence: take an active role in measuring and challenging pay practices and systems to close pay gaps and, most importantly, address structures of inequality that drive pay gaps.

Chapter 17 in summary

- Inclusive leaders focus on how their behaviour proactively dismantles systems of oppression, distributing power, ensuring equitable treatment, and levelling the playing field.
- Although legislative progress in addressing unfairness and inequity at work has been made, structures of inequality are still present at critical levels and can be easily observed by analysing pay gaps and the frequency of sexual harassment in the workplace.
- There is a range of barriers that reinforce systems of oppression, and inclusive leaders play a critical role in recognising and dismantling these barriers.
- Allocating work is a problematic context for equity and fairness because we are influenced by biases that limit our ability to be objective and fair. When there is an inequitable allocation of work, marginalised groups may be denied access to experiences that can enable them to demonstrate the capability needed for career progression.
- Managing pay is an important outcome measure that reveals unfair systems. Many rely on the merit-based pay argument to respond to evidence of pay disparity. However, merit is only possible when there is a level playing field free from systems of oppression, such as sexism, racism, and ableism.
- Pay gaps are one of the most visible indicators of workplace inequality. Inclusive leaders go beyond reporting pay gaps and addressing individual disparities, they actively work to close pay gaps at a structural and intersectional level, tackling the root causes that create them.

Notes

1 TUC (Trades Union Congress). (2023). *New TUC poll: 2 in 3 young women have experienced sexual harassment, bullying or verbal abuse at work.* Accessed from https://www.tuc.org.uk/news/new-tuc-poll-2-3-young-women-have-experienced-sexual-harassment-bullying-or-verbal-abuse-work#research-analysis. Retrieved 3 February 2025.
2 ONS (Office for National Statistics). (2024). *Gender pay gap in the UK: 2024.* Accessed from https://www.ons.gov.uk/employmentandlabourmarket/peopleinwork/earningsandworkinghours/bulletins/genderpaygapintheuk/2024. Retrieved 4 February 2025.

3 ONS (Office for National Statistics). (2022). *Ethnicity pay gaps, UK: 2012 to 2022.* Accessed from https://www.ons.gov.uk/employmentandlabourmarket/peopleinwork/earningsandworkinghours/articles/ethnicitypaygapsingreatbritain/2012to2022. Retrieved 16 April 2025.

4 Tomaskovic-Devey, D. (2014). The relational generation of workplace inequalities (p. 52). *Social Currents, 1*(1), 51–73.

5 International Labour Organization. (2018). *Care work and care jobs for the future of decent work.* Accessed from https://www.ilo.org/publications/major-publications/care-work-and-care-jobs-future-decent-work. Retrieved 13 February 2025.

6 Henley Business School. (2025). *The four-day week.* Accessed from https://www.henley.ac.uk/the-four-day-week. Retrieved 13 February 2025.

7 Chung H. (2022). A social policy case for a four-day week. *Journal of Social Policy, 51*(3), 551–566.

8 Chung, H., & Yuan, S. (2025). Did COVID-19 level the playing field or entrench it? Comparing patterns of homeworking by ethnicity, gender and migration status, before, during and after COVID-19 in the UK. *Industrial Relations Journal,* 1–15.

9 Villamor, I., & Aguinis, H. (2024). Think star, think men? Implicit star performer theories. *Journal of Organizational Behavior, 45*(6), 783–799.

10 Sieghart, M. A. (2021).*The authority gap.* London: Penguin Books.

11 Harrison, M. (2024). *Gender equality in leadership: Is 2024 the start of a downward tend?* Access from https://www.veriangroup.com/news-and-insights/gender-equality-2024-downward-trend. Retrieved 23 February 2025.

12 DiTomaso, N. (2013). How social networks drive black unemployment. *New York Times.*

13 Neugart, M., & Zaharieva, A. (2024). Social networks, promotions, and the glass-ceiling effect. *Journal of Economics & Management Strategy,* 1–33.

14 Schein, E. H. (2010). *Organizational culture and leadership.* Hoboken, NJ: Jossey-Bass.

15 Rivera, L. A. (2012). Hiring as cultural matching: The case of elite professional service firms. *American Sociological Review, 77,* 999–1022.

16 Kochhar, R. (2023). *The enduring grip of the gender pay gap.* Accessed from https://www.pewresearch.org/social-trends/2023/03/01/the-enduring-grip-of-the-gender-pay-gap/. Retrieved 6 February 2025.

Practising allyship   **18**

Practising allyship is about purposefully collaborating with marginalised groups to actively promote equity through supportive and collaborative relationships, which includes actively listening to accounts of bias and mistreatment, acts of sponsorship, speaking out against bias, advocating for new opportunities for marginalised professionals, and public advocacy with the purpose of driving systemic change.[1]

Allyship is a process or the ongoing practice of actions and, for those actions to be considered allyship, they must be seen as so by the group they are intended to support: "put simply, people are not allies; people do allyship".[2] Just as one single healthy behaviour does not constitute a healthy lifestyle, engaging in a single act of allyship does not constitute being an ally.

Unpacking the criticism behind allyship: performative and self-serving

The concept of allyship is not new. Several social justice authors introduced the idea of engaging privileged groups in supporting marginalised groups to dismantle structures of inequality a long time ago. The process involved privilege awareness,[3] solidarity,[4] advocacy, and accountability.[5] Although the term allyship was not explicitly mentioned in the work of these influential authors, we started to see an alignment between these principles and the term allyship in the 1980s and 1990s when activists called on heterosexual allies to support LGBTQ+ rights. Since then, scholars have elaborated on the concept

DOI: 10.4324/9781003598022-24

of allyship, highlighting how allyship is not limited to standing in solidarity but is an active process of learning about privileges, unlearning stereotypes, redistributing power, and driving systemic change.

However, recently, there has been growing criticism that most allyship activities are performative,[6] self-serving,[7] have no impact on systemic inequalities, overlook injustices with only superficial attention,[8] and in many cases perpetuate dependency of marginalised groups on dominant groups as opposed to fostering autonomy and empowerment.[9] As a result, some have distanced themselves from the term "allyship" altogether, arguing that it has become associated with virtue signalling, such as sharing content on social media, without any real change in behaviour. For allyship to be meaningful, we need to return to the foundations laid down by the original scholars who clearly highlighted several aspects of supporting social justice, including self-reflection about one's own privileges, understanding of systemic oppression, listening and amplifying marginalised voices and power, and being accountable and committed, rather than centring one's involvement in the cause to receive credit. Changing the terminology will not stop concepts from being misused or weaponised. A more robust approach is to reposition the concept back to the roots of social justice and ensure that when someone says that they are an ally, we encourage them to reflect on what this means and how they are living up to their commitment.

There are several challenges to practicing allyship. These can include the fear and anxiety linked to social discomfort, the desire for self-preservation and retention of privileges, the lack of awareness and biases, the gap between perception of allyship and actual impact, and an absence of accountability and support from the wider system. Below we address two challenges that we often observed across multiple clients.

The first significant challenge is that people often think that they are better allies than they really are. For example, research on allyship from 1,150 participants in mid-sized to Fortune 500 companies across industries in the United States demonstrated significant gaps between how men and women view men's allyship behaviours.[10] Particularly concerning was the gap at the executive/C-suite level where 77 per cent of men felt that men were "active allies and public advocates" for gender equity compared to just 45 per cent of women working at this level. The danger with an awareness at C-suite level, is that the C-suite consists of those who have the power to allocate resources and distribute power. If they perceive allyship not to be an issue, they are unlikely to allocate resources to improve it. It is not just at the C-suite level either, the gap persists at all management levels.

So why is there such a large gap between perceptions of allyship? Most allies do not measure the gap between their intentions and the structural changes they influence. Sometimes, leaders might believe that being supportive in principle and expressing their inclusive and fair values are enough. They might also deliver low-impact actions such as showing solidarity online when convenient and feel that they have done enough; or remain silent when it is risky to voice an opposing opinion and take action. Allyship is not only about believing in social justice; it is about *doing* social justice. Doing social justice is an ongoing process, informing your actions to drive meaningful and impactful change. For example, reflect on the following questions to self-assess your own allyship impact:

- How are you sharing power and opportunities with marginalised groups?
- Have you ever held back from challenging bias due to fear of conflict or social discomfort?
- How do you ensure learning leads to action rather than only intellectual awareness?
- What actions (rather than words) would your marginalised colleagues cite as examples of your allyship?
- If you left your position tomorrow, what changes to the system and culture would remain because of your allyship (for example, in removing barriers in hiring, promotion, and pay equity)?

The second challenge to engaging in allyship is the anxiety that leaders may feel about engaging in allyship initiatives. When clear and compelling reasons for the allyship initiative are not provided, processes supporting the initiative are not implemented, and visible role models for allyship behaviour are not present, leaders can experience a high level of anxiety about participation in the allyship initiative.[11] As anxiety is an inhibitor of learning and change, this can cause the leader to disengage with the initiative and potentially become defensive, closing down their curiosity and openness. As individual leaders, we can notice when we start to become anxious about something (such as efforts to increase allyship) by tuning into our somatic responses, emotions, and thoughts. When we start to switch from being curious to learn to becoming defensive of our position and actions, that can be a cue for us to pause and notice what is happening and to reflect on why this might be the case.

Practising allyship describes a series of ongoing actions and inclusive leaders can be allies in virtually every work context. In this chapter, we focus on two key work contexts that illustrate the importance of practising allyship for inclusion: dismantling systemic barriers to career progression and advocating for balanced representation.

Dismantling systemic barriers to career progression

In Chapter 17 we described the many, varied barriers that serve to make our workplaces unfair and inequitable. These systemic barriers hinder the career progression of marginalised groups. In practising allyship, inclusive leaders proactively dismantle these systemic barriers. This dismantling can take many forms and will vary depending on the individual leader's seniority and access to resources.

Allies engage in both critical self-reflexivity and critical reflexive practice to raise awareness of and then dismantle systemic barriers to career progression.[12]

Critical self-reflexivity involves examining our own biases and underlying assumptions that can contribute to exclusion. This involves centring marginalised voices and experiences by seeking input to create insight into marginalised lived experiences. This may result in the awareness that we have, at least at some point in the past, been a perpetrator, affiliate of a perpetrator, or bystander in practices that oppress marginalised groups in the workplace. Critical self-reflexivity involves recognising the privileges that we have: the opportunities, resources, and power that have been automatically afforded to us as a result of aspects of our identity, as well as the privileged role that we play in the organisation. With a high level of awareness of our own power and influence, we can be mindful that rather than perpetuate inequalities, we use this position of power to address them. Critical self-reflexivity is the first step to help leaders to see barriers that are frequently invisible for those who have unearned privileges within a system.

With critical reflexive practice, the focus turns away from ourselves and involves reflecting on what is taken for granted, assumed, or not acknowledged, from a systemic and cultural point of view, and the impact this may be having on those around us, especially marginalised groups. This involves questioning social structures that create and sustain inequalities by reinforcing oppression, so power and resources privilege some but not all. In the work context, this includes the assumed neutrality of concepts such as skill, talent, and merit, and instead acknowledging the socially constructed nature of how we define who or what we see as having skill, talent, and merit. Action following critical reflexive practice will include working alongside marginalised groups to advocate for structural change that addresses systemic inequities. It challenges and transforms oppressive systems as opposed to merely understanding them. This can include changing formal policies and procedures, informal work practices, norms and patterns of work, narratives and language, and informal patterns of social interactions that contribute to inequality at work. Many examples of these actions are covered throughout this book.

Case example: Witnessing the negative systemic impact of performative allyship

Early in my career in EDI, I worked with a senior white leader, James, who saw himself as a strong advocate for diversity. He regularly spoke about the importance of inclusion and fairness, proudly stating that his team operated on a meritocratic basis. "If you work hard, you'll get ahead here," he often said. On the surface, James seemed like an ally. He attended EDI events, mentored junior employees from diverse backgrounds, and expressed frustration at the slow progress of diversity efforts in the organisation. However, when we reviewed the data, a different picture emerged. James's team consistently struggled to retain talent from underrepresented backgrounds. Employees praised his open-door policy, but many left after a few years – not because they lacked ambition, but because their career progression had stalled. When I raised this with him, his response was familiar: "I don't see barriers here. The best people rise to the top naturally." I pushed him to look deeper. As we analysed his team's promotion history, patterns became clear. Those who progressed most quickly had been informally tapped for stretch assignments, high-visibility projects, and influential sponsors – opportunities that were rarely extended to employees from diverse backgrounds. Without meaning to, James had been reinforcing the very barriers he thought he was fighting against. I suggested structural changes: transparent criteria for promotion, sponsorship accountability for senior leaders, and a more intentional approach to talent development. James nodded along but seemed unconvinced. He preferred to focus on individual performance rather than systemic barriers. A year later, I caught up with some former colleagues and heard a familiar story: talented employees from underrepresented backgrounds were still leaving James's team. But they were not leaving the company, they were being promoted elsewhere, under leaders who had created environments where they could truly thrive. James wasn't a bad leader, nor was he resistant to diversity. He genuinely believed he was doing the right things. But his story reflects a common challenge: performative allyship without real structural action leads to frustration, disengagement, and ultimately, the loss of great talent. Sometimes it is much harder to get through to people who believe that they "get" equity, diversity, and inclusion than people who are new to their journey of becoming more inclusive.

Advocating for balanced representation

To advocate for representation means to push for diverse representation in any given work context (such as meetings, decision-making, leadership composition, when hiring, or in the team generally). Inclusive leaders who practise allyship recognise the importance of representation in ensuring that all voices are heard and perspectives are not overlooked due to a lack of lived experience. Representation of diversity is critical for innovation as it is our diverse lived experiences that enable us to experience the world very differently and consequently bring a different perspective to any given challenge.

Practising allyship does not mean speaking on behalf of someone from a marginalised group. If we are not a member of that group, we do not have the lived experience to understand what it is truly like to be a member of that group. Therefore, even with the highest levels of awareness, we still need to ask people from that marginalised group to share their insights. When we are being "helpful", we have a tendency to believe that, as the helper, we know best. We can speak up on behalf of people not in the room (or even, sometimes, they *are* in the room, but we might decide they need our help to ensure their view is heard, so we speak up for them). In the pursuit of being helpful, we are centring ourselves as the helper rather than centring the groups we are intending to support. Therefore, to avoid slipping into helper or saviour mode, we should use our position of privilege and take action as an ally to advocate for representation. This means that we are not speaking on behalf of marginalised groups. Instead we are highlighting where representation is not present, why this is a problem, and the action which can be taken to adjust this. In this way, we are honouring the lived experience of marginalised groups. Recognising they are perfectly able to speak for themselves, they do not need our "help" to speak for them.

White saviour mentality and allyship

An important area to highlight when we consider practising allyship and specifically when we think about advocating for representation is what is known as "white saviour mentality". "A white saviour is a white person who 'comes to the aid' of a Black, Indigenous, or brown person. In the mind of a white saviour they are doing good, noble work".[13] Often, being a white saviour is associated with performative allyship, taking action against racism, for example, to enable the saviour to feel good about themselves and present a positive image to the world. The negative association between allyship and white saviour mentality is another reason why many have moved away from using the term allyship.

White leaders can avoid becoming white saviours (or any other type of saviour for that matter) by reflecting on how they view marginalised groups in the context of themselves. Social justice work refers to solidarity as a partnership of equals, focused on an active commitment to support and stand by marginalised and oppressed groups. Help implies superiority of some sort, reinforces power imbalances, and it can feel patronising. Where there is a helper, there is often a person who is helpless. When we are "helping" we are often holding on to an underlying assumption that "I have to help all these others because they're not able/good enough to help themselves".

We can engage in critical self-reflection to bring to the surface and understand our deepest beliefs and assumptions about different identity groups in the context of their need for our "help". When we view others as our equals and whole, resourceful people, we switch from wanting to help to practising allyship. Allies do not need to be helpers. Allies engage in allyship behaviours to dismantle systemic barriers to oppression. They do it even if no one else ever recognises or becomes aware of the work they are doing.

You may at this point be feeling somewhat confused. Haven't we spent most of this book describing how difficult, challenging, inequitable, and unfair the world is? Doesn't this mean that to address these inequities and unfairness, leaders from dominant groups must help? Yes and no. The *way* that dominant groups take action is what is critical here. Inclusive leaders recognise that the most valuable help they can provide is in addressing the systemic barriers that exist. Using their privilege and platform as a leader to speak up and take action. To normalise conversations about inclusion and exclusion. It is not about helping marginalised individuals. As soon as we start to see ourselves as someone who helps individuals, it keeps the power firmly rooted in the dominant group (the helper) and consequently only serves to perpetuate the very systems of oppression that we may be working to dismantle.

A final point here is to recognise that representation does not mean one person of that identity in the room. For example, an executive team of 12 members with 1 woman and 11 men does not have a balanced representation. When someone is the only person of that identity (a token), it increases the burden placed on that individual to represent everyone of that identity.[14] Tokens tend to experience high levels of emotional labour with greater impact on mental health, stereotype threat, high pressure to conform, scrutiny, and lack of support.[15] Without a critical mass of representation, the voices of those in the marginalised group will be unlikely to be heard or taken seriously, they cannot form collective, organised forces, and the power of action can only be generated when there is a coherent and united will of a social group. Research suggests around 30% of represetation is often necessary to shift dynamics in a group.[16] However, most groups can be underrepresented in society in general, making the risk of tokenism even more problematic.

Case example: Driving representation in leadership recruitment from the top

When I worked for a financial firm, I noticed that despite having a diverse workforce, leadership roles were still predominantly occupied by people like me, white men – there was a severe lack of representation at the top. The company published an EDI report annually and promoted its "allyship programme", but I questioned what they really meant by "allyship". In my first year in the company, I challenged HR as efforts to promote allyship weren't translating into real representation at senior levels. I suggested upgrading the mentoring scheme, which was part of the programme, to a sponsorship programme, where high-potential employees from underrepresented backgrounds would be paired with senior leaders who could actively advocate for their progression, particularly during talent review committees. I also pushed for diverse hiring panels and set clear representation targets for leadership roles in my area, which created pressure on others to follow suit. Over time, this led to more equitable promotions. HR were thrilled because, for years, they had been trying to foster real allyship, but no one from the executive team had been willing to take meaningful action until then. Executive teams have a lot to answer for when it comes to performative allyship. Too often, they talk about inclusion without taking the actions that actually shift representation. Now their executive team is made up of 30 per cent women and they have two people of colour. It was a great achievement in three years.

What can inclusive leaders do?

In the pursuit of social justice, allyship has emerged as a powerful tool to support access to resources and the fair distribution of power. To achieve this, allies focus on dismantling barriers to access and advancing representation in leadership and decision-making so systems can be reformed to serve all, not only a few. Verbal commitment and efforts without measuring impact are not enough. While a desire to be an ally is often rooted in good intentions, actions must drive real change. To measure the effectiveness of your allyship you must seek feedback from those you are supporting. The actual experiences of marginalised individuals will be the true barometer of success.

Below are some considerations on how to practise allyship when dismantling systemic barriers to career progression and when advocating for representation.

Dismantling systemic barriers to career progression

- Define what allyship means to you and how you are going to measure your impact. Consider broader and lasting changes to processes and policies.
- Seek input and feedback from those you aim to advocate for to inform your allyship actions.
- By driving objectivity, challenge systems of privilege in hiring, access to resources and development, and promotion and pay equity. Evaluate

practices to identify barriers for marginalised groups and consider what intentional, positive, and conscious efforts you can put in place to dismantle these barriers.

- During career conversations, allocate extra time with colleagues from marginalised groups to understanding their lived experiences, explicitly discuss barriers to career progression, and explore your role in identifying and removing such barriers.
- Actively amplify marginalised voices by increasing their contribution in meetings, presentations, projects, and social spaces. Remember, it is not about speaking on their behalf, it is about bringing them to the table and creating a safe space for everyone to be heard.
- Lobby for institutional reforms or influence wider societal structures with pledges or roles outside employment, such as boards and voluntary work if possible. Also stand in solidarity and participate in collective action like advocacy campaigns and grass-root movements.
- Support and take part in inclusive leadership programmes.
- Confront biases and address microaggressions. Small everyday microaggressions have a cumulative impact on reinforcing oppression. Learn how to become an active bystander so that you are not caught by surprise when microaggressions occur and instead know how to constructively interrupt microaggressions without making the marginalised person feel singled out. This includes addressing the behaviour not the person and including the group in the process of critical reflexivity. For example, someone might say "It is not that bad, you are just being overly sensitive" to a colleague, which invalidates someone's lived experience. The ally might say, "I understand that it might not seem like a big deal to some people, however it is helpful for us to understand that what's not bad to one person can be very hurtful to another. Let's try to listen and understand other perspectives, even if different from our own."
- Engage in continuous learning and reflection. Reflect on your own role in perpetuating inequalities and challenge your own biases and self-preservation decisions to protect privileges.

Advocating for representation

- To address representation, encourage the rest of your leadership team to promote equity, not just equality, when supporting individuals to compete for leadership roles. Marginalised groups will need differentiated treatment to be able to compete fairly (the ability to compete fairly is the equal outcome). This can involve supporting talent acceleration programmes and schemes for marginalised groups and offering sponsorship.

- Consider intersectionality (different layers of oppression towards certain identities, i.e., sexism, racism, ageism, etc.) when endorsing candidates for promotion into leadership roles and consider how intersectionality translates into career barriers. For example, Black women are less likely to receive promotion than white women. If underrepresented employees are overlooked for promotion, set aside time to reflect on and assess why this is the case and encourage decision-makers around you to do the same.
- Be a critical friend during talent review committees to decide who to appoint into leadership roles and when succession mapping. For example, during the process of calibrating and moderating the input of others, drive objectives while also identifying and addressing bias.
- Take an active role in advocating for fair practice in hiring and promotion – this might include supporting people to review recruitment and promotion practices.
- Talk to your inner circles about the knowledge you have gained about underrepresented groups in leadership and decision-making and share how others can advocate for them.
- Promote inclusive decision-making with consultation in areas where balanced representation is in progress by involving underrepresented voices in strategic meetings.

Chapter 18 in summary

- Practising allyship is about purposefully collaborating with marginalised groups to actively promote equity through supportive and collaborative relationships, with a series of impactful and ongoing actions.
- Verbal commitment and good intent are not allyship. Allyship behaviours must drive real change and impact needs to be measured. Gather feedback from the group the ally is supporting.
- Allyship means learning about our own privileges, unlearning stereotypes, distributing power, and advocating for marginalised groups without centring or benefitting ourselves.
- Performative and self-serving allyship has given the term "allyship" a bad name, leading many people to reject it. However, the essence of allyship was never meant to be performative, so it's important to reposition and challenge what is actually being done when practising allyship. Simply

changing the terminology will not stop those who are not genuinely interested in social justice from misusing concepts to benefit themselves.

- Practising allyship is about engaging in both critical self-reflexivity (internally focused) and critical reflexive practice (externally focused) to raise awareness of and then dismantle systemic barriers to career progression.
- Allies advocate for representation by challenging homogeneous leadership groups and pushing for diverse representation in any given work context, particularly in hiring and promotion, as well as in decision-making processes through active consultation.

Notes

1 Creary, S. J. (2024). Taking a "LEAP": How workplace allyship initiatives shape leader anxiety, allyship, and power dynamics that contribute to workplace inequality. *Academy of Management Review*, 49(4), 848–878.

2 De Souza, L., & Schmader, T. (2025). When people do allyship: A typology of allyship action (p. 5). *Personality and Social Psychology Review*, 29(1), 3–31.

3 McIntosh, P. (1989). White privilege: Unpacking the invisible knapsack. *National SEED project*. Accessed from https://www.nationalseedproject.org/key-seed-texts/white-privilege-unpacking-the-invisible-knapsack.

4 Lorde, A. (1984). The master's tools will never dismantle the master's house. In *Sister outsider: Essays and speeches* (pp. 110–114). Trumansberg, NY: Crossing Press. Accessed from https://monoskop.org/images/b/be/Lorde_Audre_1983_1984_The_Masters_Tools_Will_Never_Dismantle_the_Masters_House.pdf.

5 Crenshaw, K. (1991). Mapping the margins: Intersectionality, identity politics, and violence against women of color. *Stanford Law Review*, 43(6), 1241–1299; hooks, b. (2000). *Feminism is for everybody: Passionate politics*. New York: South End Press.

6 Kutlaca, M., & Radke, H. R. (2023). Towards an understanding of performative allyship: Definition, antecedents and consequences. *Social and Personality Psychology Compass*, 17(2), e12724.

7 Westra, J. C. (2021). Towards an understanding of performative allyship: Definition, antecedents, and consequences. *Social and Personality Psychology Compass*, 15(2), e12724.

8 Creary, S. J. (2024). Taking a "LEAP": How workplace allyship initiatives shape leader anxiety, allyship, and power dynamics that contribute to workplace inequality. *Academy of Management Review*, 49(4), 848–878.

9 Becker, J. C., Radke, H. R. M., Iyer, A., & Becker, J. C. (2020). Beyond allyship: Motivations for advantaged group members to engage in action for disadvantaged groups. *Personality and Social Psychology Review*, 24(4), 297–315.

10 Smith, D. G., Johnson, W. B., Lee, K. G., & Thebeau, J. (2022). Men are worse allies than they think. *Harvard Business Review*. https://bit.ly/3Zds0my.

11 Creary, S. J. (2024). Taking a "LEAP": How workplace allyship initiatives shape leader anxiety, allyship, and power dynamics that contribute to workplace inequality. *Academy of Management Review*, 49(4), 848–878.

12 Creary, S. J. (2024). Taking a "LEAP": How workplace allyship initiatives shape leader anxiety, allyship, and power dynamics that contribute to workplace inequality. *Academy of Management Review*, 49(4), 848–878.

13 Jackson, R. & Rao, S. (2022). *White women: Everything you already know about your own racism and how to do better* (p. 135). New York: Penguin Random House.

14 Norman, L., & Simpson, R. (2023). Gendered microaggressions towards the "only" women coaches in high-performance sport. *Sports Coaching Review*, 12(3), 302–322.

15 Kanter, R. M. (1977). *Men and women of the corporation*. New York: Basic Books.

16 Dahlerup, D. (2006). The story of the theory of critical mass. *Politics & Gender*, 2(4), 511–522.

Promoting uniqueness   19

In Chapter 1, we explored the importance of valuing diversity and uniqueness as a core element of what it means to be an inclusive leader. Embracing uniqueness, originality, and non-conformity and not being afraid to stand out are often characteristics of people who drive progress and innovation.[1] Instead of conforming to established norms, these individuals tend to create new paths that contribute not only to their own happiness but also to an improved society.

However, there is also a tension that exists between promoting uniqueness and our psychological need to belong to a shared social identity. On the one hand, we want to be seen and valued for what makes us unique while, on the other, we all have a need to connect and belong, which is often based on aspects of our identity that we share with others. To reconcile this tension, we must consider how organisations, and societies, can foster an environment where differences and uniqueness can be celebrated as the shared value of a collective identity. In other words, how can we get to a point where uniqueness is not just accepted but actively valued, where we belong together *because* we are different and unique?

Even if at a cognitive level we may appreciate the value of uniqueness and how this can positively contribute to the work that we do, such as enhancing innovation and problem-solving, in practice, almost every aspect of our individual psychology and societal norms reinforces the opposite! In Chapter 1, we highlighted how we all tend to hold implicit stereotypes of what great leaders "look like". These stereotypes are influenced by historical leadership theories that suggested that effective leaders held traits such as intelligence, task-relevant knowledge, dominance, and need for power.[2]

DOI: 10.4324/9781003598022-25

More recently, extensive research explored the concept of star performers, defined as "individuals widely and enduringly perceived as possessing rare, desirable qualities through which they can produce exceptional outcomes".[3] They found that star performers are believed to have six attributes: driven, relational, extraordinary, fascinating, tenacious, and brilliant. When we evaluate the performance of someone who could be considered to be a star performer, we compare that individual to a prototype (i.e., holding typical features of that category) that we implicitly hold in our minds (i.e., that a star performer is driven, relational, extraordinary, fascinating, tenacious, brilliant) and consequently we evaluate the person based on similarity to the prototype rather than the person's actual behaviour. Therefore, as with our stereotypes of what an effective leader looks like, this research is highlighting how, when considering what makes someone effective at work, we tend to look for individuals who match our prototype of a star performer: the closer they are to this prototype, the more likely we are to easily see them as a "star". So how does this align with everyone being unique?

Sociologists have also highlighted a similar challenge to valuing uniqueness. If we reflect on the context of employment, the ideal worker concept explains how we all have a shared implicit assumption of what makes an "ideal" worker (regardless of profession or job). The ideal worker concept was heavily influenced by the Industrial Revolution and post-war work cultures, and it positioned ideal workers as those who could function as an extension of a machine. Therefore, the ideal worker concept presents idealised expectations of an undivided commitment to work, free from non-work distractions.[4] In the early twentieth century, individual thought and creativity were viewed as inefficiencies according to Taylorism, with decision-making largely reserved for a small group of managers within a strongly hierarchical system. As we have evolved as humans and as societies, and the nature of our workplaces have been adapted accordingly, our needs have changed significantly compared to those of the past century. However, despite these changes, the outdated notions of an "ideal worker" persist in our shared cultural norms. These notions of great leaders, star performers, and ideal workers generate inequalities between people, depending on how close individuals find themselves to these definitions. In the context of valuing uniqueness, these limiting concepts create an illusion of the opposite to uniqueness. This can present challenges in that the more human we are at work and the more we share what makes us uniquely us, the further we may move from aligning with these concepts and therefore the harder we may find it to "fit in" to our organisation, to be viewed as a great leader, top performer, or ideal worker.

This means that inclusive leaders need a clear awareness of the challenges they will likely face in truly valuing uniqueness. We are all working against implicit stereotypes, prototypes, and societal expectations of what great leaders, star performers, and ideal workers should look like and how they should behave on a day-to-day basis. We must reflect on these deeply held beliefs critically, counteracting them with the appreciation that each individual is unique and that this is vital for success. Therefore, inclusive leaders acknowledge that colleagues have different lived experiences, views, and strengths, and these differences are key for innovation and problem solving. As a leadership behaviour, this translates into creating an environment where people can be themselves and work in ways that play to their strengths. Inclusive leaders believe that we are all capable and able to succeed in our careers but recognise that different people need different things to do this. Most importantly, as inclusive leaders, we move beyond simply valuing uniqueness to actually promoting uniqueness: we are endorsing, encouraging, fostering, advocating, and supporting uniqueness in any way we can. In this chapter, we focus on two work contexts that illustrate the importance of promoting uniqueness: shining a spotlight and addressing performance.

Shining a spotlight

Organisations are inherently social systems: they exist because of the relationships between people that take up different roles and make up different departments and functions. Therefore, how we progress through the organisation is based on how we relate to others in the organisation. Even if we are doing an exceptional job, if nobody notices, will we ever progress? Consequently, we rely on people becoming aware of the great work we are doing as a tool to aid our career progression.

Some experiences, projects, or tasks at work can be critical in terms of exposure to senior leaders. These critical experiences often bring with them the spotlight. They are the experiences where people take notice of the work that we are doing either because of the importance of the project itself or the other, often senior people, involved in the project. These spotlighted experiences can be extremely beneficial for career advancement as they are an opportunity to showcase our skills and expertise and can mean that we are offered other experiences and opportunities that may have not otherwise come our way. Likewise, sponsorship is critical to shining a spotlight. When more senior colleagues publicly advocate and speak up on our behalf, they bring the spotlight onto us, even if we are not working on a task or project that automatically brings the spotlight with it.

However, as we explored in Chapter 17, inclusive leaders know that some groups experience more barriers than others during their working lives and have fewer opportunities to be in the spotlight, including being overlooked for critical experiences and having limited access to sponsorship. They recognise that there are many factors that will influence someone's performance during their working life and several of these factors are external to an individual's capability and merit. Therefore, inclusive leaders appreciate that marginalised groups will not automatically be given equal access to the spotlight and so will need positive interventions so that they can level with others to compete fairly. Doing nothing means perpetuating the issue. Equally, inclusive leaders will appreciate that putting a non-conforming individual in the spotlight might represent risks for the individual that need to be mitigated. For example, when an environment lacks diversity or is very rigid in ways of working, there may be an inherent lack of openness when considering new and unique perspectives. Therefore inclusive leader play an important role in this process, which might include preparing the environment before spotlighting (such as securing additional allies and sponsors), partnering with the individual to establish the best opportunity to increase visibility, and to be ready to back them with action by allocating necessary resources and support.

Case example: Being elevated after so many years of being overlooked

When I joined my new team, I was used to being overlooked. As a Black Muslim woman in tech, I had always worked twice as hard just to be noticed. Despite this, leadership opportunities always seemed out of reach. But then I started working under my new line manager, and everything changed. Unlike my previous managers, he didn't just acknowledge my work, he was deeply curious about my perspective and took the time to truly understand me. He openly appreciated that I saw things differently and encouraged me to bring that difference into every conversation. In meetings, he didn't just give me a seat at the table, he made sure my voice was heard and valued. When a major project came up, he championed me to lead it, using his influence to ensure my expertise was recognised. Within a year, I was promoted, my confidence soared, and, for the first time, I felt truly seen and valued. After working for this manager, I'm not sure how I survived all those previous years or working in an environment that had never felt like it was meant for me. His leadership didn't just accelerate my career, it redefined what it meant to be included.

Addressing performance

When we are experienced high performers, it can be very tempting to help those we work with by showing them how we have done things in the past: the best, most efficient route to good performance. We know the tried and tested techniques and ways of working. Sometimes this is helpful. Sometimes people appreciate knowing what has worked in the past and being able to experiment with this as they find their own way of working. However, what if they find that the way that worked for us does not work for them? What if they find a different way of working that suits them and their strengths better? This is the essence of the context addressing performance.

It is human nature to assume that our way of working is the best, most effective way, and therefore when we are supporting the performance of others, it can feel like the safest option is to encourage everyone to work in the same way. While sometimes there may be very little flexibility in the ways of working, there can often be more flexibility than we might first assume. A key part of being an inclusive leader is recognising that, as we are all unique and we will all have our own unique way of working.

Consequently, inclusive leaders provide colleagues with the level of autonomy they need to work in a way that is most effective for them. They will define good performance without erasing individuality, recognising and leveraging unique strengths. Inclusive leaders acknowledge that lived experiences will impact on how individuals work, find solutions to problems, and innovate. Therefore, they are able to provide colleagues with the flexibility needed to achieve good performance, balance creativity and individuality with team cohesion, while clearly communicating ethical ground rules. This means that inclusive leaders are clear in differentiating between goals and actions. Although they will clearly communicate cascaded organisational goals and offer guidance on codes of conduct, they will allow colleagues to decide what actions they will take to deliver desirable contributions.

Case example: Empowered to work in my own unique way

One of the most impactful leaders I've worked with was my line manager from my last employer, a senior director in a global consultancy who had a rare ability to drive high performance while valuing the uniqueness of every team member. From the moment I joined their team, it was clear they saw performance as more than just hitting targets, they wanted to understand what motivated each of us and how we worked best. Instead of imposing a one-size-fits-all approach, they encouraged open conversations about work styles and team dynamics, ensuring that collaboration felt natural rather than forced. They created space for people to contribute in ways that played to their strengths. At the same time, they set clear expectations around shared goals, ensuring that even as we worked differently, we were aligned in our impact. They frequently checked in, not just on deliverables but on how we were feeling about our work, adjusting processes to remove barriers rather than forcing people to conform to rigid structures. They also challenged the organisation's performance evaluation system by advocating for a more nuanced approach, pushing leadership to recognise different styles of contribution. For example, recognising not just extroverted, high-visibility leadership but also those who excelled in behind-the-scenes innovation.

What can inclusive leaders do?

As discussed earlier in this chapter, inclusive leaders need to learn to manage the tensions that exist when valuing uniqueness. This includes balancing individuality with our deep need to share a social identity to feel we belong. To address this, inclusive leaders take steps to nurture a culture where people belong *because* they are different, so their individuality is their shared value.

A further tension with valuing uniqueness is how we categorise understanding and create stereotypes to simplify what we see as good and desirable – for example, the great leader, the star performer, and the ideal worker. Inclusive leaders may navigate this tension by using frameworks such as behavioural competencies to communicate expectations, while ensuring that these frameworks are held loosely. For example, rigid competency models can sometimes reinforce bias, particularly if they have been created by homogeneous groups. By favouring dominant cultural norms rather than recognising diversity and uniqueness, biases are likely to be built in. Instead, we can strive to challenge assumptions and expand possibilities based on uniqueness, rather than solely relying on shared expectations of what is good and desirable.

Adopting a coaching approach to leadership can aid valuing uniqueness considerably: for example, when we lead as coaches we become wired to ask questions and actively listen to the answers. A coaching approach to leadership is the opposite of a one-size-fits-all approach. It focuses on unlocking each person's potential based on their unique strengths and perspectives.[5] The process of leading then shifts from telling to asking, from judging to listening, from directing to empowering and uniqueness becomes an asset, not a challenge.

Below are some recommendations on how to promote uniqueness when shining a spotlight and addressing performance.

Shining a spotlight

- Consider the whole picture when shining a spotlight on someone's contribution. Remember that privilege is not earned, it is systemically given and in many cases is invisible. Therefore, sometimes a small contribution from someone who had very little privilege during their working lives and experienced more barriers to career progression, will deserve more credit than a contribution from someone who contributed a lot but had all the tools, support, and opportunity to do so.
- Ensure marginalised groups have the appropriate resources and support if their views and ideas do not conform with group expectations. This includes mitigating for retaliation and resistance. For example, prepare the environment before spotlighting: this might involve assessing the climate and laying the groundwork by advocating for diverse contributions, ensuring difference is communicated as an asset and not a threat, and securing other allies and sponsors to gain critical mass in relation to support.
- Share the spotlight strategically: ensure each individual's contributions are linked to business impact so the value is undeniable and ensure each individual feels in control of when and how to improve their visibility.
- Challenge your affinity and proximity biases and how they might show up when shining the spotlight on others. For example, make a list of colleagues you are naturally drawn to helping with their careers. Then make a list of colleagues that are underrepresented in leadership and decision-making (i.e., because of gender, race, disability, sexual orientation, etc.). Compare both lists to see how much you are drawn to helping these underrepresented groups without needing any nudges. Then select at least one person from your underrepresented list and make a commitment to support this person with their career advancement (i.e., mentoring, sponsoring, or promoting them outside of your direct team).

Addressing performance

- Be specific about what your grounds to manage performance are and communicate them clearly. Define performance without enforcing conformity. In doing so, challenge your ideas of what is really needed for good performance, leaving flexibility for colleagues to behave in innovative ways.
- Ensure colleagues are empowered to make decisions on how they will meet their goals. Evaluate how you are able to empower good performance without being too prescriptive and restrictive, despite what is available to you in relation to performance management. Be open to listening to different ways on how to achieve the same results.
- Focus on individual strengths and motivations when managing performance. Learn how each person works best, align their outcomes to their strengths as much as possible.
- Consider cultural differences and neurodiversity and how different individuals express leadership, collaboration, and innovation when defining performance.
- Ensure that valuing difference is encouraged and integral to team goals and team performance and not just tolerated. Create opportunities for inclusive collaboration to allow diverse contributions, while ensuring alignment with collective goals and values.
- Ensure unbiased performance evaluations. Structured performance reviews are helpful to avoid subjectivity and stereotypes. Equally, if part of the structure is to use frameworks like behavioural competencies, ensure these are deployed within the context at hand. For example, "effective communication" might be part of performance criteria and defined as being clear and direct, but, in a multicultural team, this might need to be adapted to account for different communication styles, such as indirect or high-context communication. Rather than rigidly enforcing a single definition, the framework should be flexible enough to accommodate diverse approaches while still upholding core expectations.
- Encourage multi-source feedback for calibration of performance evaluations. However, be mindful of our deep need for shared social identities and the impact of this on 360 assessment. For example, individuals who are not seen as part of a dominant shared identity might be rated more harshly as group affiliations can lead to ingroup favouritism and outgroup negative bias.
- Allocate time and energy to understand the reasons behind average or below average performance. Consider the context before judging

someone's merit. Use performance data to identify patterns between majority and underrepresented groups. Avoid labelling individuals and value efforts as much as you value results.

Chapter 19 in summary

- While cognitively we may appreciate the importance of valuing uniqueness, we also have a deep need to share social identity, to feel we belong, and rely on categorisation which discourages uniqueness.
- Inclusive leaders are able to hold these tensions effectively and encourage the shared identity to be based on valuing diversity and uniqueness, therefore diversity and uniqueness become an asset rather than a challenge.
- Career progression relies on the spotlight shining on the great work we are doing. However, not everyone has equal access to the spotlight. Inclusive leaders take positive action to ensure that the playing field is levelled and marginalised groups also benefit from a spotlight shining on their unique contribution.
- Equally putting a non-conforming individual in the spotlight may represent risks that need to be mitigated, which might include preparing the environment by assessing the climate and securing additional allies and sponsors before spotlighting.
- It can be tempting to encourage everyone to work in the same way, especially in highly pressurised environments. However, inclusive leaders provide colleagues with the level of autonomy they need to work in a way that is most effective for them, recognising that lived experiences will impact on how individuals work, find solutions to problems, and innovate.
- When managing performance, context is critical. Sometimes a small contribution from someone who had very little privilege and many barriers will deserve more credit than someone who contributed a lot but had all the tools, support, and opportunity to do so.

Notes

1 Grant, A. (2016). *Originals: How non-conformists move the world.* New York: Viking.
2 Woods, S.A., & West, M.A. (2019). *The psychology of work and organizations.* Andover, UK: Cengage Learning EMEA.

3 Villamor, I., & Aguinis, H. (2024). Think star, think men? Implicit star performer theories (p. 783). *Journal of Organizational Behavior, 45*(6), 783–799.

4 Rowson, T. S., & Jones, R. J. (2025). Understanding the subjective experience of menopause at work: A systematic review and conceptual model. *Journal of Constructivist Psychology*, 1–20.

5 Jones, R. J. (2021). *Coaching with research in mind*. Abingdon, UK: Routledge.

Disrupting biases   **20**

Before we learn how to disrupt biases we first need to understand them. The topic of bias has been a regular theme throughout this book so far. In Chapter 14, we defined biases as the mental shortcuts that enable us to make fast decisions and react quickly.[1] We can think of bias as a preference or inclination that affects our judgement, such as preference (or prejudice) for or against a person, group, or idea. Biases are often based on stereotypes (generalised beliefs) or personal experience. Biases can be explicit (when we are aware of our preference or prejudice) or implicit (when we are not aware of our preference or prejudice). For example, a hiring manager might favour stereotypically masculine traits (such as assertiveness) for a leadership role and therefore they might favour a man over another gender because of this belief. They might or might not be aware of this association. Across the chapters, we have referred to a range of different types of biases that are important in the context of inclusive leadership including:

- Proximity bias: favouring individuals who are physically closer to us.
- Confirmation bias: seeking out information to confirm what we believe is right.
- Familiarity bias: preferring what is known and comfortable to us.
- Similarity bias: favouring those who share a similar background.
- Affinity bias: favouring those who we feel interpersonally connected with.
- Conformity bias: agreeing with others rather than exercising our own independent judgement.
- Empathetic bias: experiencing less empathy for people we see as being in our outgroups compared to those who we see as being in our ingroups.

DOI: 10.4324/9781003598022-26

- Cultural bias: preferring what is familiar to us in terms of the shared communication, norms, social expectations, deep-rooted conditioning, and increased sense of belonging experienced when we have a shared culture.

These biases, and many others not listed here, are barriers to inclusion and can give rise to other biases, such as racial and gender biases. They are often implicit, so we are generally unaware of their influence on our thoughts and behaviours.

However, bias is a natural part of human day-to-day functioning. Our brains rely on taking shortcuts as it is not possible to engage in deliberate thinking most of the time. In Chapters 7 and 14, we explored the work of Kahneman (2011)[2] and how his theory of system one and system two (or fast and slow) thinking, can help us to understand why bias is commonplace in decision-making. System one thinking is our default mode of thinking. It is fast and intuitive, allowing us to operate with minimal effort, but it is inherently biased, as it relies on shortcuts to make decisions quickly. On the other hand, system two thinking is slower, effortful, deliberate, and more objective. Generally, our brains prefer system one as we use less energy and it is faster. Consequently, we underuse system two thinking. Kahneman's ideas are highly relevant for this chapter as we focus on the behaviour of reflecting on biases. As we have seen, bias is primarily a product of system one, whereas reflection is primarily a function of system two, it is effortful and deliberate.

To disrupt bias, we must learn how to spot it, then deepen our understanding of its impact through reflection. This will provide us with the tools and language necessary to challenge and dismantle bias for ourselves and others. Therefore, we argue that reflection is the bridge between bias awareness and taking action to dismantle it. While awareness can come from education and courses, this can be a superficial level of awareness. Reflection is essential for developing a deeper, more nuanced understanding of how bias operates in your thoughts and actions, which in turn allows you to challenge and address it effectively. This is why bias awareness training often falls short. Most training design tends to focus only on identifying different types of biases, without fostering the deeper internal work necessary to challenge and transform them. As a result, it often fails to disrupt bias and can even reinforce stereotypes instead.

Reflection is the structured, focused, and conscious thought process that facilitates a deeper development and understanding. We can think of reflection as listening to ourselves,[3] and it is considered to be a key element in how we learn, especially when we learn from our experiences. An example of a learning theory which highlights the importance of reflection is Kolb's (1984) experiential learning theory.[4] According to Kolb's theory, learning is best facilitated by the process of reflection, which draws out a learner's beliefs and ideas about a topic so that the learner can then examine, test, and integrate these beliefs with new, more refined ideas. Learning requires the resolution of conflicts, differences, and disagreement. Therefore, in the process of learning, we are required to move back and forth between opposing perspectives. Consequently, the process of reflection involves deepening awareness of our beliefs and ideas – in other words, why we might feel, think, and behave in a particular way. By bringing this deeper understanding into our awareness as well, we are then able to act with agency and make conscious decisions as to whether to continue in the same way or seek to change our thoughts and behaviour.

However, in the context of diversity and inclusion, reflecting on and thinking about the reasons why we feel, think, and behave in particular ways can be extremely confronting. Especially if this reflection results in the awareness that we have, at least at some point in the past, been a perpetrator, affiliate of a perpetrator, or bystander in practices that oppress marginalised groups in the workplace. Sometimes the reasons why we have deeply ingrained thoughts and behaviours are not easy to acknowledge, and recognising that we may have behaved in a way that does not align with our core values can be intensely uncomfortable. Reflective thought brings all of this into our awareness. Therefore, the process of reflection can be challenging as we need to open the door to let these unconscious thoughts into our conscious mind. To learn from them, we need to consider these shortcomings.

Inclusive leaders are constantly reflecting on their own biases and the biases they observe around them. They understand that most biases are a natural part of being human. These biases are often implicit and difficult to recognise without actively seeking feedback from others. When we reflect on our biases we spend time exploring what biases might be at play in any given situation and seek to understand the root of these biases, therefore increasing our understanding of why we might feel, think and behave in that way. When we truly value diversity and inclusion, and spend time developing our knowledge and expertise in this area at a deeper level, it is not unusual to assume that we are moving beyond biased ways of thinking. However, no matter how self-aware and inclusive we become, we will always operate with bias and in denying the existence of bias, it becomes much harder to identify when biases are having a negative impact (which they inevitably will for all of us). In this chapter, we focus on two work contexts that illustrate the importance of disrupting bias: when making decisions and when addressing stereotypes.

Making decisions

Leaders have a responsibility to intentionally disrupt and address bias while making decisions. Inclusive leaders recognise that many biases are programmed by our external context as opposed to our true values, therefore they create a psychologically safe environment where bias can be brought to the surface with feedback and reflection in a non-judgemental way. Inclusive leaders empower everyone to take responsibility to address bias, picking up on social cues and recognising unspoken messages. For example, this might involve someone in the team asking the question "What are we missing?" or "Whose voice aren't we listening to?" when making decisions. This is especially important when there is a high level of group thinking, agreement, or consensus in the room: discussion and critique can be a great tool for surfacing and disrupting implicit bias. This means that inclusive leaders remain extremely vigilant to stay in the present while deliberating on evidence available to them at that moment in time to actively counteract their assumptions. This helps them to keep their system two thinking active rather than defaulting to system one thinking (with all the bias that this entails).

Disrupting bias while making decisions also takes courage as it involves explicitly shining a spotlight on bias so that it can be openly discussed, explored, and mitigated. It might lead to challenging deeply ingrained views, disrupting, confronting, and facing resistance. Inclusive leaders practise being the person who says what is unsaid and asks the difficult questions to highlight when bias might be operating. Only then can the team choose to do something about it.

Case example: Moving from "fit in" to "add to"

When I took on an executive role in HR at a business school, I prided myself on hiring the best talent. I always looked for people who would be a "good cultural fit", those who could seamlessly integrate into ways of working. Over time, I began to notice a troubling pattern. Despite our stated commitment to diversity, most of the people we hired and promoted looked, thought, and operated in very similar ways. It felt comfortable, but I started to wonder: Were we actually limiting our potential by prioritising familiarity over fresh perspectives? I took the time to reflect on this. I sought out different viewpoints, read about implicit bias, and encouraged my leadership team to do the same. Through this process, I realised that "cultural fit" had become a proxy for hiring people who made us feel comfortable rather than those who could challenge our thinking. This wasn't just an individual bias; it was also baked into our hiring and promotion decisions. The consequences of this hit home when we embarked on an ambitious internal project that required innovative thinking and a range of perspectives. We had assembled a team of high performers who had always excelled in our existing environment, yet we found ourselves repeatedly overlooking key considerations that would have been obvious to someone with a different approach. One example stood out: A team spent months planning a new partnership with a charity to provide coaching to disadvantaged groups, refining the details and getting excited about the impact. However, no one had thought to check with the legal department first. When they finally did, they discovered that compliance issues made the project unworkable. It wasn't a disaster, but it was a frustrating waste of time and energy. When we later reviewed our team dynamics, it became clear that we lacked individuals with a strong, rule-focused, detail-oriented mindset, exactly the type of perspective that could have caught this issue early on.

Addressing stereotypes

When reflecting on biases, we must also consider how much these biases have been fed by stereotypes. Stereotypes often serve as the foundation for biased thinking and decision-making and can fuel our bias in relation to designing work and forming team and organisational cultures. In Chapter 14, we defined stereotypes as generalised and simplified notions of people and things we use to make sense of the world. Stereotypes are usually associated with a group and can be based on, but are not limited to, ethnicity, age, gender, and sexual orientation. Therefore, stereotypes often lead to prejudice and discrimination.[5]

It can be easy to be lulled into a false sense of security and believe that we are operating beyond stereotypes. Particularly once we have started to work on ourselves and spent time learning about EDI and inclusive leadership. However, stereotypes are ingrained in every element of our society and no matter how aware we become, we will always hold stereotypes. For example, how often do you come across statements such as: "He has man-flu", "I'm having a senior moment", "Women don't support each other", "He did a man-look", "She's so emotional", "She's so bossy", "Boys will be boys", "Man up", "You can't teach an old dog new tricks", "The younger generation don't know what a hard day's work means", "She's the ice queen",

"Young people these days have no attention span". We could go on and on. In fact, research has shown that stereotypes are so powerful that our own internalised stereotypes about ourselves, linked to aspects of our identity, can negatively impact our performance. There are a number of studies that focus on stereotype threat: the fear of doing something that would confirm negative perceptions of a stigmatised group that we are members of.[6] For example:

- Black participants did not perform as well as white participants on verbal ability tests when participants were told that the test was "diagnostic" and a "genuine test of your verbal abilities and limitations". However, when this instruction was not given, the differences in performance disappeared.
- Men did not perform as well on a task involving the decoding of non-verbal cues if they were told that test measured "social sensitivity", which is considered a stereotypically feminine skill compared to when they were told that the test measured "information processing".
- When children from poorer families were reminded of their lower socioeconomic status, they underperformed on tests described as "diagnostic of intellectual abilities", but not otherwise.
- When women viewed only two advertisements based on gender stereotypes among six advertisements in total, in a subsequent task, they tended to avoid leadership roles, even though the advertisements had nothing to do with leadership. Consequently, demonstrating the power of stereotype threat with even very subtle triggering cues.
- Neuroscientists found that after reading a report about memory declining with age, older adults experienced neural activation corresponding to having negative thoughts about themselves. They also underperformed in a subsequent, timed categorisation task.

Consequently workplace systems and culture are often designed based on stereotypes, which are then reinforced on a daily basis. For example, through hiring practices, such as associating leadership with traditionally masculine traits. Leadership norms prioritise assertiveness, disadvantaging those from collaborative cultures, and emotional expression is judged differently based on gender. Therefore, everyday interactions reflect deep-rooted stereotypes about value and competence.

Inclusive leaders recognise the prevalence and power of stereotypes. Leaders can also be faced with their own stereotypes, observe stereotypes in others, and are aware that some situations heighten the risk of stereotypes being deployed. For example, we can respond to someone favourably because they align with a positive stereotype we hold, perhaps because they remind us of someone we hold in high esteem. Equally, we might observe that we notice a dislike for someone, perhaps finding them to be difficult or annoying. As inclusive leaders, we should be aware that, when this happens, it is a cue for us to pause and reflect on whether this response might be because that person is not conforming to the stereotype of how that person "should" behave. In recognising this, we are able to acknowledge our responses and refocus on the present. We can questions ourselves to understand:

- What assumptions am I making? What assumptions are others making?
- Would I make the same judgement if this person belonged to a different group?
- Where did this belief come from?

In staying vigilant for the potential influence of stereotypes, inclusive leaders are very aware that all opinions are subjective and that we humans tend to generalise our views, and then see them as facts. Therefore, inclusive leaders are extra careful to avoid labelling individuals and sharing their opinions of others in a judgemental way.

Case example: Counteracting stereotypes in leadership definitions

I used to facilitate talent review committees in a global technology firm. Talent from technical career pathways had always been recognised for their deep technical expertise. However, when they were considered for a leadership role, they encountered a persistent stereotype: that technical experts lack the interpersonal skills needed to manage people effectively. In leadership meetings, I often heard comments like, "They're brilliant, but are they really a people person?" or "We need someone with natural leadership instincts, not just technical skills". I started to question, was this a genuine gap, or was it an assumption based on an outdated stereotype? I took a step back to reflect and noticed a pattern. Technical leaders were often overlooked for leadership roles based on the belief that strong analytical skills and strong people skills were mutually exclusive. I used to teach leadership at university and realised, when reflecting on the evolution of leadership, this stereotype likely came from traditional ideas around leadership, which associated successful leaders with extroversion and charisma and ignored important skills such as adaptability and problem solving.

What can inclusive leaders do?

Awareness is a critical first step in disrupting biases, but it is not enough to know biases exist. Once we acknowledge that biases are present, we must engage in deep reflection, including examining the impact of bias, in order to spark meaningful change. Therefore, reflection is probably the most powerful tool one can use to disrupt bias and challenge stereotypes for oneself and others. Inclusive leaders need this reflection to develop the language and ideas necessary to challenge biases for themselves and for those around them and to implement actions to support more inclusive policies, practices, and culture.

Equally, the process of reflecting will likely increase the cognitive load and potential conflict as we become aware of what was previously unknown. This includes the awareness that our behaviours may not be aligned to our values as well as the impact of our and other people's biases and stereotypes on others. Therefore, an important role inclusive leaders play is to create the conditions necessary for reflection and personal growth to happen in the first place. For example:

- Leaders prioritise reflection as a leadership practice. Biased responses thrive in driven and fast-paced environments where decisions are made at speed, which is an ability that is often valued in leaders. Embrace the importance of slowing down and protect time for reflection.
- Psychological safety needs to be nurtured, where a culture of high intellectual friction is normalised and low social friction is prioritised. This includes establishing rules of engagement, discussing team psychological contracts, enabling connection, and team-building opportunities.
- Embed micro pauses in decision-making and use coaching for self and others to challenge and validate assumptions.
- Adopt team-based reflective practices to call out and call in biases and stereotypes. For example, leadership teams might reflect together on who is consistently getting high performance ratings? Who is overlooked and why?
- Focus on developing feedback skills for self and others as biases and stereotypes are hard to self-identify and therefore feedback is a necessary barometer, signalling the presence of biases and stereotypes.
- Finally, inclusive leaders can role-model the public demonstration of their humanity (versus striving for perfection). This includes sharing how they are reflecting, learning, and adapting. For example, an inclusive leader might say: "I realised I was initially leaning towards this decision

but, after reflecting, I noticed that it was my bias based on my previous experience and I had not spent enough time considering how the situation at hand was different from the past. This is what I found …".

Below are some practical examples of how to disrupt bias when making decisions and when addressing stereotypes.

Making decisions

- Embrace bias as part of being human. When someone calls out a biased behaviour of yours, pause and reflect on what is driving this behaviour. Then reflect on what behaviour would be more aligned with your true values. By doing this you will be able to adjust your programmed behaviours to your true values. If you stay in a defensive mode, this process does not happen, and the old programme of behaviour is reinforced as opposed to changed.
- When negotiating decisions with others, consider if you are talking "at" the person or "with" the person, if you are doing something "for" them or "to" them. If the answer is "at" and "to" them, you are probably being driven by your own biases, which will likely be dictating your assumptions on what the person needs or what is best for them.
- Proactively seek diverse perspectives before making a decision – these are great barometers to sense-check our own biases.
- Use data to spot bias patterns.
- List all your assumptions about a person or a topic before starting a meeting where decisions need to be made and mentally allow yourself to park them.
- Recognise when bias is most likely to occur in decision-making, such as when faced with ambiguity and stress, for example, so that you can integrate opportunities to pause and reflect on the process.

Addressing stereotypes

- List the three most frequent stereotypes that are likely to be influencing you at work and label the stereotype for yourself, – this makes them easier to disrupt. To do this you might like to finish sentences, such as " Men are usually …", "Women are usually …", "Leaders are usually …", "Older people are usually …" with whatever immediately comes to mind. What other sentences could you add to help bring to the surface your internalised stereotypes? Self-coach yourself as part of your reflection to challenge assumptions.

- Reframe your narrative with counterexamples – if you cannot think of any, actively research for them or seek new experiences. For example, you might assume that someone is not a natural leader because they are quiet. To counter this, recall (or seek out) examples of impactful, introverted leaders.
- Next time you experience negative assumptions related to a work colleague, pause and challenge yourself to write a list of all their possible strengths. After that, invite them for a meeting, coffee, or lunch, with the intention of learning more about these strengths. This will not only help you to counteract your assumptions but will also enable you to take a more balanced view when forming an opinion about someone.
- Commit to learning and seeking stories and examples of the lived experiences that challenge your assumptions. For example, challenge yourself to spend time with three people at work that you would not normally spend time with. This might involve making an effort to sit next to them and chat with them before the start of a meeting, or going out for lunch or a coffee. Focus your attention so that you learn something new about yourself, about the person, and about the experience. By actively learning from the experience, you will start to disrupt existing stereotypes and generalised views of things for which you do not have first-hand experience.
- In situations where there are no patterns of preferences, take a moment to check and reflect if this is a sign of openness or of something else, like disconnection. In some cases, we disconnect from what we truly think or feel because we are experiencing a sense of dissatisfaction, and exploring this disconnect can help us make meaningful improvements in our lives.
- When someone else expresses a stereotype, pause and reframe the conversation. For example, you might say "That is an interesting assumption, I'm curious to understand what makes you say that?". This disrupts stereotypes without direct confrontation.
- Ask other thought-provoking questions by using "we" to invite collective growth – for example, you might say "Would we say the same thing if this person was from a different identity group?".
- Be an upstander not a bystander. Stereotypes are socially reinforced when you do nothing, therefore address stereotypes in real time, even in informal conversations. For example, if someone says "She's too

emotional", you might want to respond by highlighting that emotional intelligence is an important leadership skill, so let's focus on impact.

- Proactively support and advocate for colleagues who are from marginalised and outgroups as they tend to be more frequently subject to stereotypes and stereotype threat.
- When there is evidence of stereotype threat (i.e., fear of conforming to internalised stereotypes), talk openly without making assumptions and explore if the person also recognises the presence of the threat. Then acknowledge systemic factors that contribute to the existence of this stereotype. Reinforce belonging by expanding the shared identity to be about valuing diversity (rather than conforming to an identity-based stereotype), with a focus on a growth mindset based on individuality.

Chapter 20 in summary

- Bias is the mental shortcut that enables us to make fast decisions and react quickly. Bias is a preference, inclination, or prejudice that affects our judgement.
- Stereotypes are generalised and simplified notions of people and they feed our biased reactions.
- Stereotypes will fuel our biases, which are barriers to inclusion and can be implicit or explicit. However, in most cases, we are unaware of their influence on our thoughts and behaviours.
- To disrupt bias, we must learn how to spot it, then deepen our understanding of its impact through reflection. We argue that reflection is the bridge between bias awareness and taking action to dismantle it –without this deep work, awareness will just reinforce stereotypes.
- When we reflect on our biases and stereotypes, we spend time exploring what might be at play in any given situation and seek to understand the root of these biases and stereotypes, therefore increasing our understanding of why we might feel, think, and behave in that way.
- Leaders have a responsibility to create a psychologically safe environment that enables reflection in the first place. This includes creating opportunities to pause so that bias can be brought to the surface and addressed in a non-judgemental way, empowering change.
- Inclusive leaders should stay vigilant for the potential influence of stereotypes and stereotype threat, and act as an upstander, counteracting stereotypes for self and others.

Notes

1 Tversky, A., & Kahneman, D. (1974). Judgment under uncertainty: Heuristics and biases. *Science, 185*(4157), 1124–1131.
2 Kahneman, D. (2011). Thinking, fast and slow. New York: Farrar, Straus and Giroux.
3 Stevens, D. D., & Cooper, J. E. (2009). *Journal keeping: How to use reflective writing for learning, teaching, professional insight, and positive change.* Sterling, VA: Stylus Publishing.
4 Kolb, D. A. (1984). *Experiential learning: Experience as the source of learning and development.* Hoboken, NJ: Prentice-Hall.
5 Allport, G. W. (1979). *The nature of prejudice* (25th Anniversary edition). Boston. MA: Addison-Wesley.
6 Zawisza, M. (2018). *The terrifying power of stereotypes – and how to deal with them.* Accessed from https://theconversation.com/the-terrifying-power-of-stereotypes-and-how-to-deal-with-them-101904. Retrieved 4 March 2025.

Being emotionally agile 21

Have you ever noticed yourself becoming defensive when someone has given you some feedback? Perhaps your automatic response was to justify your behaviour or persuade the other person to see how their perception was inaccurate. This is because, unless it is positive, feedback can be emotionally triggering. Even when feedback is constructive, it can violate our need for competence which means that it can trigger a defensive reaction. It can be difficult to see ourselves as "incompetent", and even harder to feel that others are seeing us this way. Even if, looking at it rationally, we appreciate that one piece of negative feedback does not mean that we are incompetent, in the moment of receiving that feedback, our rational thinking can often desert us and we act much more reactively, which is always in self-protection mode.

Yet feedback, when given or received constructively, is a great example of emotional agility in action and is a critical part of being an inclusive leader. As privilege is invisible, we depend on feedback to create awareness of how privilege may be operating, enabling us to address inequality and foster accountability. Therefore, we need to build our ability to be emotionally agile so that we can regulate our emotions appropriately, reducing the likelihood of defensive reactions when triggered. Equally, emotional agility is not just important for responding to feedback. When we have high levels of diversity around us, we must also be emotionally agile to create supportive environments that can foster tolerance for different belief systems and values, where everyone is able to feel that they still belong and are cared for, even when they disagree with one another.

So what is emotional agility? Understanding emotional *rigidity* can help us to understand emotional *agility*. Emotional rigidity is about fixating on

DOI: 10.4324/9781003598022-27

certain emotions and views while closing ourselves down to any new possibilities. So emotional agility is the opposite, it is all about flexibility: being flexible with the way we feel, think, and behave, allowing us to respond optimally with our emotions to everyday situations.[1] Therefore, being emotionally agile is the opposite of ignoring or denying our emotions: it is about embracing our emotions and being flexible with them.

In the context of equity and diversity it is also important to recognise emotional oppression in the context of social structures and gender roles. For example, patriarchy (a social system in which men hold primary power and dominate, subordinating women and other gender identities) can be harmful for men as it discourages vulnerability and emotional expression,[2] yet the experience of emotion is an integral part of what it means to be human – whatever your gender! Therefore, restrictive expectations of how different genders "should" or "should not" experience and express emotion is a form of oppression. Instead, by seeking emotional freedom from these systems of oppression, we can define how we as individuals want to feel and be able to express our emotions while maintaining boundaries of dignity, respect, and care for self and others.

Now let's bring emotional agility to the context of employment. There is a widely accepted unwritten rule that the workplace should be an emotion-free zone. Instead, we assume that appropriate behaviour at work is a consistently cheerful demeanour or, at the very least, a brave stoicism in the face of adversity. If we pause to really consider this shared assumption, the irrationality of it is plain to see. Humans are emotional beings: for example, it is thought that there are as many as 87 different emotions.[3] Given that we each spend an average of 90,000 hours of our time across our lifetime in work,[4] how reasonable and rational is it that we do not display at least a slightly broader range of some of these 87 emotions that we will inevitably be experiencing? Especially when we appreciate that ample research shows that attempting to minimise or ignore thoughts and emotions serves only to amplify them.[5]

In Chapter 19, we explored the concept of the ideal worker and it is likely that at least part of the explanation for this unwritten rule can be found here. The ideal worker concept highlights how we all have a shared implicit assumption of what makes an "ideal" worker (regardless of profession or job). Heavily influenced by the Industrial Revolution, it positions ideal workers as those who can function as an extension of a machine. Therefore, the ideal worker concept presents idealised expectations of an undivided commitment to work, free from non-work distractions – including emotions. The ideal worker is an efficient, emotionless working machine. This can mean that when we experience what are perfectly natural and normal emotions, we might internalise that we are failing in some way. We may see ourselves (and others who display emotions at work), as lacking control or not meeting what we expect to be "ideal" at work.

It is not unusual for individuals to believe that they are not emotional. However, this does not mean that emotions do not exist. Instead, it normally highlights that the individual has learnt to ignore their emotions. However, emotions play an important role in communicating what is going on with us and by ignoring them we are also neglecting our needs, which can eventually lead to physical and mental health issues. Emotions serve as an internal communication system that something in our environment needs attention, when we are on the right track, and when we need to take action. They also tell us not only about what is happening around us but also about our inner landscape, guiding us to change and grow, serving as important data points that signpost our needs and values.[6] For example, when we feel angry, the emotion of anger might be telling us that our values regarding fairness have been violated and we need to set boundaries. When we feel rejected or isolated, this may be telling us that our need to belong and connect is not being met. When we feel guilt or shame, this might be telling us that our action was not aligned with who we want to be. And so on. Our emotions are uniquely ours, and the emotion we experience in any given scenario will be influenced by a range of experiences and factors. Either way, they tell us something important about ourselves and our situation. Therefore, if we ignore these emotions, we are at risk of continuing in a situation that is not aligned with our values and that does not meet our needs – and, in the long-term, this is unlikely to be a situation that supports our wellbeing. By denying our emotions, it also means that we are more likely to be "hooked" by them, like a fish being caught on a line.[7] When we are hooked by an emotion, we are at the mercy of that emotion: the emotion is in the driving seat rather than the other way around. Therefore, rather than attempting to suppress our emotions, we can develop emotional agility which enables us to manage and respond (rather than react) to our feelings.

However putting this into practice can be challenging. When we feel triggered, we feel unsafe emotionally and our nervous system activates our fight, flight, or freeze response. There is nothing flexible in these states. Instead, we become fixated on a perceived threat, the cause of the "trigger", whether it is a difficult conversation, a disagreement, a criticism, or feedback. As with many of the behaviours we have covered in this book, developing emotional agility is not easy and unfortunately there is no quick fix to help us instantly become emotionally agile.

In this chapter, we focus on two key work contexts that illustrate the importance of being emotionally agile for inclusion: when responding to a negative emotional trigger for oneself and when supporting the emotions of others in difficult situations.

Responding to a negative emotional trigger for oneself

We have already touched on how easy it is to become "hooked" by our emotions and how when this happens: the emotion takes the driving seat for our reactions and consequent behaviour. This process of getting "hooked" can often happen when we feel triggered for any reason. Typical examples at work might include when we are highly stressed, which, as we saw in Chapter 7, produces a reduction in our cognitive functioning but an increase in our experience of negative emotions. Another classic example is when someone shares an opposing view or directly challenges us, particularly in a public context. In these situations, we may struggle to self-regulate our emotions. This is when a worse version of ourselves might show up and we may shut others down and dismiss their ideas without due consideration. Unfortunately, this can lead to a rupture in the relationships with those concerned, trust might be compromised, and psychological safety hindered for everyone.

Ideas from transactional analysis can help us to understand what is happening during these interactions when we find ourselves triggered. According to transactional analysis, we have three distinct modes of thinking, feeling, and behaving, known as ego-states, which are parent, adult, and child.[8] Most of the time, we are operating from our adult ego-state. This means that we rationally process what we are thinking and feeling, based on facts and with minimal interference from implicit beliefs (although, as we have seen throughout this book, even in the adult ego-state, the influence of implicit beliefs such as bias is much greater than we might assume). However, when we get triggered, a different ego-state (rather than adult) might get "hooked", meaning that instead of responding from an adult-to-adult point of view (i.e., based on facts, data, and openly communicating our needs) we might respond from our child ego-state. When in the child ego-state, we are behaving, thinking, and feeling just as we used to in childhood. This can include acting as a rebellious child, which might involve replaying childhood patterns of behaviour that are no longer appropriate to our grown-up situation, such as having a tantrum or sulking if things do not go our way, rather than expressing how we are feeling in an open, honest, and calm manner, or asking for what we require to enable our needs to be met. When we are in a state of heightened emotion, it can be easy to become hooked and respond from the position of rebellious child rather than adult.

For example, if we believe that we are being unfairly criticised, ignored, or dismissed (i.e., we are not being treated as an adult), we may experience an emotional response, and our rebellious child may be hooked into responding by lashing out or withdrawing our energy. When this happens, we are acting without agency, responding instinctively to the emotion, generally in ways that do not serve us. The key here is to not ignore the emotion, as we have seen, that emotion is an important source of data trying to tell us something. Instead, we can pay attention to the emotion as a passing experience and choose to respond in a way that will serve us better. This might include using our curiosity to ask questions to help understand the other's perspective better and then communicate how we are feeling. This means that we must practise pausing and staying with the discomfort of the negative emotion. When we are emotionally agile, we do not deny that an emotional reaction will occur, instead, we learn how to regulate ourselves when the reaction does occur.

Consequently, inclusive leaders are tuned into their emotional responses, able to pause and mentally locate their emotional responses in their bodies like in their chest, head, or gut. This process of locating and labelling their emotions forms an integral part of understanding and communicating how they are experiencing the emotions to others. This human experience allows them to be vulnerable, which means being brave enough to communicate how they are feeling, despite the risk of possible rejection or judgement. In addition to sharing how we are feeling, we also need emotional agility to park our own views and emotional needs while receptively listening to others.

Case example: Experiencing negative triggers at meetings

A colleague, who was a new direct report, frequently interrupted others in meetings and I felt that they often dismissed perspectives that did not align with their own. What made it particularly difficult was that they reminded me of someone from my past, a former boss who had undermined my contributions and left me feeling invisible. I recognised that I was being triggered not just by the present situation but by unresolved feelings from the past. At first, I tried to suppress my emotions, telling myself that a good leader remains composed, respects different personalities, and acknowledges that people, especially newcomers, often try to impress. Equally, I needed to ensure that everyone had a safe space where they could contribute, and I also needed to determine whether this behaviour was disproportionately affecting a specific group, which could indicate a microaggression requiring a more direct approach. To gain perspective, I had informal conversations with a few colleagues. Some admitted they also found the behaviour disruptive but preferred to address it directly and have had no problems since, while others were not particularly affected. This helped me separate what was rooted in my past from what was happening in the present and to establish that this probably was not a microaggression. Since the impact was not universally negative, I decided not to intervene immediately. However, my frustration did not go away. Instead, it clouded my ability to engage with this person constructively. I noticed how my body tensed whenever they spoke and how my mind jumped to assumptions about their intent. The tipping point came when a critical meeting nearly ended in a heated argument, and I shut them down entirely. Afterwards, I felt uneasy and avoided addressing what had happened. But I soon realised that avoidance was not an option. I re-engaged with the team, apologised for my reaction, and had an open conversation with my direct report. Through this conversation, it became clear that their behaviour stemmed from a combination of factors: communication skills, cultural differences, and a desire to prove their value as a newcomer. What I had not initially realised was that, from the moment I felt triggered from the very first meeting, I had unconsciously changed how I treated them. Through our open conversation, I became aware that in response to my behaviour, they tried even harder to prove themselves, creating a negative cycle where neither of us felt heard.

When supporting the emotions of others in difficult situations

When a difficult situation arises, emotional agility becomes even more critical. Not only may our own emotions be triggered as described in the section above, but all those involved in the difficult situation may also be triggered – a precarious, ticking bomb – each person hooked on their emotions. At this point inclusive leaders need to assess if they should support more directly or not. Although inclusive leaders are ready to play an important role in mediating difficult situations or even escalated conflicts, they also recognise the need to empower others to behave autonomously and with agency.

The decision of getting involved or not might be influenced by the level of emotional agility at play and how individuals involved in the difficult situation frame conflict for example. Particularly in organisational cultures where harmony is prioritised, conflict can be seen as unsettling and threatening. When parties are feeling psychologically safe and are willing to draw on their empathy and include each other's perspective, they acknowledge that even conflict is an enabler of growth. Therefore, the inclusive leader plays a critical role in reframing the situation.

Another interesting point to consider is that emotionally charged, difficult situations can become even greater when we are working in environments with high levels of diversity and low inclusion. In fact, evidence shows that low inclusion with high diversity increases tensions and conflicts, which can negatively impact team cohesion and performance.[9] However, when there is diversity with inclusion, we are more likely to experience creative friction, which leads to innovation, enhanced learning, and performance. Even in the case of escalated conflict, if handled constructively, it can deepen relationships when they are repaired following a rupture.

Case example: Mediating and reframing conflict for team growth

As a gay person, I've learned that difficult conversations are opportunities for growth, not something to avoid. However, one particular situation tested this belief when a major restructuring led to conflict between two of my senior team members. Their constant disagreements over project priorities created a toxic work environment and started to affect the whole team's morale. Instead of stepping in as a referee or forcing a resolution, I chose to facilitate a deeper conversation. I first met them separately to understand their concerns and emotional triggers. This built trust and allowed me to challenge some of their assumptions about each other. Once we had established that, I brought them together for a structured conversation, with the goal not to "win" but to understand each other. I encouraged them to focus on shared goals and to articulate the underlying needs driving their positions. By highlighting how their differing perspectives on innovation and risk management could create a better outcome, they stopped seeing the situation as a threat and started visualising possibilities, which led them to find common ground. Clear communication and ground rules for psychological safety were important in guiding the conversation and ensuring that both individuals were aligned on their shared goals. The conflict became a catalyst for transformation, strengthening our relationships and creating a more resilient team.

What can inclusive leaders do?

Inclusive leaders play a pivotal role by creating a safe environment to enable us to step out of reacting with a fixated threat response and, instead, view emotions as a passing experience detached from our sense of self, that provide us with important information. For example, when we are experiencing anger, we will often say "I am angry". However, by doing this, we are implicitly associating the emotion with our identity. Instead, a simple yet powerful change is to label the emotion appropriately, therefore, we can say "I notice I am feeling angry". By doing this, it is much easier to detach ourselves from both identifying as the emotion (i.e., I *am* angry) and seeing the emotion as a permanent, rather than passing state. This can help to calm the nervous system and allows us to pause to respond with flexibility as opposed to with rigidity.

Inclusive leaders also appreciate that to get the most from diverse environments, we need low social friction to ensure differences do not escalate, therefore they dedicate quality time to team building and bonding. They also practise open and honest communication that integrates emotional words into the professional language while detaching identity from emotions. Inclusive leaders nurture psychological safety so that people feel able to share how they are noticing and experiencing emotions safely, creating an environment that contributes to adaptive teams better equipped to thrive in a diverse environment.

Below are some practical examples of how to be emotionally agile when responding to a negative emotional trigger for self and when supporting the emotions of others in difficult situations.

Responding to a negative emotional trigger for self

- Pause and name the passing emotion, instead of saying "I am frustrated" say "I notice I am feeling frustration". Creating this psychological distance helps you to see the emotion as a passing experience, not your identity.
- After labelling your emotion, locate the emotion in your body. This mindfulness exercise, accompanied with deep breathing, disrupts the threat response and helps to calm down your nervous system.
- Practise accepting and embracing your emotions. Otherwise there is a risk that your brain will think you are not getting important information and will only intensify the experience until you get the message.
- Next time, when experiencing an emotional situation, try to embrace your emotions not only by labelling them but also by decoding what they are trying to tell you. And then communicate them constructively to others.

- Practise self-compassion to avoid self-criticism. Tell yourself it is okay to feel this way and that you do not need to react immediately.
- Check the narratives you are telling yourself, as emotions might be triggered by recalling an unpleasant experience from the past and by transferring the threats experienced then to the here-and-now. You can ask yourself "What previous experience might be influencing how I am seeing this problem?".
- Try to suspend your values temporarily so that you can perceive the situation from an alternative point of view. Only then, re-engage with your values and respond to the situation. How did suspending your values momentarily change your perception of the situation? What insights did you gain when you re-engaged with your values?
- Recognise your patterns. For example, one sign is that your thinking becomes rigid and repetitive: you feel "hooked", fixated by your thoughts and emotions.
- Reconnect with your values to help you pause and respond – as opposed to react. For example, ask yourself "What would the best version of myself do in this situation?".

Supporting the emotions of others in difficult situations

- Acknowledge emotional information as useful evidence and as a foundation for understanding one another in a difficult situation. Therefore, inclusive leaders create a safe space to explore these emotions.
- Focus on emotional needs. Most of our expectations are driven by an emotional need so when we understand what these needs are, we can be more creative in how to meet them and find common ground.
- Support those involved in a difficult situation, helping them to understand themselves first. Then create a safe space for all parties to express themselves without fear of rejection.
- Reflect on how you think about conflict first before supporting others. What comes up for you and your experiences with conflict? Helping others to reframe the meaning of disagreement and see constructive conflict as fuel for innovation and growth, helps our brains to move away from a threat response and engage the reward system. This activates curiosity, adaptability, motivation, and learning.
- Support individuals in creating the foundations to repair any relationship rupture if and when difficult situations escalate. You can do this by coaching them on how to constructively communicate with each other and helping them to get the basics in place: for example, mutually agreed

ground rules, mutual awareness of emotional needs, and psychological safety. Let them know that you are available to help in an independent manner if needed.

- Role-model emotional empathy. Remember that for people to feel heard, and to calm their nervous system, they need to experience emotional empathy. You can acknowledge how they are feeling and how the situation is impacting them without taking sides. For example, you can say "I can see this is causing a lot of distress and is really upsetting for you".
- Encourage cognitive empathy and perspective-taking as part of the process by displaying curiosity, active listening, and asking open questions to understand the situation.
- Counteract systems of oppression that shut down emotions, such as social structures that reinforce the ideal worker and traditional stereotypes of masculinity. Negative emotions are normally a sign that a need has not been met and therefore should not be ignored. You can do this by normalising emotions and sharing your own emotions if appropriate.

Chapter 21 in summary

- Emotional agility is the ability to respond to everyday situations in a flexible manner, while emotional rigidity involves fixating on certain emotions and viewpoints, thereby closing ourselves off to new possibilities.
- Emotional agility does not mean ignoring or denying our emotions. Instead, it involves embracing our emotions and being adaptable in our responses to them.
- We face emotional oppression from various social structures. For instance, patriarchy often discourages men from expressing their emotions, and the ideal worker concept views people as mere extensions of machines, lacking emotional range and depth.
- Emotions are essential, signalling what is happening in our environment and highlighting unmet psychological needs. Therefore, it is vital for us to embrace our emotions by understanding the messages they convey and communicating them effectively.
- To avoid getting hooked by our emotions, we can view emotions as passing experiences rather than defining them as our identity (e.g., saying "I notice I'm feeling angry" instead of "I am angry").
- Inclusive leaders play a crucial role in fostering emotional agility in others by creating a safe environment. They invest quality time in team building and bonding and are willing to step in to support others during difficult situations if needed.

Notes

1 David, S. (2016) *Emotional agility: Get unstuck, embrace change, and thrive in work and life*. New York: Penguin Books.
2 hooks, bell. (2004) *The will to change: Men, masculinity, and love*. New York: Atria Books.
3 Brown, B. (2021). *Atlas of the heart: Mapping meaningful connection and the language of human experience*. London: Vermilion.
4 Martin, C. (2019). *How much time do we spend at work*. Accessed from https://blog.moderngov.com/2019/02/how-much-time-do-we-spend-at-work. Retrieved 19 March 2025.
5 David, S., & Congleton, C. (2013). Emotional agility. *Harvard Business Review*. Accessed from https://hbr.org/2013/11/emotional-agility. Retrieved 7 March 2025.
6 David, S. (2016) *Emotional agility: Get unstuck, embrace change, and thrive in work and life*. New York: Penguin Books.
7 David, S. & Congleton, C. (2013). Emotional agility. *Harvard Business Review*. Accessed from https://hbr.org/2013/11/emotional-agility. Retrieved 7 March 2025.
8 Stewart, I., & Joines, V. (1987). *TA today: A new introduction to transactional analysis*. Nottingham: Lifespace Publishing.
9 Garcia-Prieto, P., Bellard, E., & Schneider, S. C. (2003). Experiencing diversity, conflict, and emotions in teams. *Applied Psychology*, *52*(3), 413–440; King, E. B., Hebl, M. R., & Beal, D. J. (2009). Conflict and cooperation in diverse workgroups. *Journal of Social Issues*, *65*(2), 261–285.

Final thoughts 22

We hope that, in reading this book, our message that inclusive leadership is integral to all effective leadership has come across loud and clear. Inclusive leadership is good for everyone. It is good for the people you lead, which means it is good for the organisation as a whole. It is also good for you as the leader. When you are an inclusive leader, you are able to show up as yourself, you do not need to hide behind an emotionless, machine-like façade. You can be human. You can form strong connections with the other humans in your team. There can be some give and take. As leaders, precariously balancing on the pedestal where we can find ourselves placed can be truly exhausting. The danger with being on a pedestal is that it is very easy to fall off. As inclusive leaders we are not on a pedestal as we acknowledge that we make mistakes. Successful business relies on successful relationships and being an inclusive leader enhances our ability to build successful relationships. Most importantly, in addition to all of this, inclusive leadership addresses the inequities and systems of oppression that mean that not everyone can thrive. The future of the human race relies on us being able to draw on the beautiful capabilities of every one of us, ensuring that all are resourced fairly to contribute and succeed.

In this book, we have attempted to simplify something complex without losing its depth, essence, tensions, and nuances. This means we have aimed to clarify the practice of inclusive leadership by using precise language and drawing on several practical applications to make the practice of inclusive leadership accessible. It is not our intention to oversimplify or minimise the experiences of marginalised groups.

In this final chapter, we wanted to leave you with some final thoughts on what we see as some of the core principles of inclusive leadership,

DOI: 10.4324/9781003598022-28

highlighting the broader picture, and finally embracing the key tensions and nuances of practising inclusive leadership.

Core principles of inclusive leadership

Inclusive leadership is not a fixed leadership style or a static state of being, it is an ongoing practice. Inclusive leaders are individuals who are committed to this practice on a daily basis. The most transformative change happens when leaders engage in this practice consistently as a long-term commitment. Leaders who truly embrace inclusive leadership are rarely driven solely by the business case for inclusion. While they acknowledge its strategic benefits, their motivation often stems from deep-rooted social and environmental values. They care about people and the planet, operating with integrity and consciousness even amidst workplace pressures. The question is not whether inclusive leaders will make mistakes and unintentionally exclude others – they inevitably will, as human nature leans towards familiarity. What defines them is their willingness to reflect, take responsibility, and grow. True inclusion is built in the small, everyday moments: the decisions we make, the conversations we engage in, and the spaces we create.

Drawing from multidisciplinary research, we know that sustained inclusive leadership requires leaders first and foremost to care for their own wellbeing in order to be able to create the biological conditions needed to be inclusive. They must also establish psychological safety as a foundation for equity, creating environments where people feel safe speaking up about prejudice and privilege, as both in many cases are baked-in and invisible to those who are privileged in a given system. Maintaining a mindset of curiosity, courage, and empathy is essential, as is fostering genuine connections while disrupting biases that hinder inclusion. Furthermore, without humility, the steep learning curve of inclusive leadership becomes even more difficult to navigate. Inclusive leaders must also become reflective learners, from seeking knowledge to drawing insights from their own lived experiences and relative privileges to understanding how social hierarchies shape workplaces. This understanding enables them to dismantle biases and reform systems so that they work for everyone. Finally, inclusive leaders must develop the ability to identify the key workplace contexts where exclusion most often occurs (such as meetings where power dynamics come into play) and implement inclusion habits to mitigate our instinct to exclude, rewiring our brains to be more inclusive as the default.

The broader picture

Throughout history, systems have been reformed by those who had access to power and belonged to dominant groups. Systems do not change on their own. They require those with influence and access to push for reform, ensuring that leadership, policies, and decision-making processes reflect the needs of all, not just the privileged few. Therefore, genuine active allyship is the foundation for the practice of inclusive leadership, which not only challenges inequitable systems but also redistributes power and ensures diverse representation in shaping a future that is fair for all. The good news is that with social reform you do not need everyone, you just need the critical mass. Furthermore, not all workplace misconduct or counterproductive behaviours are directly tied to prejudice or systems of oppression. Inclusive leaders must also consider other factors hindering inclusion, such as personality types, cultural differences, or lack of skills. It's crucial to understand that while some behaviours are rooted in social hierarchies, inclusion challenges can also stem from other factors.

Tensions and nuances

Inclusive leaders must navigate several inherent tensions. We are wired to be cautious of what is different, believing it keeps us safe, yet it is in embracing difference that we truly grow and become inclusive, so we need to teach ourselves that difference is a reward not a threat. We often crave belonging through shared identities that connect us with others, yet this same belonging fuels ingroup bias and outgroup prejudice. We want to be our authentic selves, yet we fear that authenticity might compromise our acceptance and sense of belonging. Therefore, inclusive leaders help teams foster a sense of belonging because of their differences, not in spite of them. The shared identity is built on respect and dignity, as well as a genuine care for one another, not on individual backgrounds. As a result, oppression is addressed with seriousness and accountability. While conversations about identities like race, gender, and age are important, inclusive leaders care about what truly causes harm. This includes systems of oppression, such as racism, sexism, ableism, ageism, heteronormativity (stigmatising non-heterosexual orientations), cisnormativity (marginalising transgender, non-binary, and gender non-conforming individuals), islamophobia (prejudice against Muslims), xenophobia (marginalising immigrants), and so on. Although, to avoid the discomfort the dominant group (or oppressors) might experience, we often do not talk about and we do not measure these systems of oppression, inclusive leaders do not avoid these conversations. So inclusive leaders find themselves igniting discomfort and unsettling harmony as part of their practice. Furthermore, to drive inclusion in corporate settings, we often use the business case because it speaks the language of the current decision-makers. However, this raises another tension: advocating for equity should not be reduced to a self-serving strategy. Equally, we do not want to be tokenistic. Yet, in some countries, achieving a critical mass of underrepresented groups may never be possible due to demographic homogeneity. Consequently, inclusive leaders recognise that tokenism is a real threat that often goes unaddressed. The challenge for inclusive leaders is to keep pushing forward despite these contradictions, knowing that progress is not always linear, but it is always necessary.

Closing reflections

Navigating all of this helps to illustrate why practising inclusive leadership is not easy. It is a lifelong work. Indeed, we are still learning ourselves. Therefore, we will have missed things in this book and there will have undoubtedly been perspectives we overlooked and important points we did not consider. Although, unfortunately, equity and human rights can take a step backwards and regress, the world also continues to evolve. This means that standards improve and what is acceptable changes. We embrace this and know that this means that what is acceptable behaviour now, in five, ten, twenty years' time will be considered old-fashioned, outdated and even unacceptable. This is a normal part of the challenge of being an inclusive leader – the space is in constant motion. When we can learn to embrace this as a good thing, we become open to the amazing opportunities this affords us all to grow and evolve as human beings.

Index

For Product Safety Concerns and Information please contact our EU
representative GPSR@taylorandfrancis.com
Taylor & Francis Verlag GmbH, Kaufingerstraße 24, 80331 München, Germany

www.ingramcontent.com/pod-product-compliance
Lightning Source LLC
Chambersburg PA
CBHW062024270326
41929CB00014B/2306

9 7 8 1 0 3 2 9 6 8 5 5 1